A MANIFESTO FOR CHANGE

A.P.J. Abdul Kalam
and
V. Ponraj

HarperCollins *Publishers* India

First published in India in 2014 by
HarperCollins *Publishers* India

Copyright © A.P.J. Abdul Kalam 2014

P-ISBN: 978-93-5136-172-5
E-ISBN: 978-93-5136-173-2

2 4 6 8 10 9 7 5 3 1

A.P.J. Abdul Kalam and V. Ponraj assert the moral right to be identified as the authors of this work.

All rights reserved. No part of this publication may be reproduced, stored in a retrieval system, or transmitted, in any form or by any means, electronic, mechanical, photocopying, recording or otherwise, without the prior permission of the publishers.

HarperCollins *Publishers*
A-75, Sector 57, Noida 201301, India
77-85 Fulham Palace Road, London W6 8JB, United Kingdom
Hazelton Lanes, 55 Avenue Road, Suite 2900, Toronto, Ontario M5R 3L2
and 1995 Markham Road, Scarborough, Ontario M1B 5M8, Canada
25 Ryde Road, Pymble, Sydney, NSW 2073, Australia
31 View Road, Glenfield, Auckland 10, New Zealand
10 East 53rd Street, New York NY 10022, USA

Typeset in 11/14 Electra LT Regular at
SÜRYA

Printed and bound at
Thomson Press (India) Ltd.

CONTENTS

Acknowledgements   vii

Section I: PURPOSE OF THE BOOK   1

Section II: CREATIVE LEADERSHIP   7

Section III: INDIVIDUALS AT THE GRASSROOTS   19

Section IV: INDIVIDUALS AT THE GOVERNMENT LEVEL   43

Section V: MANIFESTO FOR VILLAGE DEVELOPMENT   83

Section VI: MANIFESTO FOR STATE ASSEMBLIES   101

Section VII: MANIFESTO FOR THE NATION   147

Section VIII: VISION FOR INDIA   245

Bibliography and References   255

ACKNOWLEDGEMENTS

The aim of this book is to share our ideas to evolve a creative political leadership at all levels of governance—from village panchayats to Parliament—with a vision. The thoughts and ideas in this book have been shaped by the interactions we had with fifteen state legislative assemblies and their members, Parliament members, village panchayat board presidents, Planning Commission members and officials from the state and central governments. The classes which we took in IIMs and other universities, our visits to various R&D organizations and interactions with domain experts, scientists, technologists, bureaucrats, members of industry, media, farmers, political leaders and the youth have played an important role in shaping our thoughts in arriving at the manifesto agenda. While writing the book, we decided to seek opinions from the youth who want to enter politics and others who are connected with politics to understand their aspirations and ambitions. Also, we normally have a tendency to blame elected representatives, but the analysis of the performing MLAs and MPs has revealed how they can contribute if they have the resolve and vision to serve the people through the existing political system in a democratic environment. Also the performance of various states reveals how they progress whenever there is visionary leadership at the helm of affairs which has a percolating effect at all levels of governance. We would like to express our gratitude to many who have contributed to our effort directly and indirectly.

Our special thanks and heartiest gratitude to Major General R. Swaminathan for his unique contribution in coordinating with various state and central government agencies in collecting, collating and analysing the data for fifteen state assemblies and Parliament addresses with our research team. We appreciate the inputs given by D. Narayana Moorthi (Former Director Launch Vehicle Programme, ISRO) for his valuable thoughts while shaping many assembly addresses. We need to make a special mention of Air Cmdr (Retd) R. Gopalasamy (Former Director, BDL) for his unique contribution to evolving the Energy Independence Mission and Space-based Solar Power Mission. We thank Prime Point Foundation's Srinivasan and Ramesh Kailasham for their valuable inputs while analysing inputs from the youth and the performance of Parliament members. We appreciate the contribution of H. Sheridon and R.K. Prasad for diligently managing all the administrative aspects regarding the manuscript.

The book would not have taken shape without the untiring and dedicated efforts of Dhan Shyam Sharma in typing, giving valuable inputs and correcting the manuscript and working closely with us and Krishan Chopra of HarperCollins. We have to make a special mention of Krishan Chopra for his contribution in reviewing the manuscript and structuring the book through his constant interaction with us and carrying out meticulous editing. His colleague Siddhesh Inamdar played a valuable role in reordering and editing the chapters.

We also thank Rajinder Ganju for his suggestions and for going out of his way in helping prepare the manuscript for press in a very short time.

We also thank the editorial, marketing and administrative teams at HarperCollins for their excellent support.

A.P.J. ABDUL KALAM
V. PONRAJ

SECTION I

PURPOSE OF THE BOOK

Manifestos are usually prepared for elections and help citizens understand what every party promises to do if it comes to power. But we have prepared A *Manifesto for Change* both for aspiring politicians as for elected governments and elected members in panchayats, legislative assemblies and Parliament—as too for the people of the country to equip them with information needed to demand good performance from their representatives in these bodies.

A *Manifesto for Change* is the result of five years of research on the parliamentary system of India. I have had extensive opportunities to interact with legislators and gain an understanding of the parliamentary system. As the 11th President of India, from 2002 to 2007, I have addressed fifteen legislative assemblies and presented a deeply researched development plan for the state. We had an opportunity to interact with members of legislative assemblies, members of Parliament, ministers and chief ministers, and governors. We hope every aspiring MP, MLA or anyone with political ambitions, specially the youth, will benefit from the book, as the issues of creative leadership, people's aspirations, development, and evolving a focused, clear vision become more and more important, right from the grassroots level to the higher echelons of political leadership.

India's rich demographic dividend in the form of its 640 million youth is second to none. I strongly believe igniting the minds of the youth to dedicate themselves to the nation and contribute their best to bring a change in thinking will make this country a developed country. As I always say, 'Ignited minds of the youth are the most powerful resource on the earth, above the earth and under the earth.'

> History has proven that those who dare to imagine the impossible are the ones who break all human limitations. In every field of human endeavour—whether science, medicine, sports, the arts, technology, or politics—the names of the people who imagine the impossible are engraved in our history. By breaking the limits of their imagination, they changed the world.

I would be delighted if this book at least sows the seeds of confidence in every youth to enter and practise developmental politics.

With their innovative and creative minds and their out-of-the-box thinking, how can they integrate their performance with excellence without diluting the democratic fabric of India and strengthen the pillars of developed India? Will the pillars of democracy and performance go together? Will developmental politics and politics as we know it coexist; if so, how much? Will the youth ever think of working with integrity and succeed with integrity in this present context of corrupt politics permeating everywhere? Are the manifestos of political parties really translating into action for their five years of ruling the country or states? It is true, however, that when a visionary leader with commitment to service comes to power, the quality of development and politics improves everywhere.

> Only a visionary creative leader who has the ability to create a multitude of creative leaders in various walks of life can bring about a fundamental change in the system or society. People and the country's democratic systems have to identify and encourage such creative leaders in every walk of life, whether it is politics, executive, judiciary, industry, agriculture or services.

Purpose of the Book

The alternation between hope and disappointment has become a pattern in Indian democracy. When the present fails to face challenges with a vision, the past returns to power in a democracy in the absence of a credible new alternative. India has always been a nation of people who respect good leadership.

People are always looking for a leader who can transform their lives when their hopes are shattered. They look for another leader with the hope that he/she may bring about a change.

We feel it is an urgent need for the nation to evolve such a platform so as to empower citizens to perform globally. We need leaders in all walks of life, be it politicians, executives, judges, academics, healthcare providers, and professionals in the services, industrial and agriculture sectors. In order to become a leader for change, one should act with courage, conviction and respect to the democratic traditions of the nation.

The political system is the foundation for democracy to flourish. The nation should create political executives, political scientists and political leaders, not politicians.

The political leader is one who practises politics in such a way as to envision, explore, innovate and implement public policies which improve the quality of life of the people whom he intends to serve. He offers to enrich people's lives without expecting anything in return.

It is our attempt is to sow the seed in the minds of the leaders of tomorrow of how to make this nation great. How to bring about a change in the political system which will in turn enact laws and make the political system responsive, corruption-free, transparent and proactive to empower the people to be globally competitive; how to build the nation's strength using its core competence? How to empower people with innovative policies and agendas which will enhance their quality of life and standard of living so that they can devote their time to raising their children in a system of values for which the nation is known through the ages? How to ensure that the basic requirements of citizens are fulfilled in record time? How to address the challenges of the nation based on the pillars of democratic principles? How to build our strength in bringing about unity in diversity? That, in short, is the foundation of *A Manifesto for Change.*

SECTION II
CREATIVE LEADERSHIP

It has become crucial for us to be clear about what we can rightly expect from our leaders, from panchayat members to local councillors of municipal corporations to members of Parliament. In other words, there has to be ownership. Whether it is the panchayat member, development officer, councillor, MLA or MP or minister, they have to at least try to the best of their ability to do what they are elected to do. We need a Parliament with a vision, one which has the larger picture in mind and can rise above petty party politics. How would such a Parliament perform? What are the ways in which it can play a far more constructive role than it has in the last Lok Sabha?

Every member of Parliament should think that the nation is bigger than the individual and the party. Parliament should pass a resolution to work on a 'Vision for the nation'. Parliament does not mean the ruling dispensation alone but all its members. In the heat of an election campaign parties will try and score points against the others; it will be politics as usual, so to say. But after election, every party should ensure that they work for development in a sustained manner without wasting even a single minute in Parliament. Before bringing any bill, discussion is essential. Adopting the necessary changes proposed by MPs, even if they are in opposition, should be considered on the merit of the proposal if it benefits the nation. A conducive atmosphere has to be created to welcome out-of-the-box ideas and make it a truly inclusive Parliament. It is not enough to talk about inclusive development, we need to practise it as well. What will help inspire the 640 million youth of this nation? It is the visionary policies enacted by Parliament to make this nation great, and transform its society into a knowledge society.

How will we bring about the fundamental changes needed in

thinking and action? These are not for the government alone but for us to bring about, of course. But as far as the government goes, what we need is a visionary leadership that can lead this nation towards sustainable economic development from the grassroots to the centres of commercial enterprise.

During the last six decades of our parliamentary democracy, it's the political leadership that has made this nation great through its visionary policies. Let us take a quick glance at how, in their own way, past leaders have made a lasting difference. The list is indicative, of course, and far from complete. Thus, in no particular order, even a sampling shows the range of their contributions.

Mohandas Karamchand Gandhi is known as the Father of the Nation for having led India to independence and inspired movements for civil rights and freedom across the world. Born and raised in a Hindu merchant caste family in coastal Gujarat and trained in law in London, he first employed nonviolent civil disobedience as a lawyer in South Africa, in the resident Indian community's struggle for civil rights. After his return to India in 1915, he set about organizing peasants, farmers, and urban labourers to protest against excessive land-tax and discrimination. While independence movements around the world were bloody, he became famous for fighting for freedom with non-violent means such as civil disobedience and non-cooperation. In the months following partitition, he undertook several fasts unto death to promote religious harmoney. He is fondly remembered for making an example of the Indian freedom struggle internationally.

Pandit Jawaharlal Nehru is remembered as an architect of modern India. He is also remembered for sowing the seeds of development by initiating major projects such as dams and other infrastructure, creating great institutions in space, atomic energy, defence and scientific research, as too in education and healthcare. Nehru is considered an iconic parliamentarian. He attended Question Hour regularly and kept track of discussions in his room as well, where he had a provision for listening in on the debate, quietly going back into the House if he heard something interesting, according to R. Venkataraman, former President, at a seminar on Nehru and Parliament in 1985. He had the rare virtue of being tolerant of and patient with contrary viewpoints, seeing the merit in them and revising his own opinions where needed.

> 'Surely, there can be no higher responsibility or greater privilege than to be a member of this sovereign body, which is responsible for the fate of the vast number of human beings who live in this country'
>
> —Jawaharlal Nehru

Vallabhbhai Patel was one of the founding fathers of India. He played a leading role in the country's struggle for independence and guided its integration into a united, independent nation by persuading princely states to join the Union. As the first home minister and deputy prime minister of India, he organized relief for partition refugees in Punjab and Delhi, and led efforts to restore peace across the nation. Often known as the 'Iron Man of India', he is also remembered for establishing modern all-India services.

Bhimrao Ramji Ambedkar, popularly known as Babasaheb, was independent India's first law minister and also the architect of the country's Constitution. He earned a law degree and various doctorates and gained reputation as a scholar in spite of the challenges he faced as a Dalit.

Indira Gandhi believed India will be respected among nations only if it is made strong. She conducted India's first nuclear test and went to war with Pakistan over its excesses in East Pakistan, which resulted in the creation of Bangladesh. Her years in power were notable for many initiatives to strengthen the country's position in the neighbourhood and the world.

The Green Revolution took place under her government in the 1970s and transformed the country from one dependent on imported foodgrain to one that achieved food security. Playing a key role in this were C. Subramaniam, the minister for agriculture, and Dr M.S. Swaminathan, the eminent agriculture scientist.

R. Venkataraman, a former defence minister who later became the eighth President, initiated India's missile programme, and was responsible for shifting me from the space to the missile programme. He helped consolidate the missile activities, naming the combined body the Integrated Guided Missile Development Programme.

Jayaprakash Narayan launched the *Sampoorna kraanti* (Total Revolution). He gave the country the confidence that it can rise up against oppression and authoritarianism and thereby strengthened individual liberty.

Rajiv Gandhi will be remembered for a slew of measures to encourage science and technology. These benefited industries such as those in computers, airlines, defence and telecommunications by way of reduced taxes and tariffs. Alongside he helped take the country towards a modern mindset. One key measure he introduced was of panchayati raj to take power to the grassroots. He took telecom to the villages and showed how e-governance could bring transparency and accelerate the process of governance.

Prime Minister V.P. Singh brought social justice to the economically backward sections of the people. As chief minister of Uttar Pradesh earlier, he restored order in lawless districts of the state where banditry had become widespread. As finance minister, he took a tough stand against tax evasion. Thus, his contribution to the fight against corruption makes him stand out as a leader.

P.V. Narasimha Rao launched a process of economic transformation that continues. He became prime minister in 1991 at a time of economic crisis. By the time he left, the country was firmly in a position to become one of the world's biggest economies. He helped establish the world knowledge platform by using the core competence of partnering nations to build a world-class supersonic missile system, Brahmos.

Atal Bihari Vajpayee had the remarkable distinction of being elected to Lok Sabha nine times and to the Rajya Sabha twice. He was known for his oratory in Parliament. The nuclear test in 1998 changed the trajectory of the country's relationship with the world, making it clear that India could take tough decisions when circumstances required even at the risk of others' displeasure. His efforts for peace with Pakistan set a new benchmark for diplomacy in the subcontinent. His Golden Quadrilateral Roadways project has changed the economic face of the nation on road transportation across India.

Manmohan Singh will be remembered as a low-key leader who worked quietly and accomplished much. His tenure from 2004 to 2014 is notable for programmes for social welfare, reduction of poverty, and milestone measures to increase transparency and accountability in the government such as the Right to Information Act and the Lokpal bill. Economic growth touched high levels during his first term, from 2004 to 2009, and there was much respect for him as a leader across the world.

As we can see, every leader and every political party in India has made a contribution through their policies, programmes and by enacting appropriate laws to keep up the tempo of development of the nation. The contributions range from agriculture to science and technology, from uplift of the backward to education, so that India can be on a par with any nation in the world. The question is whether we can carry these initiatives forward to accomplish the desired results.

What Makes You a Creative Political Leader?

Today what we witness is not a leadership crisis but a crisis of the lack of emergence of creative leadership. Anybody can become the leader of a political party, or anybody can start a party. But the aspiring one should think:

- Do I have a vision for the nation or state?

- Am I able to rise above matters of caste, creed, religion, language and keep the nation bigger than the individual?
- Do I have the tolerance and respect needed for different views, ideas and thought?
- Do I have the courage to transform the vision into missions?
- Do I have the capability to win over popular support with qualities such as integrity, love for people, passion for social service, ability to work for people without any personal benefit and, ultimately am able to come up with innovative policies that will make this nation globally competitive?
- Do I have the capability to create multiple leaders within my own party?
- Do I have the ability to respect others' point of view and the patience to listen to opposing views? Am I able to accept mistakes and take corrective action?
- Do I have the good spirit to overcome my ego and give credit to others, including the opposition, for their suggestions?

A party to truly succeed has to be built on a value system. If that is not so, corruption and moral turpitude result. It could again fail if it lacks credible inner democracy or line of command. Until India becomes a knowledge society, however, it appears its politics will remain centred on either charisma or dynasty, is a view that came up in our discussions.

I will be happy if new creative leaders emerge whether from existing parties or new ones. Ultimately my mission is to generate a large number of political leaders from within the country. After all, we cannot import leaders, can we? My work will be done if the ideas of my book percolate in the minds of a few committed ignited minds in each state who are aspiring to be the leaders of tomorrow.

There have been many transformational changes in the evolution of political systems. The most important of them is democracy. I firmly believe that the fundamental principle of democracy is there to stay forever, with its aim of continuous empowerment of citizens for their betterment. India is one of the greatest and biggest democratic nations in the world. The democratic tradition of our country has worked well for more than six decades. As Mahatma Gandhi said, 'Democracy, disciplined and enlightened, is the finest thing in the world'. We are in the process of reinventing democracy to meet the fundamental goals of empowering citizens. To keep pace with the changing world, our nation and people urgently need a paradigm shift in thinking.

Nurturing the Seeds of Development Politics

An MPhil student in Presidency College, T. Sarvanan, wrote a letter to me. As its content is relevant to the subject we are going to discuss, I will quote from it. The letter went like this:

> Dear Sir, The full power of the banyan tree is equal to the power in the seeds of the tree. In a way both of us, you and me, are the same, but we exhibit our talents in different forms. A few of the seeds become banyan trees but many die as saplings without ever becoming trees.

Truly, it struck me, the seeds of a banyan tree are indeed something like the citizens of the nation. Democracy gives opportunity to every citizen to grow and perform to his capacity. Every citizen indeed contributes to the success of the few. Let the success of the Indian nation be shared by all Indian citizens. Let every seed be nurtured. Where this book is concerned, that means nurturing the leaders of the future.

On 19 January 2011, I visited Amravati to attend a programme organized by the Satpuda Shikshan Prasarak Mandal to address one lakh youth assembled over there. I gave a talk on the subject 'I am unique' in the presence of many leaders, teachers and educationists.

When I asked them to raise their hands, 99 per cent of the youth lifted their hands and said that they wanted democracy with a faster rate of growth. Here the message was: 'Youth definitely want democracy to be re-invented with faster growth'.

Many civilizations have disappeared because of the absence of a vision. It is time for India to have a creative leadership to articulate a vision in every branch of activity and make it a reality.

I have seen three dreams which have seen the light of day. The space programme of ISRO (Indian Space Research Organization), Agni programme of DRDO (Defence Research and Development Organization) and PURA (Providing Urban Amenities in Rural Areas) have become national missions. Of course, these three programmes succeeded in the midst of many challenges and problems. I have worked in all three areas. I would like to convey to you what I have learnt about leadership from these three programmes:

1. A leader must have a vision.
2. A leader must have passion to realize the vision.
3. A leader must be able to travel on an unexplored path.
4. A leader must know how to manage both success and failure.
5. A leader must have the courage to take tough decisions.
6. A leader should have nobility in management.
7. A leader should be transparent in every action.
8. A leader becomes the master of the problem, defeats the problem and succeeds.
9. A leader must work with integrity and succeed with integrity.

Let me give an example for one of the essential qualities of creative leadership: courage. I still remember a scene from May 1996. It was 9 at night. I got a call from the prime minister's residence that I should meet P.V. Narasimha Rao immediately. I met him just two days before the announcement of the general election results. He told me, 'Kalam, be ready with your team for a nuclear test. I am going to Tirupati. You wait for my authorization to go ahead with the test. DRDO-DAE teams must be ready for action.' The journey to the temple town of Tirupati was to pray for success in the election. As it turned out, the result was quite different from what he anticipated. I was busy at the Chandipur missile range. I got a call saying that I must immediately meet prime minister-designate Atal Bihari Vajpayee with the outgoing PM. I was struck by the fact that Rao was asking me to brief Vajpayee on the nuclear programme, so that a smooth takeover of this very important activity could take place. This incident reveals the maturity and professional excellence of a patriotic statesman who believed that the nation is bigger than the political system. Of course after taking over as prime minister in 1998, the first task given by Vajpayee to me was to conduct the nuclear test at the earliest. Both these leaders had the courage to take difficult decisions boldly, even though the consequences of such a decision had great national and international significance.

> Nelson Mandela (1918-2013) spent twenty-seven years in prison for fighting against apartheid in South Africa. On being released, he went on to become the nation's first democratically elected president and the most respected political leader in the world.
>
> Apartheid had offered the country's non-white majority few economic opportunities. Mandela was arrested for organizing anti-government activities and sentenced to life in prison. 'I have cherished the ideal of a democratic and free society in which all persons live together in harmony and with equal opportunities,' he said during his trial. It was an ideal for which he was prepared to die, he said. As president, he worked hard to improve opportunities for the country's large black population, and despite his long imprisonment, showed himself to be a statesman rather than let his unhappy past colour his actions. He was a true creative leader.

Hence, we need creative leaders who have these nine qualities, and a Vision to work for. The youth of our country should inherit a nation that is a leader and not a follower.

SECTION III

INDIVIDUALS AT THE GRASSROOTS

Thousands of youth are today interested in entering politics. Many, however, give up the idea, without even trying, finding it too hard a prospect. One major hurdle: today, to contest any election, whether as MLA, MP or even panchayat board president, a candidate needs to spend lakhs and crores of rupees. Based on estimates from those who have knowledge of the process, a candidate for MP has to spend Rs 8 to 12 crore to become an MP, Rs 1 to 2 crore to become an MLA, and Rs 2 to 5 lakh to become a panchayat board president. The expenses are manifold. A party and its candidates spend money on campaigning, advertising, touring the constituency and paying the support staff. If a candidate spends such large sums to become a public servant, how can we expect him or her not to indulge in various unscrupulous means, including corruption, to earn back the investment? Has public service become a business? Hence the key question is: how to reform this scenario which is at the root of all the present-day political turmoil and keeps fresh, committed talent away from politics?

We decided to get responses from a varied group of people, youth from both rural and urban areas, and people in politics. We formulated a questionnaire and created an online feedback mechanism using social media. An online and offline survey was conducted with the help of Prime Point Foundation to understand the views of youngsters on Indian politics. While the urban youth responded online, it was necessary to reach out to the rural youth on telephone and in meetings.

We kept our coverage wide. Not only youth, we also included village panchayat presidents, MLAs, MPs, some who entered politics and went back to social service, others who served as bureaucrats and held constitutional positions, to get their perspective about politics and governance. We hope this chapter will help the youth to consider and evolve their own action agendas.

Thoughts of Ignited Minds from Urban and Rural Areas

We sent out the questionnaire to around 1,000 youth in all. The people contacted were from the age group of 20 to 35. We got 90 per cent response within a week's time. We have selected some of the answers to get an idea of the general view.

Question 1: What is your perception about politics?

Positives: Politics is a sacred field and needs a great sacrifice. It is an honest place for social reformers, a place for attempting a change; don't criticize it if you cannot change it. The country needs more honest politicians and retirement age is a must.

Negatives: A place for the corrupt, a for-profit, only profession to make quick and easy money, a place for criminals.

Question 2: Do you feel politics is the right route to do public service?

Positives: It is the duty of every youngster to enter politics and contribute to cleaning it up. It is the best route for public service, Service to society will make youth responsible, contribute to constructive policies and make the country positive.

Negatives: There are other ways to do public service than politics.

Question 3: What are the challenges to entering politics?

Positives: A youth needs credentials, financial stability, time, people management, understanding of the globalized world and local realities among other things. A youth with these traits and wide-ranging knowledge will certainly venture into politics. Politics requires huge amount of sacrifice and dedication. It can't be part-time.

Negatives: The cost of politics is becoming higher, thereby

preventing genuine people from entering it. It is not a stable career option, especially for those from the middle class.

Question 4: Do you think caste, creed, religion, money and strength colour voters' perception? Or is good service respected by them?

Positives: People appreciate good service and a clean image. These, backed by an ability to attract voters and an effective outreach programme, fetch votes.

Negatives: However idealistic one may be, sadly the dominance of caste, creed, religion and money cannot be discounted in today's political scenario. Each voter, whether he is rural, urban, educated or illiterate, rich or poverty-stricken, looks at politics in a different way, and caste, etc play a major role for him.

Question 5: What is your suggestion to reduce or eliminate corruption in public life and administration?

Positives: Appealing to people's conscience is the only way forward. Intra-party democracy, ensuring the emergence of the right people and the reduction of discretionary powers is essential. Doing away with cash transactions can bring in transparency. Awareness campaigns are a must. Use of technology can bring down corruption. Zero tolerance must be the way forward.

Negatives: Corruption starts at home. Craving for a seat starts from the time a person throws his handkerchief through the window to ensure a seat for himself in the public transport bus. As long as society remains like this culturally, it is difficult to wipe out corruption. The leaders we see are a reflection of who we are.

Question 6: What are the reforms needed to make public life clean and reduce election expenses?

Positives: Elections should be a matter of state expenditure. Transparent spending and reporting models are a must. The right to reject candidates will start making an impact in the long run.

The concept of reservation should be gradually done away with. The bureaucracy also needs to be reformed.

Negatives: Not just money, but drugs, liquor and freebies are also used to entice voters. This shows a deficit of conscience among Indian citizens.

Question 7: *How do you get a political leader to consider you to be a potential candidate for elections?*

Positives: Reach out to all political leaders with your credentials. Let him know your vision, mission and plans for the people in that area and convince him about your strategic thinking and implementation capabilities.

Negatives: Without a godfather or money in the bank, it is difficult to make that happen. The chances of an ordinary citizen being considered a candidate are one in a million.

Question 8: *How do you reach out to people to do public service? Why would people look out for a leader like you presently?*

Positives: Do public service in whatever way you can. Whether you are a doctor, engineer, lawyer, accountant or social worker, contribute in your own little way. Every drop adds to the ocean. Voluntary service is the best way forward and associating with a cause is the need of the hour. People look out for a leader who is selfless and holds high moral values and practises them.

Negatives: Trust deficit is the main problem today in politics and public service. Unfortunately there is no leader without ulterior motives today.

The responses reflect the mood of the people and their perceptions about politics. Many of the responses reflect a lack of awareness about politics, with some people having high hopes and others having lost hope. Some of the responses are idealistic, confident of finding a practical solution for the challenges faced by Indian politics. In addition to the responses received by mail, we also contacted some rural leaders and voters on telephone to get a balanced view for our study. Based on the responses, we have observed the following.

1. When asked about the challenges faced by youth in entering politics, all the respondents uniformly said that money power, muscle power and dynasty are the greatest challenges for all. Educated middle class youth indicated resistance from family members, as a career in politics does not provide a regular income to maintain a family. In addition, the educated middle class youth does not want to please senior leaders to help their rise in politics. The educated youth of today generally do not accept failure and they get disillusioned when they face defeat. Hence, many middle-class youth are not venturing into politics, and political leaders find it easy to groom their own wards for leadership. This leads to dynastic politics.
2. The responses from rural leaders and workers from uneducated and low-income groups were different. Since these youngsters are already facing economic and social challenges, they are able to enter politics smoothly and get along with the leaders by following them and living up to their expectations. Money is a common challenge for both the rural and urban segments. Generally, we observed that rural youth fit into politics better than urban youth in respect of attitude.
3. When asked about the impact of caste, creed, money and muscle power on voters during elections, all respondents agreed that they dominate elections. They felt that political parties put up candidates on the basis of their caste and religion. Though candidates with a record of good social service might get an additional advantage, they did not have a winning chance if they contested as independents. They required the backing of a political party. Generally in India,

voters cast their votes based on the party and its charismatic leaders and not on the individual candidate per se.
4. When asked for suggestions to reduce corruption, all the respondents blamed the people, officials and politicians simultaneously. At the first level, the general public demands freebies in exchange for voting for a candidate or a party. Also both rural and urban people bribe officials to get their job done quickly. The majority accepted corruption as a means to get things done. They got fed up and voted out the party in power in the next election only when their work didn't get done or they were cheated even after paying bribes. The nexus between politicians and officials also adds to the problem. Though there are enough laws to punish the corrupt, due to a lack of governance and protection of the corrupt by politicians, these laws have become redundant.
5. The respondents cited the examples of honest IAS officers or government officials being sidelined by politicians and senior bureaucrats. There was a general perception that politicians and officials colluded with each other and granted licences to loot natural resources such as sand, granite and minerals and gave vague explanations to justify their government's actions. If they were caught or brought to the notice of courts, the officials who were involved in the decision-making process escaped punishment, as did the politicians. Many of the respondents suggested stepping up public awareness to nip corrupt practices in the bud.
6. Young IAS officers when they join the services with a determination to work with honesty and integrity are being made to face numerous challenges for believing in their principles. They are transferred, humiliated and put into insignificant positions. Only a few can withstand the pressure.
7. Some of the respondents felt that in the name of honesty and integrity, bureaucrats never take decisions at all! Some bureaucrats, of course, understand how to work within the

system and come up with solutions that work. A rare few come up with solutions that are innovative and change the system for the better in the long run.
8. When asked to specify any reforms that are needed to clean up politics and to avoid costly campaigns, the respondents reflected anger and helplessness. However, some respondents suggested state funding of elections, regulation of campaigns, banning freebies, and setting a retirement age for politicians as measures that help. Rural respondents felt that public awareness needed to be improved. However, since elections involve movement of workers, campaign expenses, and maintaining an office, candidates cannot avoid certain minimum expenses.
9. When asked to specify their expectations from their ward councillors, MLAs and MPs, the respondents did not have any specific idea about the role played by them. However, generally, they wanted their ward councillors to take care of water supply, sanitation and other basic amenities in the ward. They expected MLAs to take care of the roads in the constituency, bridges, water bodies, primary and secondary education, health, etc. Some respondents pointed out the difficulties faced by MLAs in the opposition due to lack of cooperation from ruling party office-bearers. The respondents expected MPs to take care of overall economic development of the constituency, planning for long-term projects and developing infrastructure. All the respondents uniformly felt that their elected representatives should be available in the constituency on the days when they were not attending the legislature or Parliament to interact with the people.

Thoughts of a Former Politician

We decided to interview someone, Dhammu, who joined politics but left it to do social service. We found one such person and asked him to respond to some specific questions.

Question: You joined politics but left it. Why?

Dhammu: I joined a party because of its ideology and the charisma of its leader. I thought I will be better able to serve society by being a party member. However, as a partyman, I found that one has no choice but to follow the programme of the party blindly and support all the actions of the leaders. The ability to listen to individual members voicing their genuine opinion on issues shows the quality of the leadership. Most parties in India have leaders who have complete control over the organization

> Any youth aspiring to join politics will have to understand that they will have to sacrifice their individuality and be prepared to go with the party's ideology irrespective of their likes and dislikes.

I realized that I could only help a few persons and not the entire society. Then I realized that the best I could do for society was to help bring about a transformation. For that I had to transform myself. My self-examination made me realize that I have hurt the feelings of many people as a politician. For me, the political dharma and spiritual dharma could not co-exist. So I decided to stay away from politics.

Politics is the collective action of a group to shape public opinion for the betterment of society. All political actions will have a direct bearing on the future of the nation and youth, hence the youth have to take an interest in politics. They need not become members of parties, but they should know how various parties approach a problem. Then they should actively support the best approach among the parties. Their involvement in politics should be issue-based and not party-based. If they keep quiet, they will stand to lose.

With the kind of connectivity possible today, candidates can easily get in touch with voters without much expense. Only innovative ideas are needed. If one is innovative, he or she can win elections without spending much money. Donations from well-

Our special thanks to the large number of youths who responded to this questionnaire, with special mention for the following who have contributed with their unique thoughts on politics in detail by email, on telephone and in personal discussions.
(Rohan Rojay <rohankumar.india617@yahoo.com>, Khetle <siddheshkhetle3142@yahoo.com>, Susan Koshy <susankoshy2005@yahoo.co.in>, Dr Arpan Mitra - <drarpanmitra@gmail.com>, Anand Bharadwaj j <anandbharadwaj.j@gmail.com>, Rameesh Kailasam <rameeshkailasam@gmail.com>, S.M. Arasu- <smarasu@hotmail.com>, Rajesh K. <kollu.rajesh@gmail.com>, Dhan Shyam Sharma<dhanshyam@abdulkalam.com>, Girish Srivatsav <girish@gnsadvisory.in>, REACH Mohammed Azad A.K. <cbeazad@gmail.com>, Suryah S.G. <suryah@suryah.in>, Karthikeyan Sivashanmugam <sivamangala@gmail.com>, Thirukkumaran Haridass <hthirukkumaran@gmail.com>, Siddhesh VANCHILINGAM ANBARASAN <anbu28@hotmail.com>, N. Rajaji <nrajaji@yahoo.com>, Tada Periyasamy, Journalist Vijayakumar <reportervijay@gmail.com>, nandineeshree sha <ekamnandushree@gmail.com>, Nagendran <southernpurabiofuels@gmail.com>, Visswanathan A. & Jaya visswanathan.a@gmail.com, Gopal T.V. <gopal@annauniv.edu>, Mani Kandan manikandan.fiery@gmail.com, H. Sheridon < hsheridon@yahoo.com>, P. Dhanapal < pdhanapal@yahoo.com>, Singapore Velmurugan <velmurugan_mariappan@yahoo.com.sg>, Hyderabad Naveen, Saleem <apjmjsaleem@gmail.com>, Andaman Venkatesh <kvenkatesa@gmail.com>, Abdul Ghani<k.abdulghani786@gmail.com>, Ravi Senthilkumar ravisenthilkumar@ctnct.in, R.K. Prasad <palghatprasad@gmail.com>, Manivannan< na.manivannan@gmail.com>, Rajendran< rselvaraj@riinc.net>, Subbiah Prabakar < sprabu2000@gmail.com>, B. Shivakumar<gfercy@yahoo.com>, R. Thiruchenduran <rthiruchenthuran@yahoo.com>, M. Vijay Anand <vijay.manivel@gmail.com>)

wishers will be sufficient to meet the minimum expenses. Leaders like K. Kamaraj, P. Kakkan and Morarji Desai did not possess much wealth. But they contested and won many elections. No self-respecting leader will indulge in bribery. The erosion of moral values is the root cause of corruption. That is why we are striving to inculcate moral values in students through the Lead India 2020 movement in Tamil Nadu.

The MLAs and MPs are presently selected by party leaders. They should be selected instead by the party's local members. Then they will become answerable to the local partymen. This may not eliminate corruption, but it will help minimize it.

The youth should be made aware of the intricacies of inner-party democracy. The lack of inner-party democracy is the root cause of nepotism and favouritism.

In most countries, youth leaders progress to become national leaders. But for this to happen here we should insist on inner-party democracy. The youth should follow their passion. If they have passion for politics and would like to do social service, then they can enter political arena.

Thoughts of an Opposition MLA

C.H. Sekar entered politics after studying engineering and was elected as an MLA of an opposition party. He represents Gummidipoondi for the DMDK (Desiya Murpokku Dravida Kazhagam) in Tamil Nadu.

Question 1: As a member of the Tamil Nadu assembly, what is your contribution to your constituency and also to the nation?

I want to be a role model for young MLAs in the country. I take up constituency issues in the legislative assembly and also with the district collector. I focus more on health, education and generating employment for youngsters.

Question 2: How did you spend the MLALAD (MLA Local Area Development) funds for the development of your constituency?

I have used the funds for the construction of fifteen community halls in the villages and plan to complete at least fifty such halls before the end of my term. I have used MLA funds for the construction of ten PDS shops. I plan to construct another twenty during my tenure.

I have provided for water filtration in ten schools out of the thirty in my constituency. This benefits 15,000 students, who get to drink clean water. I have also obtained permission from the Sports Authority of Tamil Nadu to construct a stadium in my constituency. Now, I am on the look out for a five-acre plot for it. After we find a site, a stadium will be constructed to benefit youngsters.

Question 3: Will you be able to fulfil the promises made in your manifesto? If so, to what extent?

I had promised to set up a bus depot in Gummidipoondi taluk. This has been the dream of my constituency for more than thirty years. The bus depot has been sanctioned now. I had promised to set up a sports stadium in our locality and I have got the approval for it. Identification of a suitable site is in progress. The fishermen in our constituency do not get the benefits which fishermen in other parts of Tamil Nadu do. I have already raised the issue in the assembly. I am facilitating an awareness programme for farmers with the help of agriculture department officials, so that our farmers can use better techniques. I have already completed three such major programmes. I plan to conduct another four programmes during my tenure. I am also working out a plan for a 'job mela' for the unemployed youth in my constituency. I am already in discussion with the various companies in and around my constituency. I will organize five such 'job melas' during my tenure.

Question 4: How do you prepare yourself for debates in the assembly?

Before I participate in a debate, I discuss the issue in detail with my constituents, media persons and subject experts and gather their views. Probably I am one of the few MLAs in the country to make use of the services of PRS Legislative Research based in Delhi for data inputs relating to other states and countries. I have so far attended three seminars organized by PRS India. I also participate in other professional seminars, like the Sansad Ratna Seminar.

Question 5: As an MLA, what is your advice to the youth who want to become political leaders or would like to enter politics?

If any youngster wants to enter politics, he/she should start working with the people at the grassroot level for a minimum of two years, so that he/she understands the real issues of the common people. Social media activism may not yield any results.

Thoughts of a Junior Scientist Who Created a Model Village

Kuthampakkam Ilango Rangasamy (who can be reached at panchayat@yahoo.com) worked as a scientific assistant in the Central Electro Chemical Research Laboratory in 1983. He was the elected panchayat president for two terms from 1996 to 2006. In 2006, he took up the cause of women's reservation, and one of his close associates was elected unanimously as panchayat president. When she completed her term in 2011, another woman candidate was elected. But he continues to work towards improving panchayat functioning in Tamil Nadu and trying to network the good performing ones through a panchayat academy programme. He has been establishing models for viable village-level industries with the use of local resources.

Question 1: How did you decide to run for panchayat president in spite of being an engineer?

I was born in a middle-class family and was better off compared to other villagers who didn't have the same access to food, shelter, health and education. I saw a huge difference between Chennai, which is 40 km away, and my village, since development had not reached there even long after independence. I was inspired by the model village Kundrakudi developed by Kundrakudi Adigalar. His inspirational words had penetrated my mind and I opted to quit my job and decided to contest for panchayat president despite stiff opposition from my family to my leaving a permanent government job. I worked with the community from 1994 to 1996. When the panchayat election was conducted in October 1996, I contested and was elected president.

> 'There are plenty of Elangos who will take care of science and technology, but Elangos are not available to work in their villages. Even one Elango can make a big change and it will be a start.'
>
> —Kundrakudi Adigalar

> A panchayat president has to establish himself. Office-bearers observe whether the president is working for his own benefit or his functioning is at fault. If they find him above reproach, they are forced to change their negative mindset and he wins their respect.

Question 2: How are you able to bring about a consensus on development issues in the panchayat?

Generally, in panchayats, ward members get polarized due to reasons of caste, political affiliation, or personal interests. They try and group with like-minded ward members or they join forces with the vice president to create trouble in the functioning of the panchayat. Often the president himself may not know the rules well enough and get entangled in their machinations.

Another important factor in village panchayats is the gram sabha, which is nothing but the village community gathering. In most villages, the community is able to sit together and arrive at unanimity on some decisions despite there being disparities in social status or other differences. In my case, I made use of this opportunity and pushed my proposals through the gram sabha in a very transparent manner. If the ward members bring a positive agenda to the table, the panchayat will pass that and the gram sabha will endorse it. If the agenda is negative, the panchayat will ensure that the suggestions are discussed in the gram sabha.

> Right from the beginning, the plan preparation, plan approval, funds allocation, monthly and day-to-day expenses were placed before the gram sabha and total transparency was maintained in Kuthambakkam.

This is not applicable to Kuthambakkam panchayat alone. It is a constitutional mandate and law. But panchayats are yet to understand that they are constitutional bodies. By maintaining transparency, personal integrity and simplicity, I was able to garner the support of all the sections in a couple of years.

A SUCCESS STORY

The panchayat had to construct a stormwater drain which was a long-felt need of the village, particularly of the Dalits, as the rainwater flowed through their area. Every time it rained, the water stagnated over a long stretch, creating unhealthy conditions. When the panchayat prepared an estimate with the support of block-level engineers, the cost came to more than Rs 4 lakh, whereas the panchayat limit was Rs 1.5 lakh. With my experience in working with some of Kerala's state panchayats, I considered some innovative ways of reducing the cost. Instead of collecting rubble from the quarry, we decided to approach the nearby granite cutting and processing factory and collect the waste pieces. On the company premises itself, we employed people from our village and broke the pieces collected into smaller ones suited to our requirements. Just by spending one-fourth of the estimated cost on the stone, we were able to fulfil our need of this raw material. The transportation was facilitated by the tractor-owning farmers. Labour cost was also kept low through subsidy and voluntary work.

Then, the problems started. The block engineer objected to our use of rubble from the quarry. I, our panchayat and the villagers argued about the quality, the low cost, waste utilization and wage benefits of our process, but he rejected our argument. Despite the block engineer's objection and with the approval of the gram sabha, we started constructing the drain and completed it in a month and a half. The drain was completed at a cost of only Rs 1.6 lakh, which was almost one-third of the estimated cost and brought a lot of benefit to the people living along the drains.

However, the block engineer's objection went to the Collector and, without hearing us, the Collector suspended me under section 205 of the Tamil Nadu Panchayat Act. He proceeded further to remove me from my post. I met him and explained the whole process of decision-making but he wouldn't listen. My financial powers were taken away and the panchayat was kept in abeyance for three or four months. In the meantime, I had created enemies with some of my other initiatives like stopping the brewing of arrack and illegal quarrying. On the personal front, my family was annoyed with me for having lost my job, my money and my standing. All I had left with me was my honesty.

I met the press and explained the sequence of events and also my future plans. I even placed a challenge before the district collector that the matter could be discussed in the gram sabha and we could let it arrive at a decision. In this regard, I met the higher officials of the rural development department like the director and the secretary. The objections from the collector's side were read out in front of the director of rural development and I was given a chance to answer them. I explained the whole process and its advantages. When the block engineer raised doubts about the strength of the construction, the villagers took the officials to the site and demonstrated how solid it was. My suspension was withdrawn in the gram sabha itself and I was re-instated.

> There are many examples of good work in Tamil Nadu, such as that done by Odandurai panchayat in Karamadai block of Coimbatore district. There Mr Shanmugam, who is the president, undertook a number of development initiatives. He found an innovative way to tap water from the Amravati river, treat it and distribute it to the hamlets under the panchayat. This was the first panchayat in Tamil Nadu to make use of biomass waste to meet electricity needs. He connected the community toilets and individual toilets to feed a biogas plant. The electricity generated was supplied to the community. Another interesting initiative of this panchayat was setting up a 350 kW windmill. The power generated is sold to the grid and the loan is repaid with the help of the earnings. Likewise there are a number of panchayats, more than seventy in Tamil Nadu to my knowledge, that are showing similar initiative.

Question 3: It is said that only 10 per cent of the government programmes reach the bottom of the pyramid. Is it true? If so, how can we ensure that the delivery of services reaches the bottom of the pyramid consistently?

There are plenty of schemes and programmes flowing from central and state governments. Many of the schemes are implemented on paper only. They don't yield any benefit to the community. This is because the panchayat is unable to drive its own plan and schemes. Or the government does not recognize the fact that the panchayat can design its own plans. These are always designed at the government level, even given a name and forwarded to the panchayats to implement. Since they are neither panchayat programmes nor are they generated by the people but are simply implemented because of pressure from above, people don't identify with them or realize their value.

> **⇨ A MESSAGE FOR THE VILLAGE PANCHAYAT BOARD PRESIDENT AND THE GOVERMENT**
>
> The panchayat board president should be aware of his constitutional responsibilities and should have a vision for village development that he implements with honesty, integrity and team spirit. The government, instead of thrusting its programmes on village panchayats to implement, should help them evolve their own developmental plans which would be approved by their panchayat boards and gram sabhas. Certainly if such an ambience is created, the panchayat board president can bring about significant change.

In Kerala, the process of village-level planning and integrating it with the district-level planning is in progress. The state allocates funds to meet the requirements of the bottom of the pyramid. It is the gram sabha and the panchayat which implement the schemes. Shortfalls are compensated by contributions from the village community. So the panchayat system works as per the spirit of the panchayati raj there. The Kuthambakkam panchayat tried the same, but it was a struggle. More panchayats need to function like the Kerala ones.

> The gram sabha and village panchayat should have the right to plan and spend.

Question 4: *Does panchayati raj enable funds to reach directly to the panchayat? How can village panchayat revenues be improved?*

The Panchayat Raj, 73rd constitutional amendment, which provides for power and financial devolution to villages, remains on paper. In reality, the government is simply treating the panchayats as implementing agencies for state and central government schemes. Of course, exceptions like Kerala are there. The money that comes from the Centre is totally tied up with some grant, that is, it comes with the name, form, shape and duration of a scheme. And the village panchayat simply implements the scheme. Likewise, most state government schemes are sanctioned for the village panchayat, but they are implemented by block- and district-level authorities. So there is no close involvement of the panchayat. It has become easy for many panchayat board presidents to go along with this method of operation. On average, the amount that comes from the Centre is Rs 5 to 6 lakh/year/panchayat in Tamil Nadu. The state government fund also works out to be as much. But the panchayat has to struggle a lot to meet the essential expenditures like providing drinking water, maintenance of streetlights and sanitation. For that itself, the money is insufficient. Most panchayats struggle to meet the basic needs. And when corrupt practices enter the picture, the results can be imagined.

Panchayats should be educated about their functioning and they should feel that they are institutions of self-government as emphasized by the Constitution of India. When this happens, the village community will understand its priorities, and issues like sanitation will be resolved.

A Unique Self-Help Group Model

On 31 October 2013, V. Ponraj had attended a function to plant more than 1,00,000 tree saplings in Gopalasamuthiram in Thirunelveli district of Tamil Nadu, organized by film actor Vivek's Green Globe and Abdul Ghani of Youth Exnora and Grama Udhayam, an NGO operating in Thirunelveli and Tuticorin districts. I was astonished to learn about the quiet achievements of Grama Udhayam in bringing about a transformation in the lives of the people in these two districts. Grama Udhayam was started on 15 August 1999 with seven women members under the leadership provided by an ordinary citizen, V. Sundaresan. He started this NGO primarily to help the people affected by high-interest private finance (kandhu vatti, meter vatti).

Today it has 1,45,000 members from poor families and serves more than 5 lakh people in the two districts of Tamil Nadu covering

1,042 villages, thirty-four city units, 8,400 centres, and 14,620 self-help groups.

This SHG has not received even a rupee from the government or a private or any donor organization. But it has evolved a unique model that helps people save amounts ranging from Rs 10 to Rs 500 or more. Loans can be availed against savings such as for income generation, agriculture or for emergencies at an interest rate of 6 per cent. Even a rural development bank does not give loans at 6 per cent to villagers and farmers. What was not possible for established institutions to do, a simple man has achieved with his innovative idea and determination. With the accrued interest and return of loans by villagers, this model becomes a sustainable model.

So far small loans have been issued to 2,80,000 people and they have achieved 100 per cent return of loans. All their accounts are open to inspection. They have rescued 34,640 families from the trap of high and accumulated interest they owe to private financiers, and 26,000 women were given training and helped to start small companies. Through its social security scheme so far, Grama Udhayam has helped 186 families conduct last rites for their kin. It has brought many government services and schemes within the reach of people of these two districts, imparted literacy to women and helped youth in development of skills in the areas of law, banking and other occupations. It has conducted many medical camps, benefiting more than 25,000 people.

Sundaresan is a very simple and unassuming personality, who has enriched the quality of life of more than 1,00,000 families without any government support and private funding or donation. He is a role model for many panchayat leaders. His example shows that with honesty, commitment, integrity and a vision someone can make a dramatic change in people's lives. We need many more such leaders.

Work with Integrity and Succeed with Integrity

Ponraj recently met a young and energetic youth, Naresh Kumar, from Coimbatore. He was amazed to hear from him how he could get work done from government departments using the concept of the '0' rupee note proposed by 5th Pillar, a social service organization, to eliminate corruption.

He went, for instance, to the RTO office, and found that the application forms were issued outside by brokers at a cost instead of making them freely available to the people. He was told that if he wanted to get the application form for the licence directly from the RTO, he would have to wait for a week. When he approached an officer for the application form, the officer became agitated and accused him of being oversmart. No forms available, he told him. As a 5th Pillar-trained person, however, he maintained his cool and politely told the officer that this was the first time he was approaching the office with the confidence that he could get his work done without any middlemen. He should not be made to return disappointed. The official didn't budge, so he approached the PA to the regional transport officer and wanted to lodge a complaint with the collector and the vigilance commissioner about the state of the RTO. Hearing him out, the officer offered help and issued the forms, asked him to take the driving test, and ensured that he got good service at the office. He also assured him that all the forms would be made available and thanked him for bringing the matter to his notice.

Naresh Kumar could get all the work done thanks to the training imparted by Vijay Anand of 5th Pillar.

Reflections About the Emergence of Alternative Political Parties

What we witnessed in the December 2013 elections to the Delhi assembly has changed the perception of politics for many. The elections proved that the people of Delhi opted for the politics of development rather than traditional party loyalties and ideologies.

People love the leader who shows honesty and integrity, acts with courage in taking a decision, fights for the rights of the people, and has a vision for the future. Whenever such a leader takes charge, development takes its rightful place. In the absence of such creative and popular leadership, a fragmented mandate leads to a leadership constrained by narrow political alignments. Growth suffers, and progress is reversed.

SECTION IV

INDIVIDUALS AT THE GOVERNMENT LEVEL

India has several examples of model parliamentarians, such as the ones discussed in the section on 'Creative Leadership', though, of late, the country's focus has shifted to politicians with criminal records entering Parliament. National Election Watch (NEW) and the Association for Democratic Reforms (ADR— www.adrindia.org, www.myneta.info), two organizations that track political parties and elections in India, have analysed that 1,102 out of the 6,727 candidates (17 per cent) who stood for the 2014 general elections from Phases 1 to 7 had criminal cases against them.

The malaise affected all parties, with some having a high percentage of such candidates. It did not exclude even parties which were campaigning strongly against corruption.

However, while the criminalization of politics is certainly a cause for concern and is now being combated in a firm way, it is important to bear in mind there are a good number of parliamentarians who work diligently and have rendered great service. We need to appreciate their work.

Performance of MPs

The performance of MPs in the Lok Sabha is assessed on four parameters: (a) debates participated, (b) questions raised, (c) introduction of private members bills and (d) attendance. Generally, the top performing MPs in the Lok Sabha did well in their constituencies too.

In this regard, the Prime Point Foundation and PR-e-Sense, two non-governmental organizations, have been honouring the country's top performing MPs every year since 2010 by bestowing them with 'Sansad Ratna' awards. They analysed their performance on the basis of their attendance, the number of debates they participated in, the number of questions they asked and the number of private member bills they introduced. Following is a break-up of the top-performing MPs in 2013-14 with respect to different parameters.

Questions—15th Lok Sabha

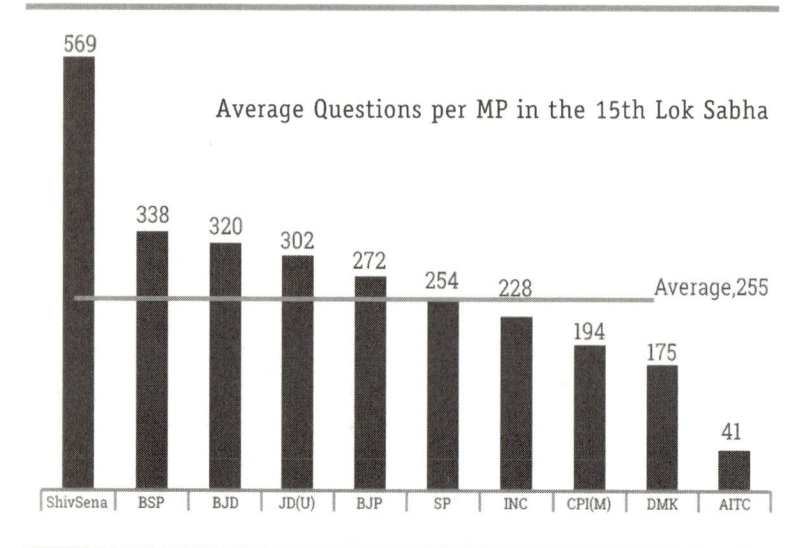

Average Questions per MP in the 15th Lok Sabha

ShivSena	569
BSP	338
BJD	320
JD(U)	302
BJP	272
SP	254
INC	228
CPI(M)	194
DMK	175
AITC	41

Average, 255

TOP 5 MPS BY QUESTIONS

Name	State	Constituency	Party	Questions
Anandrao Adsul	Maharashtra	Amravati	Shiv Sena	1,266
Gajanan Dharmshi Babar	Maharashtra	Maval	Shiv Sena	1,176
Asaduddin Owaisi	Andhra Pradesh	Hyderabad	All India Majlis-E-Ittehadul Muslimmen	1,129
Pradeep Kumar Majhi	Odisha	Nabarangpur	Congress	1,101
Shivaji Adhalrao Patil	Maharashtra	Shirur	Shiv Sena	1,082

TOP 5 MPS BY PRIVATE MEMBERS' BILLS

Name	State	Constituency	Party	Private Member Bills
Hansraj Gangaram Ahir	Maharashtra	Chandrapur	BJP	31
Jai Prakash Agarwal	Delhi	North East Delhi	Congress	23
Arjun Ram Meghwal	Rajasthan	Bikaner	BJP	20
Mahendrasinh Pruthvisinh Chauhan	Gujarat	Sabarkantha	BJP	18
Adhir Ranjan Chowdhury	West Bengal	Baharampur	Congress	18

In terms of attendance, 110 MPs scored more than 90 per cent, with K.P. Dhanapalan from the Chalakudy constituency of Kerala and Ramesh Kumar from the South Delhi constituency of Delhi registering 100 per cent.

The following MPs were the top performers overall:

OVERALL TOP PERFORMERS (DEBATES + PRIVATE BILLS + QUESTIONS)—TOTAL TALLY

Sl.	MP	Party/State	Total Tally
1	Anandrao Adsul	(SS, Maharashtra)	1,208
2	S.S. Ramasubbu	Cong, Tamil Nadu	1,141
3	Gajanan Dharmshi Baba	SS, Maharashtra	1,109
4	Arjun Ram Meghwal	BJP, Rajasthan	1,109

Eight MPs scored a total tally of more than 1,000. The other four MPs were: Asaduddin Owaisi, Hansraj G. Ahir, Pradeep Kumar Majhi and Shivaji Adhalrao Patil.

Top performers among women MPs: There were sixty-three women MPs in the 15th Lok Sabha. Among them, the top three performers overall were:

1. Supriya Sule (NCP, Maharashtra)—752
2. Ratna Singh (Congress, UP)—664
3. Rama Devi (BJP, Bihar)—652

Performance of the 15th Lok Sabha

The 15th Lok Sabha passed the lowest number of bills. It passed 177 out of the 326 bills listed for consideration in its five-year term, as per PRS Legislative Research Data. The 13th Lok Sabha passed 297 bills and the 14th Lok Sabha passed 248 bills. What is expected from every parliamentarian is purposeful, involved discussion to legislate and enact laws and pass the bills which will help bring in inclusive development. The 15th Lok Sabha adopted the Lokpal bill, an issue which had been pending for the last four decades. The food security bill, which seeks to provide cheap food grains to 67 per cent of the poor people of the country, was cleared during the tenure of the Lok Sabha. The land acquisition bill, which will give a better price to the farmer for his land and also a say in the matter, was also adopted by the House, even though it doesn't have the scope to make the farmer a partner in any commercial venture involving his land. The other important bills passed were: the Street Vendors (Protection of Livelihood and Regulation of Street Vending) Bill, 2012; the Civil Liability for Nuclear Damage Rules, 2011; the Right of Children to Free and Compulsory Education (Amendment) Bill, 2010; the Agricultural and Processed Food Products Export Development Authority (Amendment) Bill, 2008; the Right to Information Act (RTI), 2005.

But often bills don't get passed smoothly in Parliament due to divisions on party lines, and a majority-vs-minority, coalition-vs-individual parties or regional-vs-central approach. If not these, there are other issues like scams and controversies over public policy and external affairs.

Hence, seeing all this, if we are to truly work towards creative leadership, what does the performance of MPs tell us?

Reflections of Top-performing MPs

When we analysed the performance of Parliament and its members, we felt we should hear from the MPs of the 15th Lok Sabha about the nature of their role, performance and challenges. This might give an insight to the youth into how they can pursue development politics. Hence, based on the PRS Legislative Research study and the Prime Point Foundation's Sansad Ratna Award, we sent a questionnaire to the best MPs and got their answers. We also had discussions with them on the challenges that they have faced during their political careers.

Question 1: As an MP, what is your contribution to your constituency and also to the nation?

Answer 1: Hansraj Ahir, MP (BJP) from Chandrapur, Maharashtra

I tried to do justice to my position and fulfil the expectations of my constituency. I would like to mention the issue of giving increased rates for the land of farmers which was taken for coal mines and for other projects of the government and private companies. The rate was previously Rs 20,000 to Rs 1 lakh per acre. It has now become Rs 6 lakh for barren land, Rs 8 lakh for non-irrigated land and Rs 10 lakh for irrigated land. Besides this, the PAP (Project Affected Persons), including women, are to be given jobs as per their education. Among other efforts, I opened a museum, made treatment free for sickle cell anemia patients from tribal areas and obtained travel concession on trains for them.

Answer 2: S.S. Ramasubbu, MP (Congress) from Thirunelveli, Tamil Nadu

As an MP from Thirunelveli, I have performed well in all my endeavours on the floor of Parliament and outside the House as well. Due to my efforts in Parliament, more than fourteen new trains, new railway lines, electrification of the line from Kanyakumari to Madurai and construction of bridges, railway stations, and a railway reservation centre was undertaken in my constituency. Employee State Insurance Corporation and beedi workers' hospitals were established and educational assistance to beedi workers of Rs 11 crore per year has been sanctioned. I brought the onslaught of dengue in my constituency to the notice of the PM and arranged immediate medical assistance to stop the outbreak. I helped to create massive awareness in support of Kudankulam nuclear power project through a campaign. I requested adequate funds for Tamiraparani and Chitthar river development. The four-lane project from Tuticorin to Thirunelveli was pending for a long time. Funds from Kadayam to Mukkudal and Athiyur to Surandai for Rs 22 crore were also sanctioned.

I have helped poor people suffering from serious ailments get financial assistance from the Prime Minister's Relief Fund. More than 125 patients were benefitted and the amount of assistance was in the range of Rs 50,000 to Rs 3 lakh.

Answer 3: Arjun Ram Meghwal, MP (BJP) from Bikaner, Rajasthan

My major contribution was to raise constituency-related issues in Parliament and its committees and forums.

For example: at the time of my election in 2009, there was no rail connectivity from Delhi to Bikaner. I raised the issue many times in Parliament and ultimately Bikaner got not only a direct train from Delhi but now it is also linked with Chennai, Puri, and Hyderabad. In respect of national interest, I raised the issue of construction of a dam on the Brahmaputra river by China. There is strong evidence that China has begun constructing a dam on the Brahmaputra river which it calls the Yarlungzangbo (better known as Yarlong Tsangpo to the Tibetans). The matter has received serious attention and the government has taken some important initiatives to protect the Indian interest. There are many other examples of my raising matters of national interest in Parliament.

Answer 4: Anandrao Adsul, MP (Shiv Sena) from Amravati, Maharashtra

The questions I have raised pertain to my constituency as well as my state and the nation. The questions are relevant to all sections of society. I have secured the no.1 position for raising questions both in the 14th Lok Sabha and the 15th Lok Sabha (till the latest monsoon session 2013).

Question 2: How did you spend the MPLAD funds for the development of the constituency?

Answer 1: Hansraj Ahir

In case of the use of the MPLAD fund, I give priority to local problems like supply of drinking water, approach roads in remote areas, internal roads where the government does not sanction funds. There is no criterion of caste, religion, creed while distributing the development funds.

Answer 2: S.S. Ramasubbu

There are many assurances given to the people during election campaigns and I am trying my level best to fulfil those. I cannot say to what percentage they have been done. Many problems crop up even after getting elected and I try to solve them and meet expectations as best as I can.

Answer 3: Arjun Ram Meghwal

MPLAD funds are meant for development schemes. I generally convene meetings in the villages and ask the people what they would like done. After getting unanimity in the village meeting, we decide on the scheme and I sanction the MPLAD fund accordingly. In the urban part of the constituency the same procedure is followed. Mainly the amount is used in construction of facilities like a community hall, schools, compound wall for a cremation ground, tubewell in a rural area and so on.

Answer 4: Anandrao Adsul

I used my MPLAD fund to meet urgent needs like roads, samaj

mandirs, or small drinking water schemes. More than 25 per cent of the fund is used for computer labs in primary and secondary schools. Some portion of the funds is used even for computers for use in jail.

Question 3: *Will you be able to fulfil the promises made in your election manifesto to the people of your constituency? If so to what extent?*

Answer 1: Hansraj Ahir
Assurances are given to the people during elections and I am trying my level best to fulfil the assurances. But many problems crop up even after getting elected to the post of MP and I honestly try my level best to solve the problems and live up to the expectations of the people and my assurances.

Answer 2: S.S. Ramasubbu
In order to enhance the per capita income of rural people, the Mahatma Gandhi National Rural Employment Act (MGNREGA) has been made use of, helping the rural poor, and particularly women, in getting regular employment. The result is reflected in the purchasing power and the savings, which have increased spectacularly.

Answer 3: Arjun Ram Meghwal
Two types of promises are made by candidates while campaigning. One is related to the party manifesto, the second to local issues which require personal attention after election. One promise I made was that if elected the process of closing the Bikaner Railway Workshop will be discontinued. After meetings with railway authorities, I could fulfil that promise.

Answer 4: Anandrao Adsul
I have very much been able to fulfil the promises which I made in the election manifesto as I have completed the 138 km Amravati—Narkher rail line. I also succeeded in completing the 160 km Nagpur—Amravati stretch of NH6. I helped to run the Finlay Mill by allotting 8.5 acre of land for the boiler for the mill. I have taken

Individuals at the Government Level

steps to start Akashwani Kendra, which was not running for want of a transformer and staff.

Question 4: How do you prepare yourself for debates in Parliament?

Answer 1: Hansraj Ahir
Two types of bills are submitted in the House, government bills and private member bills. Government bills need extensive preparation. While presenting a private member bill, discussion with colleagues, government officers and senior leaders is beneficial.

Answer 2: S.S. Ramasubbu
I make full utilization of the opportunity given by my party to participate in the discussion on various bills. I regularly read newspapers, magazines and interact with people to update myself. I collect reference materials from the Parliament library. Before entering a debate on any issue, I thoroughly study the contents and concepts of the bills.

Answer 3: Arjun Ram Meghwal
The general practice is that the Lok Sabha secretariat sends the bills in advance to the MP. I read the provisions of the bills carefully and try to get reference material from the Parliament library reference desk. Nowadays, one can take advantage of the internet, electronic and print media and the bill-briefing sessions of PRS legislative research. I prepare a point-wise note for the pros and cons of the bill that helps me debate it in Parliament.

Answer 4: Anandrao Adsul
For any discussion on any subject or any new bills or amendments, I have taken the help of old records from the library and also the internet.

Question 5: As an MP, will you be able to discuss and bring change in the policy for public good?

Answer 1: Hansraj Ahir
To bring about a change in policy, we have different avenues:

question hour, zero hour, starred questions, un-starred questions, private member's bill, stop motion and so on. Besides this, I am a member of six different standing and consultative committees and these committees can also be used for framing policies and discussion.

Answer 2: S.S. Ramasubbu
I suggest necessary changes in policy matters based on the overall good. On MGNREGA, I urged the government to utilize the services of the people who are willing to work under this scheme, in the agricultural field. Similarly, I have urged the government to fix a minimum support price (MSP) for agricultural produce like vegetables, fruits, etc, thereby ensuring their continued supply to the market while meeting the interests of their producers. Our fishermen are being attacked, killed by a neighbouring navy frequently. They are arrested and their vessels and fishing materials captured. They have to brave natural calamities also. They face several difficulties and challenges in their day-to-day lives. Keeping their interests in mind, I have several times urged the government to address the genuine grievances of the community. I have also introduced a private member's bill on the floor of the Lok Sabha, called the 'Fishermen Community Welfare Bill'. I have been demanding for long the setting up of a separate Ministry of Fishery. This will help provide adequate funds for the welfare of fishermen and also in redressing their grievances.

Answer 3: Arjun Ram Meghwal
There may be some more examples related to changing public policy while debating in Parliament, but I am giving three concrete ones related to compensation of unorganized workers. For example, while I was speaking on the Workmen's Compensation (Amendment) Bill, 2009, on 25 November, I raised the point that you are providing compensation in the proposed amendment only if somebody falls from a height of 20 feet, whereas in the desert area of Rajasthan or some other parts of the country houses and buildings

are usually ten to eighteen feet high only. The minister made it clear while replying to the bill that somebody falling from a building one storey high or twelve feet or more would also be eligible for compensation.

There have been constructive inputs on other issues too such as safety measures for safai karamcharis.

Answer 4: Anandrao Adsul
There are so many challenges which prevent me and other politicians from working for the nation. Like corruption in all sectors, whether it is education, health, telephone department, even in sports, or coal where thousands of crores are misappropriated by the persons who are in power. If that money had been utilized for development, our country would be a world power. No employment problems, no below or above poverty line, good education, good health schemes, good means of transportation, better irrigation. So many things would have taken place.

Question 6: What are the challenges that prevent you from fulfilling your vision for the nation? What are the factors that limit your performance, whether it is corruption, nepotism, biased approach or anything else that you come across? If so, how do you overcome that?

Based on MPs' responses: Genuine, development activities are quite often stalled due to the lackadaisical attitude of the officials of the ministry concerned. Even though one wants to be an honest and sincere politician, the people around one, for example, partymen, expect undue favours in some form or the other. If their wishes are not fulfilled, they are ready to turn against the politician and switch their loyalty. Some unscrupulous people are even ready to purchase votes. Society seldom recognizes honest people.

A leadership is needed that can bring a change in the policies which are hampering growth. Policies which are approved by Parliament or reforms suggested by its committees should be implemented properly and monitored.

Question 7: As an MP, what is your advice to the youth who want to become leaders or would like to enter politics?

In essence, the answer of Hansraj Ahir summed it up. The youth need to enter politics. The present generation is educated, has vision, these people are the need of the nation and the present time. The youths who want to enter politics must come and serve the motherland.

S.S. Ramasubbu says, 'If we work genuinely for the cause of the public, they will give us repeated opportunities to serve them. After all, honesty, sincerity, service motive and perfection are the prerequisites for entering politics.'

TIPS FROM POLITICIANS

- The youth ought to start from a clean slate and move on to give their best to the people.
- A youth should be a committed social worker always ready to work for the betterment of the society. Then only can he become a perfect leader in politics.
- Though caste, creed, religion and money power play a very important role in politics, even so any youth of this country, if he has a good character, good knowledge, technical and mental capability, can change the political scenario.
- Politics is no business or industry but sheer public service, service to the motherland. Youth can enter it and take it to a stature where it will be seen with respect. The youth must have willpower and have resolve while working in this field.

Question 8: Do you feel that bureaucrats/ministers are cooperative and responsive to the demands of the public in delivering good governance and services on time?

Answer 1: Hansraj Ahir
Ministers, bureaucrats, the administrative system—they are all

meant for the betterment of the people. Sometimes we have to pursue an issue with those concerned and change their view and then only the work gets done.

Answer 2: S.S. Ramasubbu
The ministers and bureaucrats are normally cooperative while discharging their official duties. The irony is that they follow cumbersome procedures which delay the decision- making process relating to the developmental works. Nepotism, favouritism and red-tapism have played roles in obstructing the functioning of the government greatly. If the genuine and immediate demands of the public are to be addressed, quick action needs to be taken at the levels of both the political and permanent executives. Then only the voice of the public can be appropriately heard and concrete action will be visible in our public policy.

Answer 3: Arjun Ram Meghwal
It differs from person to person. Some bureaucrats are very good and some ministers too in delivering the services. I have seen some cases where the ministers and bureaucrats are not complementary to each other, but these are the stray cases. If they are not delivering good governance than it is the fault of the system, not the individual. We must improve the system and the governance would automatically improve.

Answer 4: Anandrao Adsul
In today's politics, I found, very few bureaucrats and ministers are sensible and responsive to the demands of the public in delivering services. It is a reflection of the lack of timely response that we are facing corruption, price rise, terrorism, suicide of farmers, insecurity on the borders, shortage of power and so many things.

Conclusion: From the responses of the MPs it is clear they are able to perform amidst all the challenges and deliver their best to the nation and their constituency. Many achievements of today such as the Green Revolution, White Revolution, IT and software revolution, achievements in defence, space, atomic energy and scientific capability are possible because of political leadership, executive leadership, scientific and technological research, leadership at community level, all coming together to achieve a vision and realize mission targets. To make the nation great, visionary political leadership is essential at all times. The youth should understand the importance of electing a wise leadership.

Reflections of Bureaucrats

We spoke with two former CECs (chief election commissioners) who had an impeccable record as bureaucrats about the state of the political system and some key aspects of the present electoral system.

T.S. Krishna Murthy (TSK) conducted the 2004 general elections and introduced electronic voting machines in all 543 constituencies. His recommendations for electoral reforms are with the government. He is an advocate of state funding of elections.

Needamangalam Gopalaswami (NG) conducted the first few phases of the 2009 general elections. He strongly advocates inner-party democracy in real terms and transparent party funding.

Question 1: Once a candidate spends money to do social or public service, how can we expect him not to indulge in corruption to get the money back?

TSK: Money plays a very important role in an election, be it a panchayati or parliamentary election. Once a candidate is required to spend large sums of money, he or she will willy-nilly raise funds illegally. Further, such persons will have to compromise in policy matters while holding elected office by extending favours to those who funded them. In fact, in my book, *The Miracle of Democracy*, I have clearly stated that political corruption is the starting point of corruption elsewhere. When the leaders make money, bureaucrats high and low also find it convenient to make money on the sly.

Individuals at the Government Level

NG: The first question is itself misplaced. The answer is in the second question.

Question 2: Has public service become a business?

TSK: Unfortunately, public service has indeed over the years become a business. Those who contest in the elections consider the expenditure as an investment for making quick income. This was confirmed by some parliamentarians in their speeches, telecast by electronic media. A careful study of the wealth of the successful legislators will prove that politics is the most lucrative business in many developing countries.

NG: Corruption is indulged in not because a candidate spends money on social or public service. It is the enormous public spending that governments do now combined with lack of transparency, absence of an effective system of accountability, and an overburdened, archaic legal system that can be evaded practically forever, making quick retribution for wrongdoing by public servants virtually impossible, that leads public office-holders to indulge in corruption uninhibitedly. Politics is now the quickest way to become rich. So the candidate, in expectation of enormous return on his investment, spends money in social service (not public service) to build a loyal clientele. Yes, public service, barring a few honourable exceptions, is a business for most.

> Rules allow candidates to spend Rs 70 lakh on campaigns for a seat in Parliament but the real cost of winning is about ten times that, thanks to spending on rallies, fuel and media campaigns that often include payments for coverage. The Election Commission estimated that the 2014 Lok Sabha elections cost the exchequer Rs 3,500 crore. That's about 150 per cent more than the amount spent for the 2009 polls (Rs 1,400 crore). This does not include the expenses incurred on security and the amount political parties will spend.

> The corporates/industry could be allowed to contribute to a new fund, called the National Election Fund, and such donors could be given 100 per cent tax rebate from their taxable income to incentivize such donations.

Question 3: How can we reform this scenario, which is the root cause of political turmoil and keeps the youth away from politics?

TSK: In my opinion, the remedy lies in snapping the nexus between the corporate/non- corporate donors and political parties. What is happening today is that as permitted under the Company Law provisions, profit-making companies are free to make donations to political parties within certain limits. They are allowed a tax rebate of 50 per cent on donations made to political parties which have to be reported by the parties quarterly to the Election Commission of India if each donation exceeds Rs 20,000. In turn, the Election Commission is required to place these details on its website for the benefit of the public. The donor companies very often placate political parties, both the ruling party and Opposition party, by giving donations so that they do not become persona non grata with whoever comes to power. Sometimes, I believe, donations are made in cash by certain corporates without routing them through their books of account. My suggestion is to ban all donations to political parties by corporate or non-corporate donors. The only funding to the political party should be from among their own members, for which an individual ceiling can be there for each member and his family, as is prevalent in Canada. The advantage of such a proposal is that political parties need not curry favour with the corporates for donations and reward them later with compromises in policy matters. The second benefit of this is that the entire fund obtained by the National Election Fund could be used by the Election Commission for conducting elections by suitable allocation of funds and/or benefits in kind like petrol coupons, poster papers of prescribed size, etc. Initially, the funds could be used only for Parliament and legislature elections and the local elections could be covered later in a phased manner.

Under such a scheme all candidates will have a level playing field and there will not be any huge disparity between one candidate and another in the campaign expenditure. It is true that in the initial years we may not get substantial donations to such a fund and the deficiency in the total election expenditure will have to be met by the central government. This deficiency can be borne by the Centre or the state as the case may be if the election is held for Parliament or state legislature separately and shared equally if the elections are held for state assemblies and the Parliament simultaneously. Over time, the donations will be substantial partly because of the 100 per cent tax rebate and partly because of people's increasing faith in free and fair elections with no role for money power. The allocation of funds to the candidates will be done by the Election Commission on the basis of guidelines framed in consultation with an all-party advisory board consisting of representatives from national and state parties only.

Question 4: How can we increase the voting percentage to above 90 per cent?

TSK: As regards increasing the voter turnout from the present average of 60 to 65 per cent to 90 per cent, it has to be a multi-pronged strategy. The Election Commission has to encourage voluntary organizations to promote voter education and awareness about the elections by suitable incentives, monetary and otherwise. Secondly, political parties can be compelled by law to provide for certain expenditure in educating the voters about the election process through media publicity/election literature. The Supreme Court judgement providing an option for voters to express their displeasure with the candidates put up by parties by choosing not to vote for any candidate will certainly enthuse some indifferent voters to turn up at the polling booth on Election Day. Some innovative incentives could be considered through voluntary agencies, such as by providing incentives to all those participating in voting, as is done in some countries. Internet voting could be selectively introduced under supervised booths in notified places for senior citizens, handicapped persons and those in uniformed services like the army, the police and Central paramilitary forces. While some persons may advocate compulsory voting, it is not feasible in a country like India as of now because even with about 70 per cent voter turnout, the election officials will be obliged to chase the remaining 30 per cent, each one of them individually, which is a time-consuming exercise. In Australia it is successful because 95 per cent of the voters exercise their vote and only 5 per cent are to be pursued for not exercising their franchise.

NG: There is no 'right' methodology that can be an answer for all the ills. But perhaps the following may help in attracting high voting percentage:

1. Compulsory voting;
2. First past the post (FPTP) to decide the winner but with the stipulation that the winner should have a minimum of 50 per cent plus 1 vote out of all the polled votes (including the ones under 'NOTA'), failing which a re-run should be carried out;
3. If 'NOTA' scores more votes, the re-election should be with a new set of candidates;
4. Those candidates charge-sheeted in any crime out of those listed under the 'disqualification' of members under section 8 of the Representation of People Act, 1951, should be deemed as ineligible to contest;
5. Full state spending support to candidates for election campaign;
6. Transparency in party funds;
7. Inner-party democracy in reality (and not as practised now)

With these conditions in place the electorate, especially the young, respond with greater enthusiasm to vote for candidates of stature and integrity.

Question 5: What is your suggestion for the youth to enter politics?

TSK: One important suggestion for promoting the participation of youth in politics is to provide by law that certain posts within the party will be filled up only by persons below the age of forty or fifty. Second, we have to provide that one-third of the posts in the council of ministers should be filled up only by youth below forty. Thirdly, there can be an age ceiling for candidates contesting the elections. For example, we can provide that persons above the age of seventy cannot contest elections but can hold advisory posts in the party. Another possible change could be that the candidates for the election should be selected by the members of the party in each constituency (as in the party primaries in the US) instead of the Central Election Committee of the party nominating candidates on various questionable grounds.

NG: In my view, expecting youth (those under 30–35 years of age) to be in politics is too idealistic. An average young person is bothered about completing his studies, acquiring education that can provide sustenance for him and family and only after he is sure he has the wherewithal can he think of contributing actively in politics.

The idealistic youth who want to enter politics at a very young age, braving indigent circumstances, are too small in number. At one extreme are the children of the politicians and the well-heeled who do not need to worry where the next meal is coming from, and at the other extreme are the no-good, undereducated, good-for-nothing whose only qualification is muscle power and being able to do the dirty work for their boss who can afford to enter politics at a young age. Hence the phenomenon of dynastic rule in most political parties. No amount of wishful thinking can bring the youth to politics in a big way. It should suffice if the youth become aware and do not shirk their responsibility to exercise their franchise regularly. There is a need for serious reform in the functioning of parties to make these democratic, giving precedence to merit and not accident of birth.

Conclusion

The responses from the former CECs of the Election Commission make it clear that reforms are needed in the election system to make the political system transparent, vibrant and competent to make this nation great. There are good suggestions such as: state funding of elections, banning donations to political parties by corporates and industry, multi-pronged strategies for more than 90 per cent voter turnout, setting more than 50 per cent of the polled votes as a mark for victory, and reforms such as recall, referendum, rulemaking and financial autonomy to the Election Commission, and that MPs and MLAs should carry the responsibilities of passing the laws in Parliament and in creating political awareness among the youth. Suggestions included steps to reduce the election expenditure and set up a system which can help reduce influencing voters through money power. The Election Commission should be empowered to implement the measures to reduce the election-related expenditure.

   a. First, the existing First-Past-The-Post system of voting needs to be changed as it has resulted in proliferation of parties based on caste, creed, language, etc., and multiplicity of candidates by which even a person with 15 per cent to 20 per cent of votes polled can get elected. This results in a distorted democracy as a person with 20 per cent of votes is expected to represent the whole constituency. Moreover, such candidates very often lack national outlook/vision. There are many alternatives like proportional representation, the list system with preferential voting, etc.
   b. A separate law needs to be enacted for regulating political parties providing therein for regulatory measures in respect of their formation, functions, internal democracy by rotation of posts, transparency in financial matters, resolution of disputes within the party and other subjects.
   c. The criminals charged by courts of law with heinous offences

should be disqualified from contesting during the pendency of the case in the court until acquittal.
d. The model code of conduct should be given a statutory shape provided the enforcement/punishing power such as monetary penalty or disqualification of candidates/voters is with the Election Commission.
e. Need to do away with by-election after three years tenure of the House by giving out an option either to the party to nominate another party representative or declare the person who was at no.2 in the votes polled as the interim representative. Also, ensure that election petitions are disposed of within a period of one year from the date of filing of the petition.
f. The alternative of Proportional Representation (PR) system is not a panacea. It has its advantage in so far as it gives the loser parties representation too (as against the winner-take-all FPTP system) and thereby a voice to the other voters (those who voted for the losing side). But this will work well only if the number of parties is small. In the current scenario where there are as many as fifty to sixty 'serious' parties and another 100 or so parties involving themselves in the electoral arena (at the last count the number of registered political parties was over 1,250, but barring 150-odd, the rest are not serious contenders), PR system may, if not formulated tightly, lead to unwieldy coalitions making governance impossible.
g. In the PR system, the party is the focus. While there can be doubts about parties selecting the right kind of candidates, the risks/uncertainties are not higher than is the case today where parties select dubious candidates on 'winnability' criteria. In the PR system it is the party's performance and image that is primary and the people have the choice to vote for those candidates of the party who are perceived to be better. Since the list will not be a surprise and is known to the voters, the chances that the right candidates will not be selected will be just as much as in the FPTP system.

h. Reduce the number of days for canvassing to seven to ten from the date of declaration of the candidates who are contesting by the Election Commission
i. Electronic media, newspaper, FM radio, mobile phones and local TV channels may be used for election campaign effectively at subsidized rates prescribed by the government.
j. Candidates can distribute pamphlets to individual homes containing their manifesto for the constituency and state.
k. Each village panchayat board working with the local government should arrange a platform for the parties to come and seek votes in a common place or they can use mobile vans and jeeps for meeting the people and convey their action plan for the constituency.
l. Booth slips should be distributed only by the government agencies. No door-to-door canvassing by the political parties to influence the voters by cash or other forms of influence should be allowed.
m. No parties should set up booth tent near the polling station in a 2,000 metre radius to reduce the booth expenditure by the candidates.
n. In case of the death of an elected MLA or MP, the holding party should be able to nominate their own eligible candidate, to minimize the wasteful expenditure by the government as well as the parties.
o. Bringing synchronous elections to panchayat, state assemblies and Parliament should be the ultimate aim to reduce the multiple expenditure all through the year.
p. Making the UIDAI or national ID once established mandatory for voting and curb expenditure on duplicating the work done already by issuing fresh voter ID. Allow online voters to register their ID and make UIDAI/national ID mandatory for all registrations.
q. Create a secured online voting portal. Mobile app for voting under the E-voting Cloud system which can connect the

polling stations through the robust and secured ICT system such as the electronic voting machines to avoid duplicate voting. Since we follow a postal voting system, certainly we can adopt this online voting system which will be accessible only once for a voter if he or she has successfully voted.

r. Ultimately introducing the right type of election system such as Proportional Representation or any other that is appropriate to our conditions which helps represent 80 per cent of the constituency with full state funding of elections.

Parliament Members Are Nation Builders

As I had indicated earlier, I undertook many initiatives to realize the mission of propagating Developed India Vision 2020. After brain storming, we had finalized a methodology by which I would make use of every opportunity I got as President to spread the message. We had designed many programmes whereby I would interact with the Prime Minister, Opposition leaders, Parliament members, governors, chief ministers, state legislators, media and the people. I believe Parliament is the supreme body to build the nation. Hence my first focus was to interact with MPs. Let me narrate how the breakfast meeting with MPs evolved.

Breakfast Meeting with Parliament Members

One of the highlights in the early days of my presidency, I consider, was inviting the MPs state-wise for a breakfast meeting at Rashtrapati Bhawan, so that I could get firsthand knowledge about the status of development in our states and Union Territories. These meetings were held during a period of about three months, commencing from 11 March 2003 to 6 May 2003. Their impact on me continues even today. While the duration of the breakfast meetings was about an hour, the objective for the series of meetings was well laid out and I and my team had several weeks to prepare for them. Power Point presentations were made with accent on three areas (1) Vision for developed India (2) Heritage of the state (3) Core competence of a state. It goes without saying that to achieve overall development of the nation, the process has to start from developing the state. Hence a fourth aspect was also prepared: selected development indicators for each state. It was enriching to prepare these presentations and interact with the honourable MPs cutting across party lines. I gained an intimate knowledge of each state and its strengths and all the MPs became familiar to me and my friends irrespective of their party affiliation.

Before each meeting, about four weeks of research and compilation on the competencies and development requirements of each state was carried out. The information was collected from the Planning Commission, government departments—central and state—various national and international assessments of the state and other relevant documents. They were analysed and put in a presentable form of graphics and multimedia.

Our first meeting was with MPs from Bihar. I was encouraged by the enthusiasm of the MPs. As they felt that the time allotted was too short, we extended it from 60 to 90 minutes. We had the pleasant experience that even after the breakfast meeting was over, after all the Q&A sessions, many members continued to show interest in the visual presentation about their state. A document titled President's Breakfast Meeting with Members of Parliament was brought out.

Personally I relished every moment of the meeting. It was a real education for me on the needs of each state. The preparations were complemented by the field-level inputs of the members. Many of the members also told me that such comprehensive preparation was useful for them. As a matter of fact, these details and discussions have continued to be a major communication bond between me and the MPs throughout my presidency and beyond. Even now, when I meet them while travelling or at a gathering, development becomes a basis for discussions.

Vision 2020, which evolved with inputs from many experts, led me to focus on various aspects of societal transformation. The

Individuals at the Government Level

breakfast interactions gave me further ideas on paths to progress. When I presented any aspect of the India 2020 Vision in Parliament, I would have talked at least nine times on this vision in Parliament and addressed fourteen state assemblies on missions to prosperity of a state. The type of questions and suggestions I received in the breakfast meetings paved the way for consolidating possible requirements of a state's development such as in respect of waterways, employment generation, activating the public health centres, improving connectivity in the rural areas and enriching the education system. This database became a reference tool to illustrate how the India 2020 vision could be achieved in my addresses to national and state chambers of commerce and industry, management associations and technical institutions. Later, as a logical outcome the ten pillars of Vision 2020 evolved that I speak about with professionals, leaders and researchers from different fields.

Besides these interactions, I had an opportunity to address MPs from the Lok Sabha and Rajya Sabha over ten times. At a commemorative function to celebrate the 150th anniversary of our movement for independence, I had conveyed a message which brings out the responsibility of Parliament members to their constituency, to their state, and to the nation. I said:

> Our movement to true freedom and independence is still incomplete; our story is still unfolding. The global environment, however, is still dangerous and India's freedom won by suffering and sacrifice has to be alertly guarded, strengthened and expanded. Freedom and independence must be our continuing quest, and in such a manner as to accelerate our evolution as a free nation through bold and swift development. Can we keep this perspective while we celebrate the 150th anniversary of the freedom movement? The time has now arrived for Parliament and legislative assemblies to emerge with a new vision and leadership to make our nation not only

enlightened, united, harmonious, rich and prosperous, but above all, a safe nation, invulnerable forever to invasion and infiltration across its borders.

National leadership for realizing and sustaining the distinctive profile of a strong and prosperous India which I have discussed can emerge only when there is coherent, orderly and effective leadership from our Parliament and legislative assemblies.

Roles and Responsibilities of Member of Parliament

Each MP represents over two million constituents. Each year, Parliament passes an average of sixty bills. Thus, MPs are required to legislate on a range of issues over a short period of time.

But the people's perspective about MPs is as follows:

- What did you do for the constituency?
- Why have you not desilted our village tank?
- Why have you not given a water connection to my street?
- Why have you not set right the drainage issue in our village?
- Can you help my son get a job in the railways?
- Can you get a transfer done for my daughter?
- Why have we not seen you after the election?

Common people do not differentiate between elected representatives, whether they are MP, MLA or panchayat president. For them their immediate concerns have priority, hence whoever comes as a people's representative is expected to help sort out their local and domestic problems. They do not expect major reforms, societal transformation and other change in the political system. They have faith in one or the other individual, a charismatic or powerful leader at the national or state level. They believe that such leaders will do well for them and remain confident that they will enrich the quality of life of the people.

Question Hour Disrupted

Parliament starts with Question Hour at 11 a.m. daily. The government is forced to give reply to many of the issues raised relating to the states and constituencies. When there are disruptions, the purpose of Question Hour gets lost and the ministers escape having to clarify important issues. This is a very sorry state of affairs. Disruption and cancellation of Question Hour is against the interest of the people and wishes of our Constitution-makers.

> The Member of Parliament is generally expected to perform roles such as:
> - Making laws and bills,
> - Oversee the working of the government,
> - Scrutinize and approve the budget and
> - Represent the voters in Parliament.

BUSINESS DONE IN LOK SABHA

QUESTIONS: The first hour of every sitting is for answering questions.

HALF-AN-HOUR DISCUSSIONS: Discussion on matters arising out of an answer to a question.

ADJOURNMENT MOTIONS: Motion for an adjournment of the business of the House for the purpose of discussing a definite matter of urgent public importance.

LEGISLATION: Bills originating in the House, introduction and publications of bills.

BILLS SEEKING TO AMEND THE CONSTITUTION: These bills can be introduced in either House of Parliament. If sponsored by a private member, the bill has to be examined in the first instance and recommended for introduction by the committee on private members' bills and resolutions before it is included for introduction in the list of business. Motions for introduction of the bills are decided by simple majority.

PETITIONS: Any matter of general public interest and on the bills published or introduced or any matter pending before the House.

PRIVATE MEMBERS' RESOLUTION: A member other than a minister can move a resolution.

MOTIONS: Discussions on matters of public interest.

SHORT DURATION DISCUSSIONS: Discussion on a matter of urgent public importance.

CALLING ATTENTION: Speaker calls the attention of a minister to any matter of urgent public importance.

FINANCIAL BUSINESS: Budget.

PRIVILEGES: Raise a question involving a breach of privilege either of a member or of the House or of a committee.

SUBORDINATE LEGISLATION: A regulation, rule, sub-rule, bye-law etc. framed in pursuance of the Constitution or of the legislative functions delegated by Parliament to a subordinate authority is laid before the House.

RULE NO 377: The rule is meant to bring to the notice of the House a matter which is not a point of order.

MEMBER OF PARLIAMENT LOCAL AREA DEVELOPMENT FUNDS (MPLAD): Under the scheme, each MP has the choice to suggest to the district collector works to the tune of Rs 5 crore per annum to be taken up in his/her constituency.

It is the responsibility of the leaders of the various political parties to ensure that the Question Hour is used productively and run smoothly. How much money is wasted by such disruptions? What are the actual sitting hours?

Individuals at the Government Level

A day in Parliament

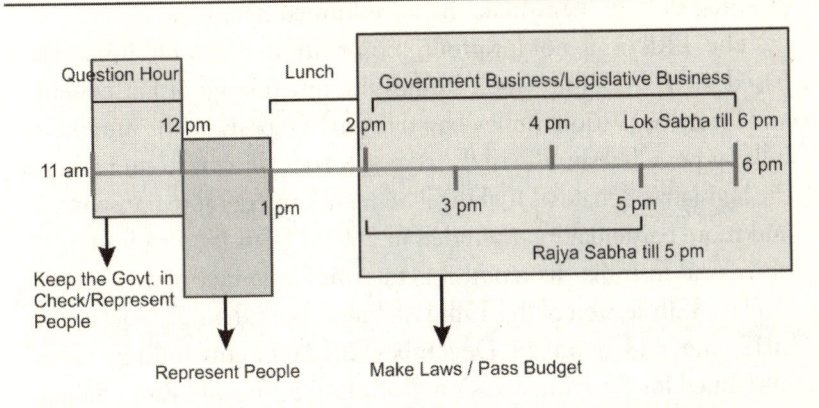

```
Question Hour           Lunch      Government Business/Legislative Business
              12 pm            2 pm              4 pm      Lok Sabha till 6 pm
11 am                                                                    6 pm
                           1 pm          3 pm          5 pm
                                                Rajya Sabha till 5 pm
Keep the Govt. in
Check/Represent
People
              Represent People    Make Laws / Pass Budget
```

Source: http://www.prsomda.org/

TOTAL SITTINGS FROM 1ST TO 14TH LOK SABHA

1st	1952-57	677	8th	1985-89	485
2nd	1957-62	567	9th	1989-91	109
3rd	1962-67	578	10th	1991-96	423
4th	1967-70	469	11th	1996-97	125
5th	1971-77	613	12th	1998-99	88
6th	1977-79	267	13th	1999-2004	356
7th	1980-84	464	14th	2004-09	332

The media is running a campaign to mobilize public opinion against such disruptions of Parliament's time. Voters have to bear in mind while voting that they elect a member who helps Parliament conduct its business, smoothly. Parliament is run for about eighty days in a year. So if we divide the budget allocation over these eighty days and for six hours a day, per minute expenditure in running our Parliament is Rs 2.5 lakh, according to some estimates.

In such a context, support for their work in Parliament becomes essential to help them make better informed decisions.

The PRS is a not-for-profit, non-partisan research initiative based in New Delhi, which studies the functioning of Parliament and brings out various policy-based research reports on the proposed bills, as per Chakshu Rai of the research body. It aims to strengthen the legislative debate by making it better informed, more transparent and more participatory. Founded in 2005, PRS is the first initiative of its kind in India. Its report makes some important points.

The 12th session of the 15th Lok Sabha started on 22 November 2012 and ended on 20 December 2012. Twenty sittings were scheduled for the winter session. Both Lok Sabha and Rajya Sabha were disrupted on many occasions due to the FDI issue, reservation issue, Delhi gang-rape issue and others. The Lok Sabha lost nearly 47 per cent of the scheduled hours of business in the winter session. Similarly, the Rajya Sabha lost around 50 per cent of the allocated time.

Parliament meets for fewer days

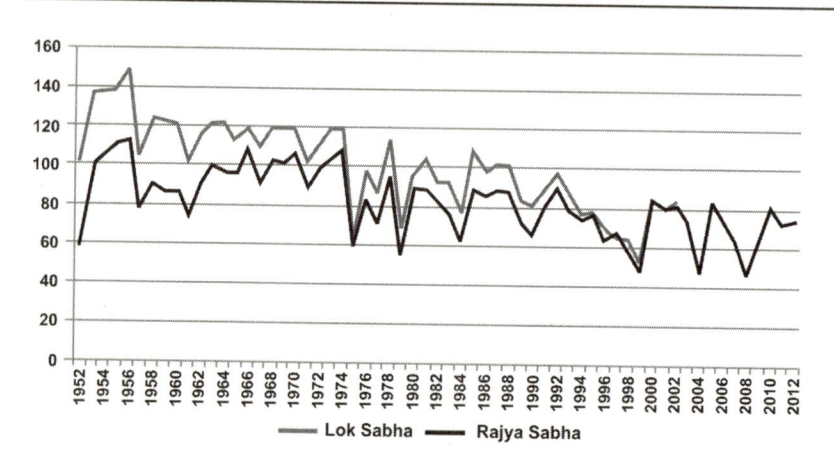

Source: http://www/prsomda.org/

15TH LOK SABHA—PERFORMANCE AT A GLANCE
TIME WASTED DURING DISRUPTIONS

Session	Planned	Actual sitting	% (Hours Lost)	% (Productive)
Budget 2009	156	162.1	-4%	104%
Winter 2009	138	105.5	24%	76%
Budget 2010	210	138.0	34%	66%
Monsoon 2010	144	136.1	5%	95%
Winter 2010	144	7.6	95%	5%
Budget 2011	138	116.6	15%	85%
Monsoon 2011	156	103.8	33%	67%
Winter 2011	126	85.0	33%	67%
Budget 2012	210	187.0	11%	89%
Monsoon 2012	120	24.4	80%	20%
Winter 2012	120	63.9	47%	53%
Budget 2013 (first half)	126	90.8	28%	72%
Total	**1788**	**1220.8**	**32%**	**68%**

Source: PRS Legislative Research Business conducted in Lok Sabha

The Lok Sabha passed seven bills during this session. The banking law amendment bill, the Companies Act, 118th Constitutional Amendment were important bills that were passed during this session. Issues relating to FDI in retail and the gang-rape in Delhi were also discussed in detail. Some of the discussions on the private members' bills were also highly useful and informative. Although the government planned to get twenty-six bills passed, due to disruptions only seven bills could go through. The government introduced nine bills of the eleven bills planned in this session.

Decline in number of bills passed

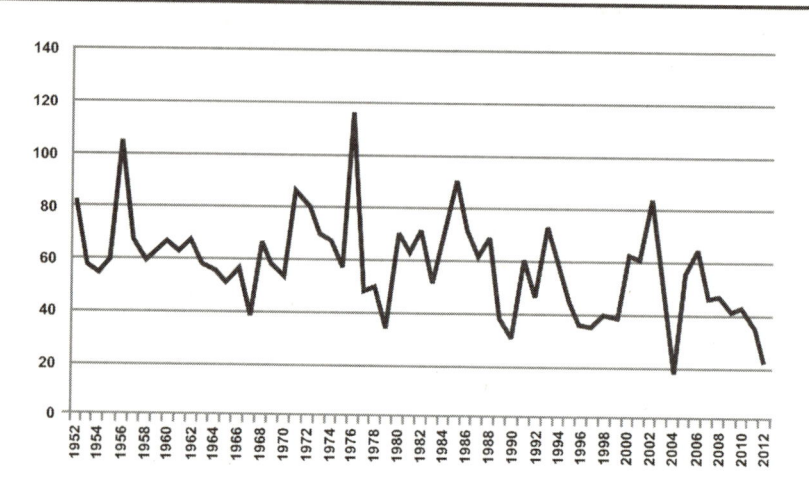

Source: http://www.prsomda.org/

15TH LOK SABHA—PERFORMANCE AT A GLANCE: BILLS PLANNED, INTRODUCED AND PASSED

PERFORMANCE OF MPS

Session	Bills introduced Plan	Performance	Bills Passed Plan	Performance
Budget 2009	29	12	13	3
Winter 2009	62	19	26	14
Budget 2010	64	28	27	6
Monsoon 2010	35	23	33	21
Winter 2010	32	9	31	0
Budget 2011	34	9	33	3
Monsoon 2011	34	13	37	10
Winter 2011	24	28	32	15

Individuals at the Government Level

Session	Bills introduced Plan	Performance	Bills Passed Plan	Performance
Budget 2012	30	17	39	12
Monsoon 2012	16	6	30	4
Winter 2012	10	8	25	10
Total	**370**	**172**	**326**	**98**

Note: Financial and Appropriation Bills are not included

Most Important Concern of All the Citizens of India

The most important concern of every citizen is the disruption of Parliament for one reason or other. When India is growing, we expect that the Parliament should conduct its business without disruption. The ruling and opposition parties should find a way to use 100 per cent of Parliament's time for national development. We even suggest that members who disrupt the Parliament should be denied some of their privileges and allowances. The power to do this should be vested in the Speaker.

On an average an MP can raise around 255 questions per Lok Sabha period. An MP gets approximately 1,400 documents per session in the form of bills, budget, documents, and reports for discussion. They have to study, debate and analyse the documents, and evolve a consensus within their party and then participate in the discussions.

In India, we have an adequate mechanism for doing research-based study, analysis and then formulate an action agenda for discussion. Parties are today discussing only some of the key or burning issues of societal relevance which affect the public directly. In the process, many bills, such as the finance bills, are passed without having a proper discussion. Sometimes, the government also goes for an ordinance due to the disruptions, an example being the food security bill.

MPs get 1,400 documents per session

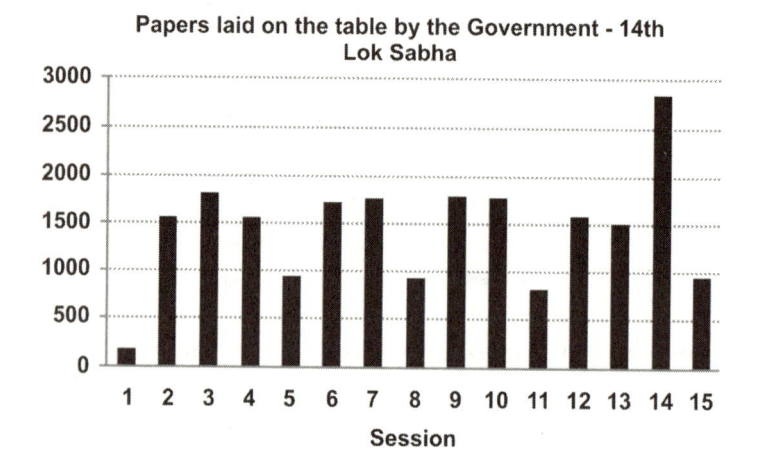

Papers laid on the table by the Government - 14th Lok Sabha

It is not a question of qualification either: the number of graduates, post-graduates and doctoral degree holders who are MPs has gone up. The number of graduates from 1952 to 2009 is on the rise, but the performance has not improved commensurately as we have seen so far.

The performance is a reminder that our MPs and political parties have no mechanism to conduct research, they don't have any staff for the purpose, lack office space, and they are run with very few intellectuals among their decision-makers. A strong research capacity would be of help in giving depth to proposals while crafting a progressive public policy for the development of the nation.

One of the suggestions to the MPs would be to have students from different disciplines, humanities, science and technology, engineering, medical, management, economics, political science, sociology and other as their interns to help with research and give inputs for the discussions in Parliament. That will at least improve their performance in terms of knowledge inputs for the better functioning of Parliament.

How educated are our MPs?

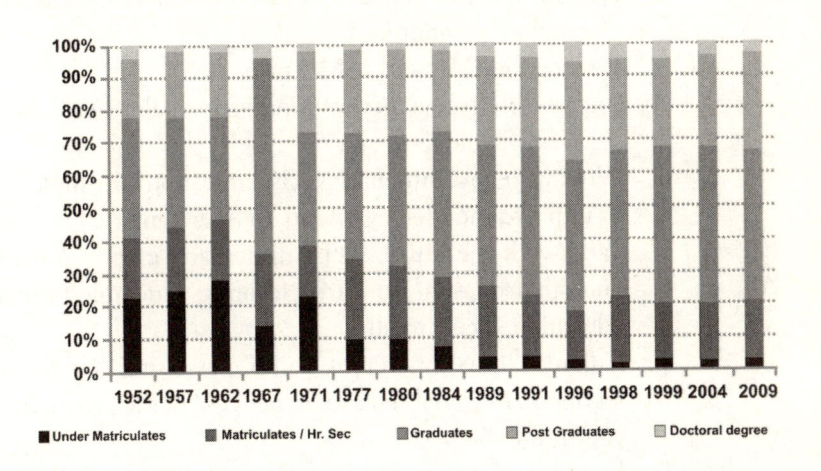

[Chart: Stacked bar chart showing educational qualifications of MPs from 1952 to 2009, with categories: Under Matriculates, Matriculates / Hr. Sec, Graduates, Post Graduates, Doctoral degree]

Vision Manifesto of an MP

A vision manifesto for Parliament members could be similar to the one given below.

1. Make use of question hour, zero hour, adjournment motions effectively to represent the issues of the people of my constituency, matters of urgent public importance and bring out the socio-economic and political issues concerning the people whom I represent.
2. Work towards maintaining parliamentary democracy by peaceful decision-making and avoid disrupting Parliament for frivolous reasons.
3. Undertake research about my constituency based on the development indicators with the help of an academic institution and use the development radar and monitor the progress of my constituency. Work with the central and state governments in enacting policies and programmes to improve the following:

a. Uplift the people living below poverty line (30 per cent to 50 per cent improvement)
b. Double the per capita income through employment-generation programmes
c. Reduce the IMR and MMR rates
d. Improve life expectancy by bringing in quality healthcare services reachable to all
e. Work with government, NGOs, educational institutions to improve the literacy rate to 100 per cent
f. Work with the HRD, social justice and empowerment and other relevant ministries to bring affordable formal education access to all
g. Enhance the number of youth possessing top flight techno-managerial skills to 50 per cent of the productive youth force
h. Provide entrepreneurship training to potential young entrepreneurs
i. Ensure the availability of safe drinking water through a programme of desilting of ponds, lakes and tanks and connect these with the rivers with the help of the state government and the people
j. Identify the societal conflicts and issues and help resolve them through building consensus and creating awareness among the people
k. Work for establishing clean, green industries through public and private partnership
l. Help develop the core competence of the people of my constituency
m. Work for establishing at least twelve PURA clusters in my constituency for bringing sustainable development
n. Work for making the constituency a carbon-neutral and pollution-free constituency and encourage usage of bio-degradable items for consumer market
o. Ultimately work for enriching the quality of life of the people

4. Promote the socialistic, secular ideals of the party and follow the path of developmental politics.
5. Work towards formulating inclusive economic and political policies for sustained growth of the nation.
6. Work towards introducing the necessary constitutional amendment bills for removing the social ills of the society which hold us back from becoming a knowledge society.
7. Identify all the challenges in the existing laws of the land which need to be modified or reformed to empower Indians to be competitive globally.
8. Set an example for inspiring the people and the youth to follow our principles, ideals and our way of life and attract the young to come forward to contribute using their expertise for national development. By excelling in every action continuously and winning the confidence of the people, pave the way for creating future leaders.
9. Vow to always keep the nation bigger than the individual, party and organization.

SECTION V

MANIFESTO FOR VILLAGE DEVELOPMENT

*'You cannot build nonviolence on a factory civilization,
but it can be built on self-contained villages.
The soul of India lives in its villages'*
—Mahatma Gandhi

When I think of Gandhiji's statement, I am reminded of a beautiful poem written by Mahakavi Subramania Bharathiyar, which is given with a rough translation.

காணி நிலம் வேண்டும் பராசக்தி காணி நிலம் வேண்டும் - அங்குத் தூணில் அழகியதாய் நன்மாடங்கள் துய்ய நிறத்தினவாய் - அந்தக் காணி நிலத்திடையே ஓர் மாளிகை கட்டித் தர வேண்டும் - அங்குக் கேணியருகினிலே தென்னைமரம் கீற்றும் இளநீரும்

*Oh divine mother, I need a piece of land, a piece of land
Where help me to build a white palace of purity,
A beautiful balcony with four pillars,
In the vicinity of a small pond with a tender coconut tree.*

பத்துப் பன்னிரெண்டு தென்னைமரம் பக்கத்திலே வேணும் - நல்ல முத்துச் சுடர் போலே நிலாவொளி முன்பு வரவேணும் - அங்குக் கத்தும் குயிலோசை சற்றே வந்து காதிற் படவேணும் - என்றன் சித்தம் மகிழ்ந்திடவே நன்றாய் இளந்தென்றல் வரவேணும்

*I need ten or twelve coconut trees nearby
There should be moonlight in front of me resembling the
    shine of a pearl
The melodious voice of beautiful nightingales to pass my
    ears
And early morning breeze enlighten my mind with
    happiness . . .*

பாட்டுக் கலந்திடவே அங்கே ஒரு பத்தினிப் பெண் வேணும் - எங்கள்
கூட்டுக் களியினிலே கவிதைகள் கொண்டு தர வேணும் - அந்தக்
காட்டு வெளியினிலே அம்மா நின்றன் காவலுற வேணும் - என்றன்
பாட்டுத் திறத்தாலே இவ்வையத்தைப் பாலித்திட வேணும்

> Need a virtuous wife to enjoy the music of life,
> Blossoming beautiful poems.
> Oh! Divine mother, protect us in this beautiful forest environment
> To enlighten this world with the knowledge of my songs.

When I think back on my childhood, memories of my village come back to me. Everywhere it was green, and on the roadside there were fruit bearing trees. Medicinal plants, coconut and banana trees grew in almost all the homes. There was a pond in the centre of the village near the temple which used to fill up whenever there was rain. The village was on an island hence there was sea all around. Birds crisscrossed the sky noisily, while cows settled down idly on the paths wherever they fancied. It was a self-contained village. In every street there was a place for domestic, kitchen and animal waste disposal which was re-used as fertilizer for agriculture and farming. Boat building, fishing and selling the catch and other produce in the village market were the common occupations.

We had no electricity nor cable television, so our streets were not congested with wires. There were no drains but no waterlogging either in the streets. We had no plastics, hence no pollution. We had mud silos at our homes to store the harvest so there was no wastage of foodgrains.

We lived in a beautiful environment, where the village buzzed with various activities, fishing, handloom, buffalo and sheep rearing, pot making and much else to make for a thriving economy. The traditional bonds of a well-knit family system, where love, affection, mutual help and service were the prevailing emotions, bound us all together.

India is still predominantly rural, over 70 per cent of its people live in villages. As of 2011, out of the total population of 1.2 billion, the urban population has increased to 377 million but an overwhelming majority of 833 million is still in villages, big and small. India, it has been said, lives in her mid-sized villages, with as many as 485 million people living in villages with a population ranging from 1,000 to 5,000. Additionally, 103 million people live in villages of 500-1,000 population, and 47 million people in villages of less than 500 people.

India's least urbanized states are 1) Nagaland, 2) Manipur, 3) Uttarakhand, 4) West Bengal, 5) Andhra Pradesh, 6) Haryana, 7) Punjab and 8) Karnataka. India's most urbanized states are 1) NCT–Delhi 2) Goa 3) Mizoram 4) Tamil Nadu 5) Kerala 6) Meghalaya 7) Gujarat. Due to the rapid pace of urbanization, rural life is also being transformed. Villages are getting fewer and bigger across the country. As cities become bigger, neighbouring villages are merging with them. Increased road connectivity and highways are also bringing change to the villages which fall alongside. All these factors lead to reduced land for cultivation and irrigation, encroachment of ponds and lakes and ultimately villages becoming congested like cities. At the same time, the village and municipal amenities are not getting developed, village infrastructure is not adequate, lack of employment opportunities still leads people to look for jobs in urban areas. Lack of quality infrastructure, lack of quality education, lack of quality healthcare facilities still makes life hard in many villages.

The picture emerging makes it clear that India's aspirations are increasingly directed towards its cities. The obvious challenge before our nation is therefore twofold: to avoid large-scale migration from rural to urban areas by providing urban amenities in rural areas. What makes this challenge all the more pressing is that about 30 per cent of the population of the country still lives below the poverty line, and nearly 80 per cent of those below the poverty line are located in rural areas, according to the ministry of rural development.

What we need to do is to take responsibility for our own wellbeing and develop our society consistent with our heritage, values and capabilities. We need to aim very high and work for removing poverty, providing proper services, and cleaning up the degraded environment.

Fundamentally our economic growth strategy would be to enhance wealth generation from the services sector. Our vision for sustainable development has set a target for a service sector contribution to be 64 per cent of the GDP whereas in 1980, it was in the region of 36 per cent. We have crossed the 50 percentage mark for the service sector. While this is happening, the contribution of agriculture is gradually going down.

According to the response to an RTI query from Mr Om Prakash Sharma, the Food Corporation of India (FCI) has confirmed that as much as 1,94,502 metric tonnes of foodgrain worth crores of rupees was wasted in India due to various reasons between 2005 and March 2013. The response details that of the damaged stock, around 84 per cent (1,63,576 MT) was rice and 14 per cent wheat (26,543 MT).

Around 40 per cent of India's fresh fruit and vegetables worth about $8.3 billion per year spoils before reaching consumers. Every year, about 21 million tonnes of wheat rots because of improper storage. India has only half the amount of cold storage facilities (6,300) with an installed capacity of 30 million tonnes compared to what it actually needs. It is estimated that investment of Rs 55,000 crore is needed by 2015-16 to keep up with growing fruit and vegetable production levels.

In order to effectively distribute the agricultural produce and make optimal use of it we need high quality expertise and a developed infrastructure in food processing and supply chain management. It will ensure a balanced contribution to the GDP from the agricultural sector including food processing sector which will reach a value of 12 per cent by the year 2020. Similarly the contribution of manufacturing sector, that is, industry has to further increase to attain 28 per cent by 2020.

The first priority for societal transformation of India is accelerated rural development. The key here is that all developmental actions have to be sustainable and should be activated in 600,000 villages which have missed both the industrial revolution and information technology revolution and in fact even the first Green Revolution in many of the states. How do we together go about achieving this? The transformation of our rural areas to a knowledge society is therefore our key to rapid growth. In such growth, our large population would itself turn out to be an enormous competitive advantage for India by generating wealth. Such a process of using one billion people has a multiplier effect. The population is then not a problem—it becomes a multiplier factor leading to a larger GDP for the country as a whole. The knowledge society which we look for is created through wealth generation and a societal transformation. The rural development focuses on the process of improving the quality of life and the economic well-being of people living in relatively isolated and sparsely populated areas.

India has gone through several Five Year Plans. Yet there is always a question mark on whether the intended benefits have reached the people, whether the plans have made available the necessary basic amenities in the rural areas such as access to safe drinking water, quality food, habitat, sanitation, electricity, education, healthcare, employment opportunity and agriculture infrastructure. All these are essentials. But, while some of the states have achieved remarkable improvement, many are still trying to achieve the threshold level in these aspects.

Sustainable Development

The allocation for rural development has seen steady increase. For rural development and panchayati raj the 11th Plan realization is Rs 3,97,000 crore, against the planned allocation of Rs 2,91,000 crore, which accounted for 25 per cent of the total central budget plan provision, whereas the 12th Plan projection for allocation is Rs 6,73,000 crore (18 per cent of the total central budget plan provision, which is a 69.31 per cent increase over the 11th Plan). The annual outlay of the Ministry of Rural Development has increased from Rs 33,900 crore in 2008-09 to Rs 80,194 crore in 2013-14.

Rural employment programmes cover employment through the Mahatma Gandhi National Rural Employment Guarantee Act (MGNREGA) and the National Rural Livelihoods Mission, housing via the Indira Awaas Yojana and other state schemes and bank support, sanitation through the total sanitation campaign, provision of drinking water via the National Rural Drinking Water Programme, social security through the National Social Assistance programme, watershed development via the Integrated Watershed Management Programme, road connectivity through the Pradhan Mantri Gram Sadak Yojana and electrification via the Rajiv Gandhi Grameen Vidyutikaran Yojana.

According to the 2011-12 revenue expenditure, the top five states focusing on rural development, spending around 8 per cent of total revenue expenditure on it, are Jharkhand, Bihar, Rajasthan, Chhattisgarh and Madhya Pradesh. The states spending 2-5 per cent are Odisha, West Bengal, Meghalaya, Andhra Pradesh, Sikkim, Assam, Karnataka, Himachal Pradesh, Uttar Pradesh, Haryana, Arunchal Pradesh, Uttarakhand, Nagaland, Gujarat and Maharashtra. The states that are spending less than 2 per cent are Manipur, Tripura, Goa, Tamil Nadu, Kerala, Mizoram, Jammu & Kashmir, Puducherry, Punjab and NCT (Delhi).

The spending of 2 per cent to 8 per cent of the total revenue expenditure has not brought sustainable development to the villages so far. The fragmented approach to the development of rural areas through multiple state and central government schemes is one cause of this.

Over the last six years, MGNREGA has generated Rs 1,200 crore person days of work at a total expenditure of over Rs 1,66,760 crore. Diverse tasks were undertaken related to watershed, agriculture, livestock, fisheries, drinking water, sanitation, irrigation among others. But, overall the large proportion (80 per cent) of the works under MGNREGA are focused on soil and water conservation-related tasks. Largely the works are undertaken independently, and are not completely in sync with the overall village development plan of the district.

Perception differs on the benefits of MGNREGA. Criticisms include that farmers are affected due to non-availability of farm workers for operations during pre- and post-harvesting, and that wages have increased, making farming unviable.

Against this backdrop, I would like to discuss in this section the system of decentralization adopted by India so that development reaches every district, taluk and panchayat in the country and outline a manifesto for the development of India's villages.

Did the empowerment of people through panchayati raj have any impact? Did the crores of rupees spent on rural development in plan after plan bring about any kind of change?

> Gandhiji was a strong votary of electrification of every village in India.
>
> 'I would prize every invention of science made for the benefit of all,' he said.
>
> Sadly the goal of electrification has still not been achieved. Nearly one lakh out of the six lakh villages in our country have no electricity, a deprivation whose true severity can be gauged from the additional fact that 56 per cent of rural households in the remaining five lakh villages that are supposed to be 'electrified' have no electricity.
>
> —Sudheendra Kulkarni
> *Music of the Spinning Wheel*

Empowerment through Panchayati Raj

The vision of Panchayati Raj Institutions (PRI) is to attain decentralized and participatory local self-government by the people, for the people. Empowerment, enablement and accountability of PRIs to ensure inclusive development with social justice, and efficient delivery of services are their objectives. The aims of the Panchayati Raj ministry are: Empowerment of the PRIs through various government schemes, capacity building of the panchayats to prepare rural development plans and financial support to the state governments through backward regions grant fund (BRGF) programme.

On 24 April 1993, the Constitutional (73rd Amendment) Act 1992 came into force to provide constitutional status to the Panchayati Raj Institutions. Panchayati Raj is a system of governance in which gram panchayats are the basic units of administration. It has three levels: Gram (village, though it can comprise more than one village), Janpad (block) and Zilla (district). It paved the way for the establishment of the scheme of 'democratic decentralization' which finally came to be known as Panchayati Raj. India has around 2.4 lakh (2,38,054) panchayats.

Establishment of a three-tier Panchayati Raj system with the powers and responsibilities delegated to panchayats at the appropriate level is meant for:

- Preparation of the economic development plan and social justice plan.
- Implementation of schemes for economic development and social justice in relation to twenty-nine subjects given in the Eleventh Schedule of the Constitution.
- To levy and collect appropriate taxes, duties, tolls and fees.

For the benefit of future people's representatives of the Panchayati Raj Institutions, we should understand the role of each of the stakeholders.

Role of Village Panchayats: Rural local bodies have the duties of providing basic amenities and civic services to the rural population. The rural local bodies are empowered to collect taxes to raise their own resources to perform their duties. However, the funds collected through their own revenues do not suffice. Therefore, the government (central and state) devolves part of its own tax revenues to the rural local bodies to meet their needs.

Role of Panchayat Samiti at the block level: This body works for the villages of the tehsil or taluk that together are called a Development Block. The functions are: implementation of schemes for the development of agriculture, establishment of primary health centres and primary schools, supply of drinking water, drainage and construction/repair of roads, development of cottage and small-scale industries, and the opening of cooperative societies and establishment of youth organizations. The main source of income of the panchayat samiti is grants-in-aid and loans from the state government.

Role of Zilla Parishad at the district level: The governing system at district level in Panchayati Raj is also popularly known as 'Zilla Parishad'. The chief of administration is an officer from the IAS cadre. The main functions are: Provide essential services and facilities to the rural population, supply improved seeds to farmers and inform them of new farming techniques, set up and run schools and libraries, start primary health centres and hospitals. Also among the duties are vaccination drives, execution of plans for development of the scheduled castes and tribes, setting up free hostels for adivasi children, encouraging entrepreneurs to start small-scale industries and implementing rural employment schemes, roads and other public facilities and maintaining them. As too, providing employment. The duties, and their potential for change, therefore, are enormous.

India has two decades of experience of managing the village panchayats, panchayat unions (blocks) and zilla panchayats (district). Rural development and panchayati raj go hand in hand. But they were handled by two different ministries, which lacked synergy in implementation.

The ministries are Ministry of Rural Development and Ministry of Panchayati Raj. Two ministries can only lead to delay in implementation, besides additional expenditure. It is essential to merge the two to accelerate achievement of rural development targets. The other requirement is to implement the PURA cluster development approach. Let us look at how PURA—a unique sustainable system for rural development—provides a solution.

Unique Sustainable System for Rural Development

We stand six years away from the goal of achieving the vision for a developed India by 2020, and there has been significant progress in all directions. Each step we take towards a developed nation also opens a fresh challenge to overcome. The need of the hour is the evolution of sustainable systems which act as 'enablers' and bring inclusive growth and integrated development to the nation.

The country has achieved Green Revolution in agriculture and White Revolution in milk. It is because of the integrated approach in mission mode by stakeholders towards realizing their objectives. We need such a mission to bring overall development in the rural areas. One system which can bring about the desired transformation is the Provision of Urban Amenities in Rural Areas (PURA) for connecting thirty to fifty villages as a PURA cluster complex with the creation of three connectivities, namely physical, electronic, and knowledge, leading to economic connectivity.

PURA, in conjunction with gram sabhas, will work towards strengthening agriculture, agro processing industry, power generation, skill development, healthcare and sanitation, water harvesting and all the other such steps that will ultimately show visible improvement in development indicators.

Today PURA has graduated into a unique system for sustainable development. There are a number of PURA clusters established by many private institutions such as the Warana, Loni, Chitrakoot and Periyar PURA.

The Warana PURA complex shows how a cooperative movement has brought about a transformation in the lives of 4 lakh people in the sixty-nine villages that are part of it through value-added employment and increased income from cooperative sugar, dairy and poultry farming and agriculture. The Warana PURA shows that with better technology and sound management, the socio-economic objectives of creating a prosperous society starting from the bottom of the pyramid. The cooperative model, product diversification, process innovation and market understanding have all been distinctive features of the Warana PURA.

The message from the Loni PURA is how a medical institution has brought about a change. Quality healthcare was taken to the doorstep of the villagers through tele-medicine and improved literacy has enhanced the quality of life of the people there.

The Chitrakoot PURA shows how an institution called DRI has helped establish litigation-free villages, promoted traditional medicine for improved health and hygiene and built water management structures for promoting sustainable agriculture in 500 villages.

In the Periyar PURA, engineering institution converted the dry land into a productive green area, and promoted a sustainable development model through planting of energy crops such as jatropha for biofuel and biomass, solar and bio-digester based power generation.

Many of the flagship rural development missions do not pay enough attention to sustainability. Thus the growth they accomplish falters. But PURA is a sustainable development system for building improved infrastructure, doubling per capita income, and a better quality of life: factors that can ensure reverse migration. *Target 3 Billion*, a book I co-authored with Srijan Pal Singh, explains PURA in detail. The first priority for India is accelerated rural development.

The PURA cluster would be key to doing that. Enterprises from different parts of the nation and the world can be partners with an identified PURA cluster by acting as equity investors, exploring and facilitating market linkages and providing a technological platform for the best practices and innovative solutions to production challenges. In this way, enterprises and business units from across the world can share their core competencies to harness the resources of untapped regions. Such collaborative platforms for 600,000 villages—that is, 7,000 PURA clusters in all—offers a business opportunity of Rs 8,75,000 crore if one estimates that each cluster offers an opportunity worth Rs 125 crore.

> **ISELTWALD VILLAGE IN SWITZERLAND— A PURA-LIKE MODEL**
>
> I visited a small fishing village named Iseltwald in Switzerland. It is on the south shore of Lake Brienz. It is a well-known fishing village with popular lakeside restaurants.
>
> It has a small population of 410 people. The main businesses are tourism and fishing. About 5 to 10 per cent of the people go to neighbouring towns for employment.
>
> All are fully employed and with value addition to their products and services enjoy a standard of living which is equal to staying in one of the cities. The facilities available put them on a par with those living in the city. Education facilities, healthcare centres and employment opportunities are all available within the village itself, as we envisage in PURA.

I have met many aspiring entrepreneurs in India and abroad who are showing keen interest to be a part of the mission and take it forward as a viable instrument for societal change. The professionals, entrepreneurs, industry, organizations and experts can be a part of the efforts to create PURA clusters to help in skill development and job creation.

All these empowerment interventions have the potential to generate over 15 million employment opportunities at the grassroots level. This could lead to quadrupling of the per capita nominal income in five years' time. What is the most important ingredient that will enable us to realize sustainable development? This would need good governance based on problem-free and rapid clearance systems for investors, well-defined labour laws, assured safety and security of people and property, transparency in all actions, efficient and unbiased redressal mechanism, and stability in laws, policy and projects.

PURA 2.0 has been accepted as a National Mission by the government through public-private partnership mode. However, much remains in the implementation. One reason is that the government focusses only on the physical connectivity, other connectivities such as electronic connectivity, knowledge connectivity and economic development are left to the PURA agencies to evolve as a business proposition.

The PURA experience is explained at length in *Target 3 Billion*. The 3 billion refers to the rural population of the world. Today, for India and any nation, the problem is how to reach the reforms, welfare schemes and benefits to the targeted population. Based on my working with many universities in India and abroad, I have come to the conclusion that major research is needed on this issue. The village panchayat is a basic unit of PURA cluster consisting of thirty to fifty villages.

> 'Innovation is the buzz word these days. However, as far back as in 1921, Gandhi instituted a prize of Rs 5000 (equivalent to about Rs 200,000 in 2012) in order to attract invention from all over the world to improve the efficiency of Khadi production. Eight years later, he increased it to Rupees one lakh! He was obsessed with the idea of technologies, innovation that could improve the quality of life in rural India.'
>
> —Sudheendra Kulkarni, *Music of Spinning Wheel*

Evolving an Action Plan for the Development of Village Panchayats

I had an opportunity to meet the panchayat leaders on many occasions since 2002. A few months ago, I met 1,600 village panchayat board presidents during the inauguration of the Green Sakthi programme to plant trees in Thiruvannamalai district, Tamil Nadu, organized by Sri Puram and Sri Narayini Peedam from Vellore Golden Temple. After interaction with them on the role played by the panchayat in development, I had administered an oath to all the 1,600 panchayat board presidents. Extrapolating from the oath and incorporating the sustainable development missions for rural areas within the three-tier structure of Panchayati Raj Institutions, we have evolved the following manifesto for the village panchayat. It can be altered, of course, to suit the vision of leaders who stand for elections to the panchayat board.

Vision Manifesto for Village Panchayats

1. We will revive all the ponds, tanks and lakes in our village by de-silting them and clearing the inlets and outlets. We will encourage rainwater harvesting in all our homes and thereby create a sustainable water infrastructure which will assure us clean drinking water.
2. We will not pollute the environment by using plastics and other non-biodegradable items. We will lay plastic roads in the village to eliminate the pollution created by plastics so far.
3. We will segregate organic and non-organic waste and convert the waste into wealth by producing bio-degradable consumer items for the market.
4. We will ensure the sanitation in all homes through the establishment of centralized drainage facility in our village. Thereby we will generate 100 kW power from the municipal waste and kitchen waste through bio-sanitizer system in each village. We will erect community solar panels for street lights and at home and make our village self-sufficient in this respect.
5. We will plant trees in the village and its surroundings and nurture and protect them for a clean and green environment.

6. We will respect our teachers and help them teach our children well; encourage skill development at the school level; and help create a school library by donating books.
7. We will create a playground for all of our students and encourage sports and games activity. We will identify talented youngsters in our villages and create facilities for them to improve their skills and succeed in Olympics.
8. We will promote good hygiene, vaccinate regularly, conduct periodic medical checkups against disease and ensure happy and healthy living.
9. We will create an environment that helps promote peace and harmony and work for removing societal conflicts and evils.
11. We will adopt best practices in agriculture, ensure the availability of quality seed to farmers in right time with the necessary water availability for irrigation, and work towards doubling.
12. Where possible, we will work jointly for activities where pooling resources will help meet common requirements.
13. As panchayat president and people's ward representative, we will help people get rid of addictions and vices that destroy both the individual and a happy family life.
14. We will encourage development of core competence of our villages and work with industry, academia, government and banks to create young entrepreneurs.
15. We will ultimately make our village a carbon-neutral village, with a clean and green environment.

SECTION VI

MANIFESTO FOR STATE ASSEMBLIES

As the President of India, I had easy access to the latest, accurate data about the performance of a state or institution from a ministry, department, the Planning Commission or the state government itself. Another core competence we had built in Rashtrapati Bhavan was a virtual conference and meeting facility which enabled us to have brainstorming sessions with experts from different organizations located in distant areas. We conducted these virtual conferences between 8 p.m. and midnight usually, when the experts were available for consultation. My team and I then put together their and our own thoughts together to prepare missions of prosperity as also my addresses to the nation, Parliament, state assemblies and public and private sector establishments and universities.

My research team comprised Dr Y.S. Rajan from CII, Dr A. Sivadhanu Pillai (Chief Controller [R&D], DRDO, and CEO of Brahmos), Prof. N. Balakrishnan, Associate Director, IISc, and Air Cmdr (Retd) R. Gopalasamy (Director, Bharat Dynamics Limited) through conferencing connectivity and the late Maj. Gen (Retd) R. Swaminathan (Chief Controller [R&D], DRDO and OSD, Research), D. Narayana Moorthi (Director, Launch Vehicle Programme, ISRO, and OSD) and V. Ponraj, Director (Technology Interface) from the President's Secretariat. We used to collate, analyse and research the data mined from various sources and combined it with what we gleaned in our brainstorming sessions with domain experts, scientists, and technologists.

The state legislative assemblies which I addressed in special sessions are Himachal Pradesh, Bihar, Madhya Pradesh, Goa, Karnataka, Kerala, Andhra Pradesh, Mizoram, Meghalaya, Sikkim, Jammu and Kashmir and Puducherry. Apart from these, I interacted with the chief ministers and legislators of other states and addressed government and private organizations in almost all the states, detailing my vision for a developed India and the missions for realizing this vision.

When I presented these missions to a state assembly (both houses of the assembly in some cases), all members from the ruling party and the opposition participated in the discussions through question-and-answer sessions and by providing suggestions. These discussions then led to the initiation of several action-oriented programmes in the state. They also made it amply clear that a developed state alone will lead to a developed India.

On the basis of all this, in this section I present case studies of some key states to help readers understand the requirements for state-wise development. Karnataka has a population of 61 million, ranking ninth in this respect among the states, and an area of 1,91,791 sq km. It has a literacy rate of 75.60 per cent and its capital, Bengaluru, is known worldwide as a hub of Information Technology. Uttar Pradesh, in contrast, has a population of 200 million, the highest of any state, and a land area of 2,43,286 sq km. It has a literacy rate of 67.68 per cent and is known for its cultural heritage and handicrafts among numerous other things. Missions similar to the ones in these states may be replicated in others based on their respective core competences and creative leadership.

Evolving a Vision for Karnataka

I was invited to interact with Karnataka's legislators on 13 December 2008 as part of a programme organized by IIM Bangalore. Karnataka has a 224-member Assembly. There are seventy-five members in the Upper House. We designed a questionnaire and sent it to them, hoping to elicit responses regarding the vision, mission, action plans and suggestions they had in mind for their constituencies. The questionnaire asked:

1. What changes would you bring about in your constituency after two-and-a-half years and after five years?
2. Do you have plans to realize 100 per cent literacy in your constituency? If so, you may indicate your plan.

3. With what skills and expertise will you empower the members of your constituency to at least double their per capita income?
4. Will you have a plan to plant at least 1,00,000 saplings in your constituency?
5. Would you like to get all the water bodies in your constituency rejuvenated after de-silting and activation of inlet and outlet?
6. Would you like to install a sanitary facility in every home under your constituency with adequate water supply?
7. Will you plan for multi-cropping in your constituency and also for the plantation of jatropha in wastelands?
8. Will you make your constituency free of power cuts and power shortage by using renewable energy sources?
9. Will you pave the way for peaceful and prosperous living of the citizens in your constituency?

I was sceptical about getting replies from the elected representatives. But to my surprise, all the MLAs and MLCs sent their responses either by email, fax or post. I requested the speaker of the Karnataka assembly to consolidate the responses and issue an assembly report with the heading 'Dreams of New Members of the Karnataka Legislative Assembly and Council'. It really elevated my spirits when I studied the details of the action plans they had charted.

Let me now highlight some of the important points and innovative plans which I liked.

- Vishweshwar Hegde Kageri, who was minister for primary and secondary education, elaborated on 'panchasutras'—a five-point programme focusing on road, water, education, sanitation and eco-friendly tourism.
- R. Dhruva Narayana had a roadmap for doing well on certain development indicators. I also liked his motto 'No farmer with one crop and all farmers with diversified crops'. His view was that all MLAs should be treated equally

irrespective of the party they belong to when development is the focus.
- Chandrakant G. Bellad's idea of constructing old-age homes, homes for destitute women, and orphanages highlighted an important societal need.
- Shivaraj S. Tangadagi's focus was on education at the SSLC level with respect to math and English. I noted his interest in using solar and wind energy to generate electricity in his constituency.
- Dr Mumtaz Ali Khan's determination to eliminate corruption is the need of the hour. For environmental rejuvenation, he distributed 1,00,000 seedlings, and I am sure he followed up to see that they were planted and nurtured.
- Katta Subramanaya Naidu's focus was on creating a well-planned underground sewage system.
- Chandrashekhar Patil Revoor had a plan to reduce the number of dropouts and a strategy to bring about peace and amity in his constituency.
- Saravabhoum Bagali had a plan of action for BPL cards, social security schemes, literacy, income generation, and comprehensive medical insurance.
- S.K. Basavarajan worked for power generation from garbage waste at the municipal landfill.
- Dr D. Hemachandra Sagar had a plan for the rehabilitation of slum areas by building large government apartments and giving them on lease in combination with some employment generation schemes.
- Jagadish Shettar had valuable inputs about creating an international airport at Hubli, increasing the per capita income through the empowerment of international competitive skills, and creation of software technology parks in tier two and tier three cities.

I was really overwhelmed by these innovative ideas and plans. In return, I suggested the following points of action:

1. Each member should have a website/Facebook page through which he or she can communicate constituency-related progress, problems and actions to every citizen of the constituency.
2. Each member should develop certain core competencies and experience in development and discuss ideas with other legislators so that knowledge can be shared and problems tackled.
3. There must be a continuous monitoring of schemes by independent citizens to enable leaders to ensure that the benefits of a scheme reach the intended citizens and timely mid-course corrections are taken.

During my meetings with the legislators, we discussed a vision for each constituency.

Vision Manifesto for MLAs' Constituencies in Karnataka

If we look at the development radar of Karnataka, prepared by the Planning Commission in the 1990s, which remains relevant now too, there are two octagons. The outer octagon represents the top level achievements, and the inner octagon represents the minimum development. Inside these two octagons the state level parameters calculated during the 1980s and 1990s are represented, which clearly bring out how the state has performed in each of the development indicators.

In a nutshell, the purpose was every MLA's vision should be to make his constituency an economically developed one. Thus, he would be trying to achieve, the following features:

- A constituency free from poverty and crime.
- Ensuring dignity of every human in an unbiased manner.
- A constituency free from illiteracy, with top-notch facilities for skill development and higher education for the youth.
- Value-added employment for all, with enhanced per capita income.

- Provision of healthcare services to every citizen and eradication of diseases like tuberculosis, cholera, malaria, HIV/AIDS and leprosy. Mass screening and provision of a proactive healthcare system leading to a reduction in infant and maternal mortality and chronic diseases.
- A sound infrastructure for safe drinking water, drainage, sanitation, irrigation, transportation, power and tourism.
- Efficient, transparent and corruption-free administration so that every citizen receives services without having to run around.
- Aiming to make the constituency a far better place to live in comparable with the best so that there is a possibility of reverse migration. The establishment of PURA clusters in the constituency would further help in this.

In essence, the constituency should focus on sustainable development which respects the environment, and makes the leader a friend to his constituents.

Vision Manifesto for Improving the State's Urban Constituencies

Karnataka, as is the rest of India, is rapidly urbanizing, and creative leaders would need to pay special attention to urban constituencies as their needs have risen rapidly. The infrastructure in cities such as Bengaluru is already overstretched and needs to be improved on an urgent footing so that the various missions in aerospace, software, machine building, biotechnology and other fields which make the city internationally competitive in these domains do not find it hard to function there. Then there is also the requirement to develop tier two cities such as Mysore, Mangalore, Hubli, Dharwad, Belgaum, Gulbarga and Mercara, improving their connectivity and providing airports where needed. One of the major concerns is to provide a pollution-free atmosphere for healthy living in all these cities.

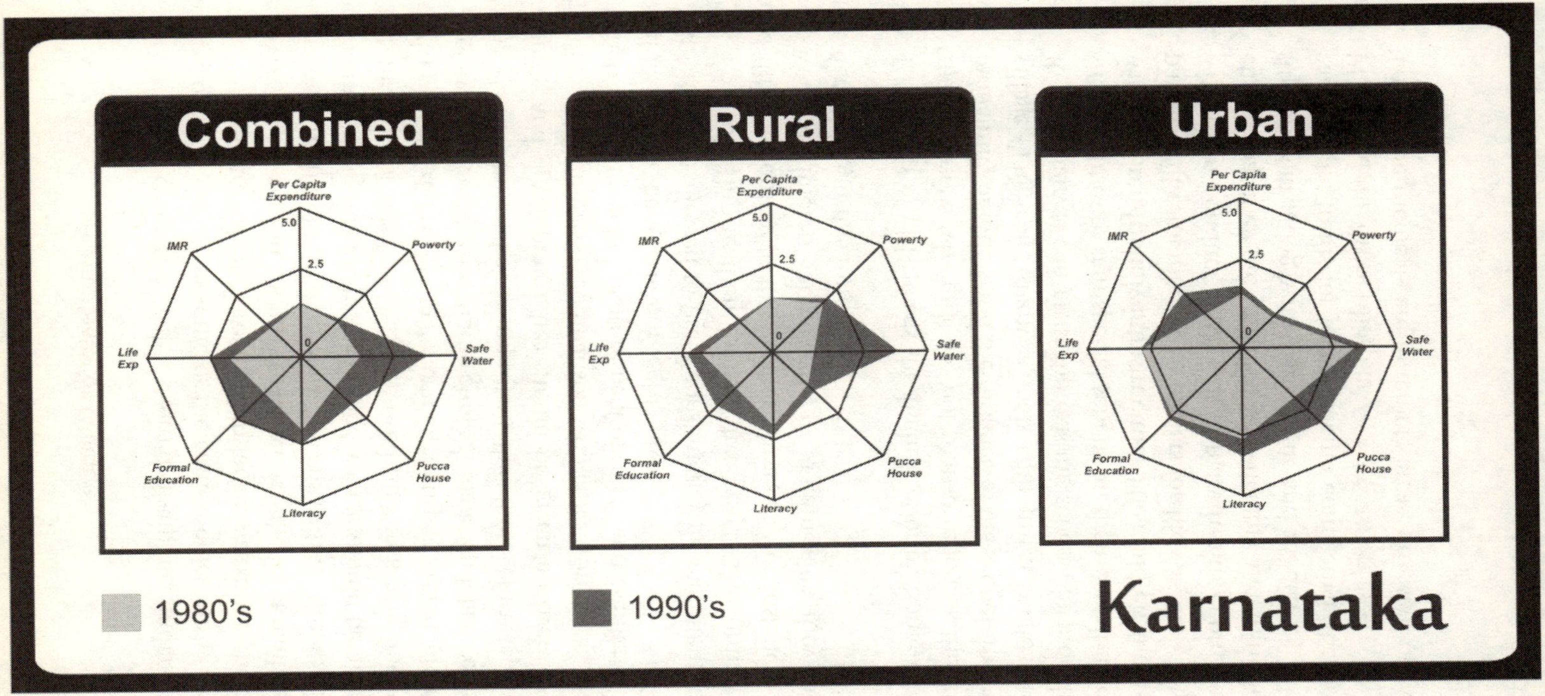

Karnataka

Combined

- Life Exp
- IMR
- Per Capita Expenditure
- 5.0
- 2.5
- 0
- Poverty
- Safe Water
- Pucca House
- Literacy
- Formal Education

Rural

- Life Exp
- IMR
- Per Capita Expenditure
- 5.0
- 2.5
- 0
- Poverty
- Safe Water
- Pucca House
- Literacy
- Formal Education

Urban

- Life Exp
- IMR
- Per Capita Expenditure
- 5.0
- 2.5
- 0
- Poverty
- Safe Water
- Pucca House
- Literacy
- Formal Education

■ 1980's
■ 1990's

Planning for cities is a highly evolved discipline. India has a long history of civilization, some of the earliest cities in the world were here, at a time when Europe, for instance, was still in the dark ages. Why, then, are Indian cities today among the most haphazard and poorly maintained, with very few providing the kind of comfortable living that a city in the modern age should be able to. City transport, for instance, has improved now in a very few with the advent of the metro, but in general the transport is characterized by smoky, crowded buses, traffic-choked roads and lack of safe driving skills. This makes it important that those entrusted with managing and developing cities should be given an overview of planning and examples of comparison with cities worldwide, many of which are far ahead of us in respect of safety and comfort. This would be of great benefit to our legislators.

All MLAs are allowed to use a constituency development fund of Rs 7.5 crore during their term of five years. The utilization would differ according to the location. In a city, for instance, the needs would be different. Some of the programmes that they could implement through this fund are:

1. Education of girls needs the highest priority. Some of the major reasons why girls are not sent to school is the non-availability of toilets and the distance of the school from the village. There are many schools with just a single room. Representatives can assist the existing schools in providing such facilities or start special schools in their constituencies with children-friendly infrastructure. The children and their parents will remember such leaders for life.
2. MLAs can conduct surveys of primary health centres and ensure that they are provided with doctors and minimum support staff along with equipment and medicines. They can allocate funds for tele-medicine connectivity between PHCs and the district hospital.
3. To provide medical-care to remote areas, provision of well-

equipped mobile hospitals could be considered. They will go to different villages under the constituency on specified dates so that the patients can be treated locally.
4. Development of skills in welding, construction, and repair and maintenance of electronic equipment will provide value-added employment to the rural youth. Legislators can organize special courses for the youth of the constituency for acquiring special skills in the polytechnic or ITI located in the constituency or the district headquarters. This will be a great opportunity to create a cadre of skilled people.
5. Organizing street plays in the constituency to create awareness about social evils such as dowry, corruption, female foeticide, gender inequality, child marriage and corruption. This will help the society inculcate good values.
6. Identifying water bodies in the constituency that need de-silting and opening of the inlet and outlet. When it rains, it is only the de-silted water bodies that will fill up and also increase the level of groundwater in the region. Legislators may also consider linking up the water bodies in the constituency.

For development missions to be successful and completed in time, science and technology have to be injected into them at the right time with the help of scientists, academicians, industry and NGOs and with committed leadership provided in each mission. The introduction of e-governance, in which Karnataka has shown leadership, will facilitate transparent management of missions. As elected leaders, MLAs can transform their constituencies into fully developed ones.

Fortunately, Karnataka is blessed with great scientific institutions such as ISRO, DRDO, IISc, HAL, BEL, CSIR laboratories, Bangalore Agricultural University, IT institutions and a number of educational and healthcare institutions. Most of the development work in constituencies needs scientific and technological solutions to accelerate development. In such situations, scientific linkages should be established with the nominated panel of experts maintained at the chief minister's office. Hence legislators should have an honorary advisory council for their development missions so that they can achieve development at a fast pace.

This is what I suggested to Karnataka's legislators during their orientation programme. Through this interaction, I got a sense of the spirit of the leaders' involvement in development activities. But will the governance system help them realize their visions for their constituencies? Will the opposition MLAs get the necessary assistance from the ruling party? The common man will benefit only if there is visionary leadership at the helm of affairs. A visionary leader is one who derives his strength from every stakeholder, including the media, and channelizes it for the benefit of the state and the nation. Our missions will be successful only if we can evolve such a visionary creative leadership in politics.

Eleven Missions for Karnataka's Development

My team and I suggested the following eleven missions:

Mission 1: Textiles

This mission will result in the export of Rs 6,000 crore worth of products and generate direct employment for 4 lakh people and indirect employment for a similar number.

Mission 2: Energy

A bio-fuel mission will generate a revenue of Rs 875 crore and provide employment to 14 lakh youth. Bengaluru city produces over 2,500 tonnes of waste per day. This can be used to generate electricity at seven power plants with a capacity of 6.5 MW each. Alternatively, it can also think in terms of having two 20 MW plants. This will not only ease the power situation in Bengaluru but also assist in the management of waste by taking its load off urban land. Similar plants can also be set up in all tier 2 cities of the state. The government of Karnataka can tie up with the CII, TIFAC and private industries that have successfully established power plants.

Mission 3: Horticulture

The main aim of this mission is to ensure an end-to-end holistic approach covering production, post-harvest management, processing and marketing to assure appropriate returns to growers and producers. This will enhance acreage, coverage and productivity. The mission will result in a revenue of Rs 10,000 crore, up from its present figure of Rs 6,000 crore, and also generate employment.

Mission 4: Agro-processing

The agro-processing industry has the potential to generate an export revenue of Rs 50,000 crore, with employment potential for a large number of rural and urban youth.

Mission 5: Water Management

Karnataka needs a water harvesting policy to ensure that enough water is stored to meet the demand during lean months, especially in certain low rainfall areas. The state should also take up wastewater recycling and reuse in a big way.

Mission 6: Tourism

Karnataka, with its myriad places of tourist interest, can definitely increase its number of domestic tourist arrivals to 40 million from the existing 21 million and that of foreign tourist arrivals to 1.5 million from the existing 5.3 lakh. This will also provide employment to a great many number of people, as international experience says that every tourist generates at least four jobs. The tourism mission will generate at least one million additional jobs and $180 million in foreign exchange. Simultaneously, the mission will lead to the development of the northern tourist circuit—which includes Badami, Aihole and Pattadakal—and the southern tourist circuit—which includes Belur, Halebid, Shravanabelagola, Melukote and Chitradurga Fort.

Mission 7: Quality Training for Paramedics and Technicians

This mission's goal should be to generate employment for and train 5,000 nurses and an equal number of paramedics per year.

Mission 8: Creation of Industries for Knowledge Products

At present, Karnataka's exports in the fields of IT, IT-enabled Services and BPO amount to around Rs 27,600 crore. These provide employment to around 3,00,000 people. Fifty-six per cent of the total BPO investment in the country is in Bengaluru. The creation of industries for knowledge products will result in the export of $20 billion worth of products and services and generate employment for 5,00,000 knowledge workers.

Mission 9: Grid Connectivities for Sustainable Growth

We need to establish 10 Gbps, multiple wavelength, fibre broadband connectivity to link the government, educational and industrial institutions in Bengaluru and tier 2 cities with all district headquarters. Villages should be linked with blocks through at least 10 Mbps Wi-Fi and Wi-Max connections. This would enable knowledge connectivity across the entire state. Can Karnataka take up the challenge of being the first state to have a seamless high bandwidth connection in any part of the state, heralding 4G systems?

Using the electronic connectivity described above, the state could connect all government institutions to create an e-governance grid; all educational institutions and R&D establishments to create a knowledge grid; and all healthcare institutions and government hospitals to create a healthcare grid. Ultimately, it could connect all rural and urban centres to create a PURA grid and interconnect it with the first three. This will facilitate government-to-citizen access (G2C), access to education through tele-education, and access to quality medicare through tele-medicine in a cost-effective manner. The government could then establish village knowledge centres, health centres, agri-clinics, agri-business and marketing centres to form a delivery mechanism for the PURA grid, enabling farmers and villagers to maximize their income potential and create a sustainable development model.

Mission 10: Establishment of PURA for Rural Prosperity

Establishment of PURA (thirteen coastal and 200 conventional) will lead to a higher employment potential in rural areas and a better standard of living for 67 per cent of the rural population.

Mission 11: Development Facilitators

Presently, the high revenue ICT industries are concentrated mainly in Bengaluru. It is interesting to note that the city occupies one per cent of the total area of the state but contains 14 per cent of its population. The situation in Mysore is similar. There is a need to distribute the economic activity equitably across the state to ensure homogenous growth, taking into consideration the core competence of each region.

This will be possible only if we develop tier 2 cities in the state around places like Mysore, Mangalore, Hubli, Dharwad, Belgaum, Gulbarga and Mercara. To improve connectivity and enable new industries to emerge, the first requirement will be to create air connectivity to and between all tier 2 cities. At the same time, there is also a need to make the development facilitators of Bengaluru world class. I have seen the city develop since the 1970s. Its economic growth has far exceeded its infrastructure. Its core attraction is slowly getting eroded.

But there is nothing to fear. My mentor, Prof. Satish Dhawan, once told me, 'If you do not have a mission, no problem will come up. But if you do have a mission or task, problems of varying magnitude will definitely crop up. But problems should not become the masters of individuals; individuals should become the masters of problems. Defeat them and succeed.'

Airports: As mentioned, Karnataka needs to set up commercial airports in tier 2 cities in a timebound way. The Bengaluru international airport should be one of the top ten airports of the world.

Roads: It is essential to create four- to six-lane roads across the state, connecting Bengaluru and all tier 2 cities with proper linkages to the rest of the country. In the next phase, the government should aim to connect all the 270 towns to tier 2 cities on the basis of the hub-and-spoke model, with at least four-lane roads, flyovers and overbridges. In addition, by passes must be created for Bengaluru and all tier 2 cities. Also, there is a need for ring roads around tier 2 cities to ensure seamless movement of traffic.

Fast Trains for Tier 2 Cities: Bengaluru's road capacity has reached a saturation point. The city needs alternatives such as a well-connected metro rail system. Enough care has to be taken while we concretize the state to ensure that it is not at the cost of the greenery which makes Bengaluru so beautiful. In addition, there is a need to create high-speed rail linkages on the lines of the Shatabdi Express between Bengaluru and all tier 2 cities.

Vision for Empowering 200 Million in Uttar Pradesh

Uttar Pradesh is India's second largest state and, in many ways, a litmus test for the country's development. It is also the second largest economy in the nation and is richly endowed with natural and human resources. With its 100 million youth, UP is home to every fifth youth in the country. Some of my expert friends have told me that, by 2016, out of every 100 skilled jobs being generated worldwide, about eight will be in this state alone.

Thus, the state poses some special challenges, and achieving progress will be a huge boost to confidence in achieving development in other difficult states where it has lagged.

My study of the state's economic profile indicates that 73 per cent of its population is engaged in agriculture and allied activities, and 46 per cent of the state income is generated by agriculture. During the Eleventh Five Year Plan period, the state recorded 7.3 per cent growth in its GSDP (Gross State Domestic Product), exceeding the 6.1 per cent target. UP has more than 2.3 million small scale industrial units. There are more than 25 lakh unemployed youth in the state, of whom 9 lakh are over thirty-five years of age.

With these aspects in mind, we need to evolve sustainable development missions for the economic empowerment of the state. This will enable the state to enhance its present per capita income from Rs 26,051 to over Rs 1,00,000, create employment for all its youth, promote a literacy rate of 100 per cent, reduce its infant mortality rate to less than 10, and eradicate diseases like leprosy, kala azar, malaria, dengue and tuberculosis.

If UP succeeds in implementing its development agenda and transforms itself into a secure, peaceful and prosperous state, it could become a working model for others to follow by adopting its best practices. I got a chance to articulate my vision for this important state thanks to an invite to address a development conclave in Lucknow on 26 May 2012. It was organized by Hindustan Times Media Ltd and aimed at drawing up a roadmap for the development of the state through discussions among experts from different walks of life. My lecture was on the topic 'Empowering 200 Million', and I would like to go over some of the missions I then proposed.

Skill-based Empowerment Mission

Uttar Pradesh is a land of rich history and culture. The carpets of Bhadohi, metal artwork of Moradabad, glassware of Ferozabad, mango products of Malihabad, leatherwork of Kanpur, and Chikankari of Lucknow are historic industries which are famous worldwide. But the question to ask is whether the fame of the product is matched by the economic activity it is able to generate? And how many relatively unknown arts, crafts and cuisines does the state have with a potential to develop into a vibrant industry with technological and marketing support?

The government needs to create a comprehensive skill map of Uttar Pradesh. This would mean mapping all the districts in the state with their core competencies in terms of skills across the dimensions of art, music, handicraft, agro products, cuisines and literature. Such a map will help the state plan policies to promote a certain skill. For example, Moradabad is known for its metal artwork industry. But it can be made more valuable with technological inputs. Similarly, Bareilly artisans have a well-known expertise in ornaments such as jhumkas. But there is scope to take their products to foreign markets to meet the international demand. Similarly, folk music and songs from the Pratapgarh region are today known only locally. They have the potential to be taken to national and international music lovers.

Such a map can provide an index to indicate the present state and the potential for each of the skills identified. It will serve as a reference tool for administrators at the district and state levels and will need to be uploaded to a website for the active participation of likely investors.

The UP government and policy makers may also consider creating a UP Skill Enterprise Corporation under a public-private partnership model. Such a body can identify young talent in traditional skills in colleges and on shop floors and invest in them so that they emerge as entrepreneurs. It can also brand its skills, products and services and assess and enhance their quality. It can further help identify markets, both nationally and internationally, for such products and also provide knowledge support to potential entrepreneurs in the domains of technology, hazard management, financial accounting, etc.

An economic map of the state, showing per capita income and

the human development index for each region and district, would also be help. The skill map could then be superimposed onto the economic map and gaps between potential and realization identified. Finally, academia, industry and administration need to come together at the district level to plan for sustainable methods to bridge the gap between economic realization and skill potential. This may require targeted training across ITIs, youth workshops, marketing and distribution support, investments in technological process enhancements and other interventions. All of this will eventually lead to the formation of industrial hubs in many areas including Lucknow, Kanpur, Noida, Meerut, Mirzapur, Bhadoi, Moradabad, Aligarh, Agra and Sonebhadra.

Empowerment through Social Entrepreneurship

Uttar Pradesh's greatest strength perhaps lies in its 100 million young people who are brimming with energy and ideas. How can we channelize this energy into constructive and creative work for the state and its people? That is the question which we must address now.

The state administration could consider launching a statewide mission of social entrepreneurship for the youth. For example, such a social enterprise can take up the task of procuring local raw materials, say mangoes in Malihabad, process them into nutrition-fortified food and make it available to the masses with a priority to the local markets, with only the necessary margins on price. In this way, the social entrepreneur will be the link between the local product, local nutritional need, technology and marketing. At the same time, the venture would be financially sustainable. The farmer will also benefit and the customer will have access to a quality product at a low cost. Because the production is local, there will be cost advantages in terms of transportation, reduced wastage and less need of storage.

This would require the setting up a total of about 1,00,000 social enterprises across the state to serve its 200 million people along the lines of:

1) Food and nutrition (about 20,000 social enterprises)
2) Access to water, both potable and irrigation (about 15,000 social enterprises)
3) Access to healthcare (about 15,000 social enterprises)
4) Access to income generation capacity (about 15,000 social enterprises)
5) Access to education and capacity building (about 15,000 social enterprises)
6) Access to quality power and communication applications (about 5,000 social enterprises)
7) Access to financial services (about 5,000 social enterprises), and so on.

Each of these social enterprises can employ about fifty social entrepreneurs who can be educated, unemployed youth with a will to be partners in the development and empowerment of UP. Industry and academia can take up the task of training these social entrepreneurs as per need. The entrepreneurs can be supported with stipends during their training. This initiative will also help find value-added employment for the 25 lakh unemployed and underemployed youth in the state and open up job avenues for others.

Infrastructure Empowerment

The government needs to prepare a roadmap for the kind of infrastructure that would be needed to make UP a preferred destination for industry both in India and abroad. For example, while the demand for power in the state is about 30,000 MW, the total availability is less than 12,500 MW. The group on infrastructure empowerment might like to specifically indicate how this gap can be filled through PPP ventures. While increasing the generation of electricity, the focus should be on non-conventional energy.

Another important issue is of ensuring all-weather, good quality roads across the length and breadth of the state to ensure speedy transportation of perishable products and passenger movement. This will also help tourism. The existing eight-lane expressway project has to be accelerated, and the expressway must in turn be connected to good quality rural roads which are maintained properly with the participation of the local community and the private sector. Another important aspect would be the provision of fast, reliable and competent emergency facilities on highways to attend to accident victims. The private sector could also participate in this venture to reduce such casualties, which should be a priority.

There is a need to modernize existing airports for tourist traffic and upgrade the ones in Lucknow, Agra, Allahabad and Varanasi to international standards and link them with high-speed rail and road networks. Development to be far reaching will have to be complemented by facilities such as good care for the underprivileged and homeless.

Comparative Development of Various States of India

Among the other important parameters for comparison of states, we give some highly informative facts and figures to show how certain states have done better than others on development.

Based on the statistics provided by the Central Statistical Organization, we the authors carried out an analysis of certain development indicators such as per capita income, gross enrolment ratio, healthcare expenditure, sanitation facilities, life-expectancy at birth, MMR, IMR, and doctor-population ratio for all the states and also at the all-India level. Then we looked at revenue expenditure on economic development, on agriculture and allied sectors, on rural development and the per capita expenditure on various sectors.

This analysis brings out the top performers, the moderate performers and the least performing states. It also shows that a state performs better overall when it spends on the development of basic sectors and focuses on enriching the quality of services. Some states show that when there is development, the government is elected again and again. In certain states, even though there is a repeated change of government, the performance on the development front is high thanks to the governance system in place.

Here is what the analysis showed: The top five states that have achieved spectacular performance in increasing the per-capita income were:

Haryana 2.4 times, Maharashtra 2.3 times, Tamil Nadu 2.5 times, Gujarat 2.3 times and Kerala 2.2 times in the period from 2004-05 to 2010-11. Tamil Nadu maintained a lead in increasing the per capita income, followed by Haryana.

States such as Punjab, Andhra Pradesh, Karnataka, West Bengal, and Rajasthan have doubled their percapita income from 2004-05 to 2010-11.

The bottom five states in this area are Bihar, Uttar Pradesh, Assam, Madhya Pradesh and Odisha. Bihar and UP are still at a low level, whereas Assam, Madhya Pradesh and Odisha have increased per capita income from Rs 31,000 to Rs 40,000 respectively, what the top five states had achieved five years earlier.

The Human Development Yardstick

The United Nations' Human Development Report 2013 says, 'India's economic performance has also been impressive, averaging nearly 5 per cent income growth a year over 1990-2012. Nevertheless, India's per capita income is still low, around $3,400 in 2012; to improve living standards, it will need further growth, since it is difficult to achieve much poverty reduction through redistribution alone at low income. India's performance in accelerating human development, however, is less impressive than its growth performance. Indeed, Bangladesh, with a much slower economic growth and half of India's per capita income, does nearly as well—and better on some indicators.'

Featuring among the top fifteen countries that have succeeded in reducing an HDI shortfall are Algeria, Brazil and Mexico, even

Per-Capita Income
Top Five States

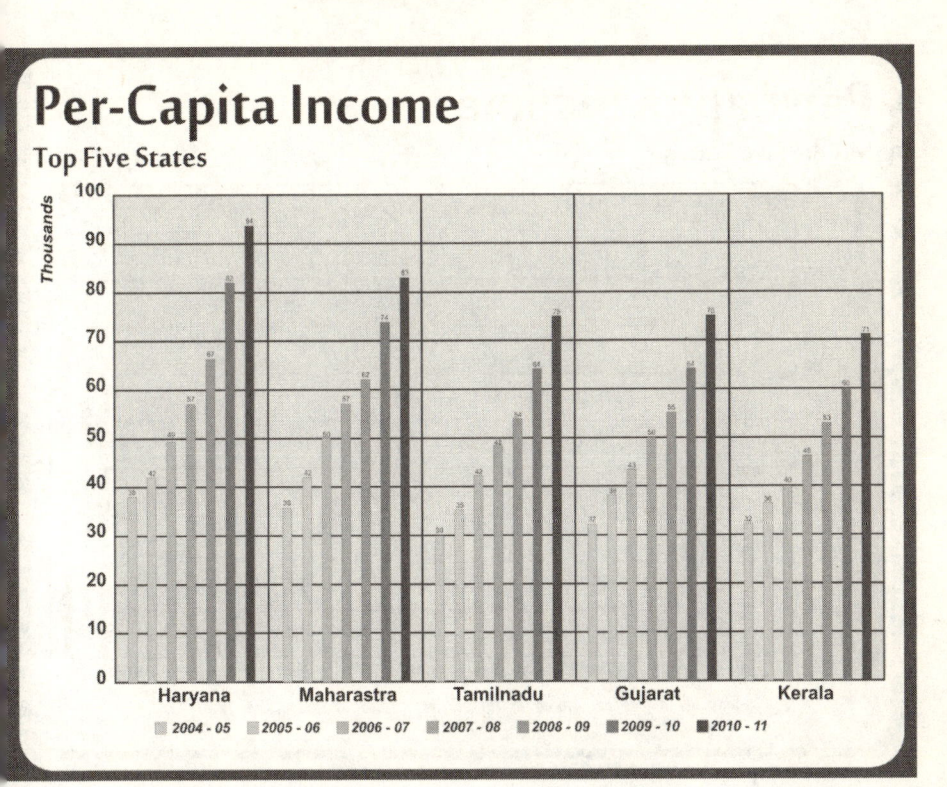

though their growth in per capita income averaged only 1 per cent to 2 per cent a year over 1990-2012. Their experience points to a broad strategy that has paid human development dividends: giving primacy to state investment in people's capabilities—especially their health, education and nutrition—and making their societies more resilient to economic, environmental and other threats and shocks.

The lesson to be learnt is that countries cannot rely on growth alone. As the 1993 and 1996 human development reports argued, the link between growth and human development is not automatic. It needs to be forged through pro-poor policies by concurrently investing in health and education, expanding decent jobs, preventing the deflection and overexploitation of natural resources, ensuring gender balance and equitable income distribution and

Per-Capita Income
Middle Five States

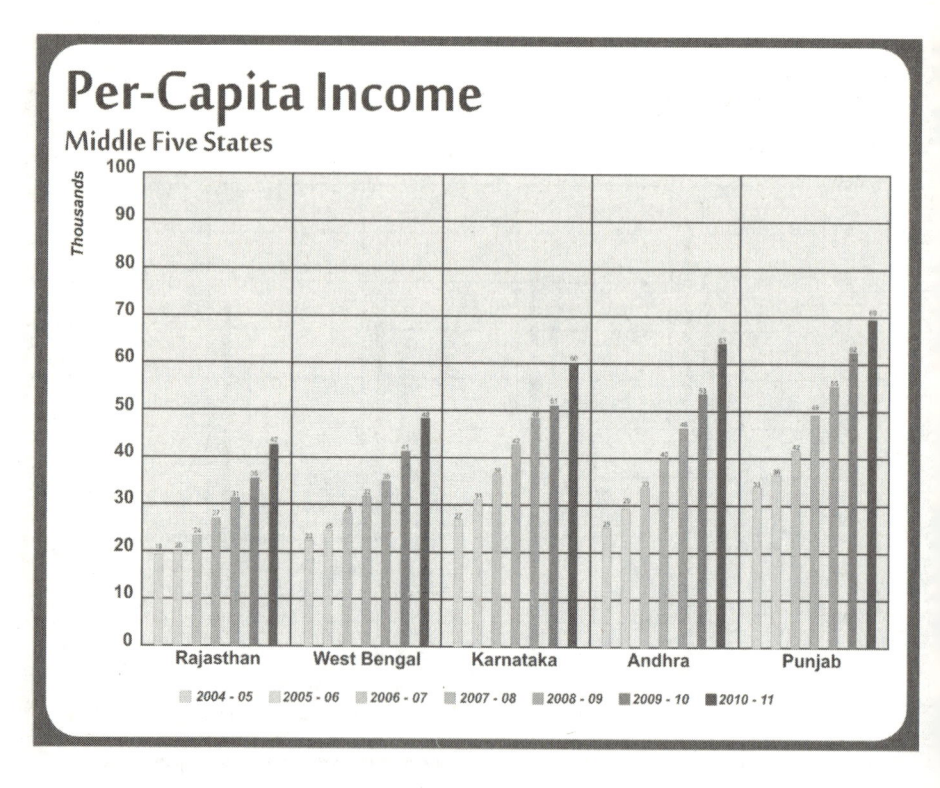

[Bar chart showing per-capita income in thousands for Rajasthan, West Bengal, Karnataka, Andhra, and Punjab across years 2004-05, 2005-06, 2006-07, 2007-08, 2008-09, 2009-10, 2010-11]

avoiding unnecessary displacement of communities. At the national level, faster economic growth can enable countries to reduce debts and deficits and generate additional public revenues to step up investments in basic goods and services, especially in health and education. And at the household level, income growth helps meet basic needs, improve living standards and enhance quality of life. Any country which is on the path of economic growth leading to sustainable development has to be built on the three drivers of transformation which, according to HDR 2013, are a proactive developmental state, tapping of global markets, and determined social policy innovation.

In this context of human development, let us look at how states concentrating on the improvement of the overall scenario in education, healthcare, agriculture and rural development have fared.

Comparative Development in Economic and Social Services by States

An analysis of the revenue expenditure of various states on economic services during 2011-12 gives an idea of how states look at their development priorities.

Agriculture and Allied services: Agriculture is the primary sector of the Indian economy and that is the core competence of India. The moment India realizes that agriculture is the backbone of the country, it will not even take a decade to become a developed country. This single change in mindset of the policy makers will brings synergy in agriculture and agro-based industry and services. Over 65 per cent of the population still relies on agriculture for employment and livelihood. India is the first in the world in the production of milk, pulses, jute and jute-like fibers; second in rice, wheat, sugarcane, groundnut, vegetables, fruits and cotton production; and is a leading producer of spices and plantation crops as well as livestock, fisheries and poultry.

The percentage of spending on agriculture and allied services, irrigation and flood control, transport & communications, rural development, special area programme, energy, science, technology and environment, industry & minerals and general economic services will give us a clear understanding of the path the state is adopting, whether it is based on the core competence of the state or political necessities.

The top ten states that spend 14 per cent to 8 per cent of the revenue expenditure on agriculture and allied activities are Mizoram, Arunachal Pradesh, Meghalaya, Chhattisgarh, Karnataka, Madhya Pradesh, Tripura, Uttarakkand, Manipur and Odisha. The other states that spend 8 per cent to 4 per cent are Himachal Pradesh, Nagaland, Sikkim, Puducherry, Kerala, Assam, Jammu & Kashmir, Tamil Nadu, Haryana, Jharkhand, Maharashtra, Gujarat, Rajasthan, Andhra Pradesh and Bihar. The following states spend less than 4 per cent: Punjab, Goa, Uttar Pradesh and West Bengal and NCT (Territory of Delhi).

REVENUE EXPENDITURE OF STATES ON ECONOMICS SERVICES 2011-2012
MAJOR STATES AND ALL INDIA

% OF TOTAL EXPENDITURE

■ % AGRICULTURE & ALLIED ACTIVITIES

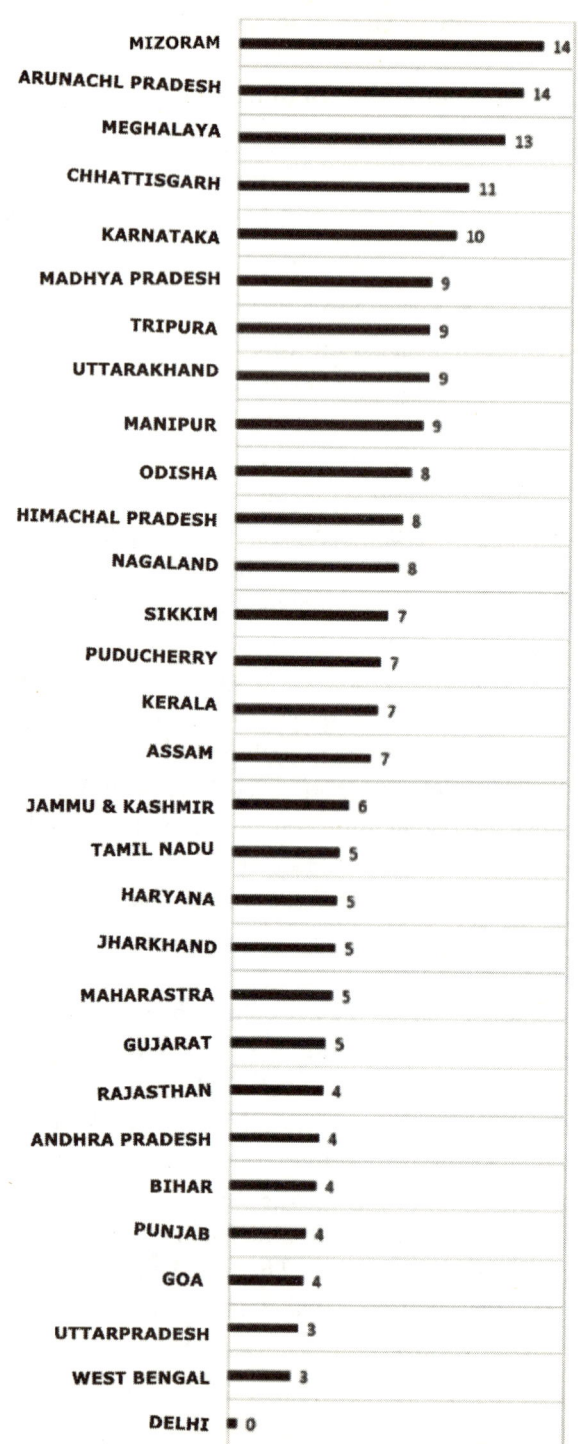

State	%
MIZORAM	14
ARUNACHL PRADESH	14
MEGHALAYA	13
CHHATTISGARH	11
KARNATAKA	10
MADHYA PRADESH	9
TRIPURA	9
UTTARAKHAND	9
MANIPUR	9
ODISHA	8
HIMACHAL PRADESH	8
NAGALAND	8
SIKKIM	7
PUDUCHERRY	7
KERALA	7
ASSAM	7
JAMMU & KASHMIR	6
TAMIL NADU	5
HARYANA	5
JHARKHAND	5
MAHARASTRA	5
GUJARAT	5
RAJASTHAN	4
ANDHRA PRADESH	4
BIHAR	4
PUNJAB	4
GOA	4
UTTARPRADESH	3
WEST BENGAL	3
DELHI	0

The Indian agriculture sector is now moving towards a second green revolution. The transformations in the sector are being induced by factors like newfound interest of the organized sector, new and improved technologies, mechanized farming, rapid growth of contract farming and easy credit facilities.

A renewed emphasis on investment in the sector will be crucial to developing states.

Rural Development: The spending of 2 per cent to 8 per cent of the total revenue expenditure for the rural development (only five states are spending 7-8 per cent: Jharkhand, Bihar, Rajasthan, Chhattisgarh, Madhya Pradesh, the rest of the states are spending only 2-5 per cent and less) has not brought sustainable development to 600,000 villages so far even after 12th Five Year Plan period. The fragmented approach to development through multiple state and central government schemes has led to leakage in every scheme and a failure to achieve the desired result in the rural areas.

Education: The GER (Gross Enrolment Ratio) of Indian states in classes I-V and VI-VIII during 2010-11 is presented in the charts in the following pages. The states that have achieved a good GER at the primary level (classes I-V) are predominantly from Northeast and Central India, such as Meghalaya, Manipur, Mizoram, Arunachal Pradesh, Sikkim, Jharkhand, Madhya Pradesh, Tripura, Bihar and UP. The rest of the states have done moderately well. At the secondary level, the states doing well are Himachal Pradesh, Tamil Nadu, Uttarakhand, Arunachal Pradesh, Mizoram, Manipur, Kerala, Madhya Pradesh, Goa, and Jammu & Kashmir.

The states that did well at the primary level fall behind and register more dropouts at the secondary level, showing that they lack a supportive school infrastructure, transportation facilities, and midday meal programmes. This is combined with other factors such as poverty, low per capita income, etc.

The states showing high dropout levels at the secondary school level are: Arunachal Pradesh, Mizoram, Manipur, Meghalaya,

Gross Enrolment Ratios
(In classes I-V and VI-VIII of Schools for General)
Focus Classes I-V – in Descending Order
2010-11

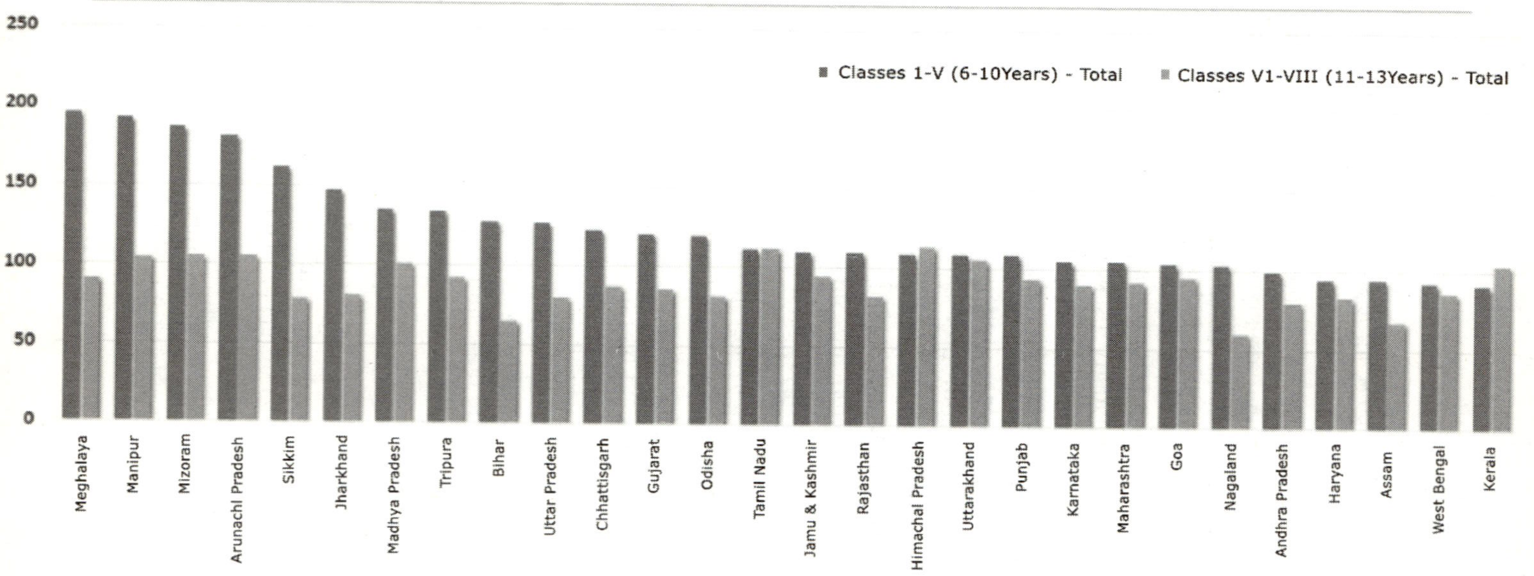

■ Classes I-V (6-10 Years) - Total
■ Classes VI-VIII (11-13 Years) - Total

Gross Enrolment Ratios
(In classes I-V and VI-VIII of Schools for General)
Focus Classes VI-VIII – in Descending Order
2010-11

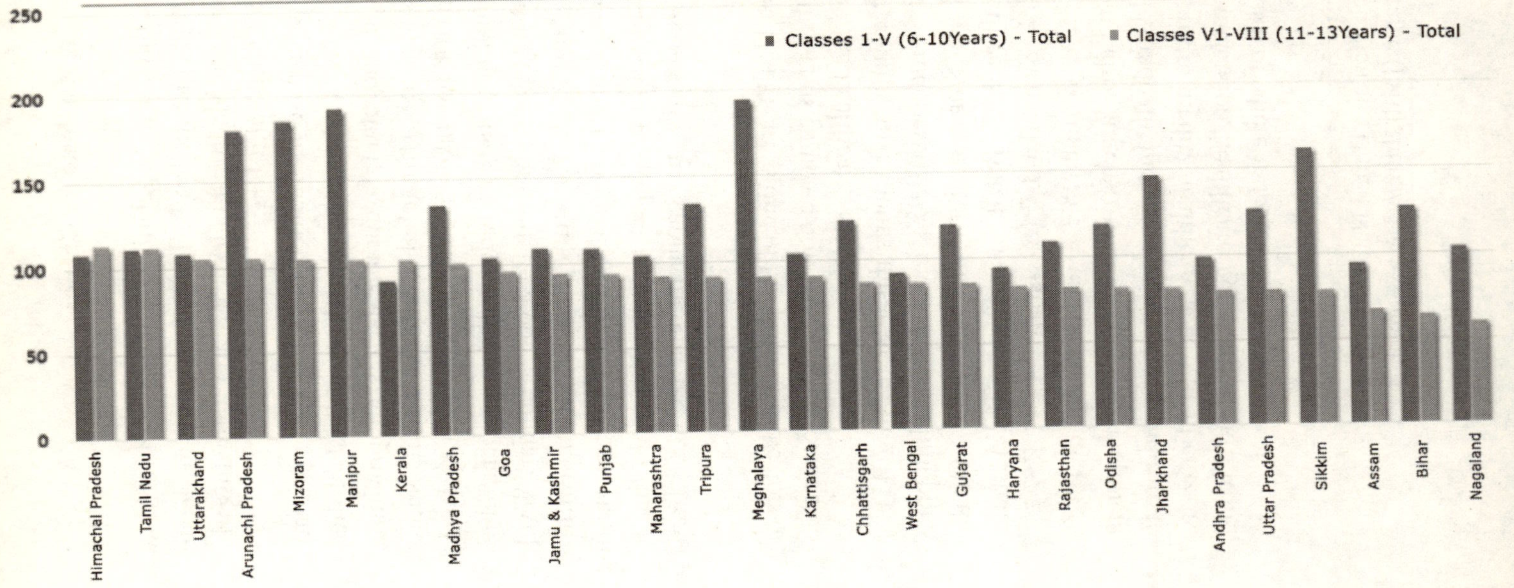

- Classes I-V (6-10Years) - Total
- Classes VI-VIII (11-13Years) - Total

Jharkhand, Sikkim, Bihar and Nagaland. They have fared very low in increasing per capita income levels. The states posting moderate numbers of dropouts are Madhya Pradesh, Tripura, Chhattisgarh, Gujarat, Rajasthan, Odisha and UP.

The following states have maintained the GER at the primary level to secondary level, showing that they have well-established school infrastructure and other favourable factors for providing education. The states are Himachal Pradesh, Tamil Nadu, Uttarakhand, Kerala (it has taken a lead at the secondary level, which shows that enrolment increase is due to the return of families from abroad admitting their children for good secondary level schooling), Goa, Jammu & Kashmir, Punjab, Maharashtra, Karnataka, West Bengal, and Haryana. Majority of these states also fared well in increasing the per capita income. We could find a direct relationship between the per capita income and GER from these two analyses.

Healthcare services: Healthcare is one of the primary indicators of human development. Let us compare how we are faring compared to other countries in the healthcare sector.

Myanmar is the country that spends the least 0.3% (2011) of GDP. Pakistan 0.7%, Indonesia 0.9%, India 1.2 %, Philippines 1.4%, Bangladesh 1.4% ,Singapore 1.4%, and China 2.9%. On the other hand, South Africa 4.1%, Brazil 4.1%, Korea 4.1%, Australia 6.2 %, Finland 6.6%, Switzerland 7.1%, Japan 7.4%, UK 7.7%, Canada 7.9%, US 8.2%, Germany 8.4%, and Netherlands 10.2% are high spenders and also, largely, much better on development indices. India should gradually increase the health expenditure to 6% before 2020 to ensure quality healthcare access to all citizens. The following parameters on healthcare compared to the world average give us an idea of where to focus.*

---

*World Health Organization and United Nations Children's Fund, Joint Measurement Programme (JMP) (http://www.wssinfo.org/).

Improved Sanitation Facilities (% of population with access)

India has only 34 per cent who have improved sanitation facilities compared to the world average of 62%.

Life Expectancy at Birth, Female & Male (years)

Life expectancy in India at birth Female 67, Male 64 in 2011 when compared to the world average of 72 for Female and 67.9 for Male.

Maternal Mortality Ratio (modeled estimate, per 100,000 live births)

India's MMR is 200/100,000 per live births, compared to the world average of 210 as per 2010 data.

Infant Mortality Rate (per 1,000 live births)

IMR in India is 36.9 compared to the world average of 47.2 in 2011.

Out-of-pocket Health Expenditure (% of private expenditure on health)

The percentage of private expenditure on health in India is 86 per cent, compared to the world average of 69.1 per cent.

Improving the Doctor-population Ratio

India ranked 67 among 133 developing nations in the case of doctor-population ratio. The doctor-population ratio works out to 1:2,000 approximately. There are around 3.72 lakh nurses in the country and the nurses-population ratio comes to 1:2,950.

According to the latest Central Bureau of Health Intelligence's survey, the number of beds in the country is 5,40,330 in 11,614 government hospitals. In the European region, there are 63 hospital beds per 10,000 people, compared with 10 per 10,000 in the African region.

New Index of Backwardness and Development

In May 2013, the Union government constituted a committee headed by Raghuram Rajan, now RBI governor, to suggest ways to identify indicators of the relative backwardness of the states for equitable allocation of funds. Central allocations are governed by the Gadgil-Mukherjee formula that places the greatest weight on the state's population, followed by other factors like per capita income and literacy.

The committee has proposed an index of backwardness composed of ten equally weighted indicators for monthly per capita consumption expenditure, education, health, household amenities, poverty rate, female literacy, percentage of the Scheduled Caste/Scheduled Tribe population, urbanization rate, financial inclusion and physical connectivity. The ten states that score above 0.6 (out of 1) on the composite index have been classified as 'least developed', the eleven states that scored from 0.4 to 0.6 are 'less developed' and the seven states that scored less than 0.4 are 'relatively developed'.

The report recommends that each of the twenty-eight states (since then one more has been added—Telangana) get 0.3 per cent of overall Central funds allocated and of the remaining 91.6 per cent, three-fourths be allocated based on need and one-fourth based on the state's improvements on its performance, to be reviewed every five years. Since states now classified as 'special category' will 'find their needs met' through the new allocations, the term 'special category' will be retired.

If the recommendations are accepted, Bihar, Madhya Pradesh, Odisha, Rajasthan and Uttar Pradesh will get a larger share of funds than their current share of Central assistance to state plans and centrally sponsored schemes, while Kerala, Tamil Nadu and Maharashtra will lose substantially. They have already raised their objections for the allocation of funds based on this report raising their genuine concern that the system would impose a penalty for their focus on development.

The performance of the states analysed by the independent agencies can help to understand their individual performance without any bias. Based on an *India Today* report, we did a detailed analysis.

Performance of the States and Where They Need to Focus

We analysed the performance of individual states based on the India Today Group and Indicus Analytics reports brought out in 2011, 2012 and 2013 which are based on nine major indicators such as Agriculture, Education, Health, Governance, Infrastructure, Consumer Market, Investment, Macro Economy and the overall performance of states. *India Today* and *Indicus Analytics* ranked the states using objective data and not perception-based qualitative information. The best performing states were ranked in nine categories by Bibek Debroy and Laveesh Bhandari with the help of Minakshi Chakraborty. The data used was from government and other credible sources with universal coverage of all states and Union Territories.

THE BEST PERFORMING STATES ACROSS NINE CATEGORIES IN 2011, 2012, 2013

BEST STATE OF THE DECADE 2003-2012

1st Himachal Pradesh	Retains the best state position since 2010
2nd Tamil Nadu	

Tamil Nadu was ranked 7 in overall performance in 2003. In 2012, Tamil Nadu displaced Punjab from second position

TOP PERFORMING STATES IN 2011-2013 IN 9 CATEGORIES

Category/Year	Big States	Small States
OVERALL		
2011	Maharashtra	Arunachal Pradesh
2012	Gujarat	Delhi
2013	Kerala	Goa
Primary Health		
2011	Haryana	Mizoram
2012	Jammu & Kashmir	Manipur
2013	Himachal Pradesh	Nagaland
Investment Environment		
2011	Gujarat	Arunachal Pradesh
2012	Gujarat	Mizoram
2013	Himachal Pradesh	Goa
Macro Economy		
2011	Maharashtra	Arunachal Pradesh
2012	Madhya Pradesh	Goa
2013	Gujarat	Goa
Agriculture		
2011	Assam	Mizoram
2012	Tamil Nadu	Puducherry
2013	Rajasthan	Nagaland
Consumer Market		
2011	Uttarakhand	Goa
2012	Maharashtra	Delhi
2013	Haryana	Goa
Education		
2011	Haryana	Puducherry
2012	Uttarakhand	Sikkim
2013	Kerala	Goa

Category/Year	Big States	Small States
Infrastructure		
2011	Himachal Pradesh	Nagaland
2012	Maharashtra	Delhi
2013	Jammu & Kashmir	Goa
Governance		
2011	Assam	Manipur
2012	Kerala	Goa
2013	Andhra Pradesh	Tripura

It was interesting to see how the small states were able to perform better in many areas whereas the big states' performance was higher in one or two sectors but lagged in many areas. What were the reasons for this? Was it related to a lack of focus, investment, leadership?

Performance of Big states (20 States)

Kerala

Kerala achieved top position in overall performance and education in 2013. The other positives were: Macro Economy—2nd, Agriculture—3rd, Consumer Market—4th, Investment—5th. The negatives: Health—8th, Infrastructure—19th and Governance—20th position.

It focused on economic and human development with growth and equity. The huge inflow of remittances from Keralites' community abroad helped the state. The key growth indicators: GDP, capital expenditure and consumer market and education sector. Its 10 per cent rise in GDP was 3 percentage points higher than the national GDP growth. Its 30 per cent rise in capital expenditure was much higher than the national average of 5 per

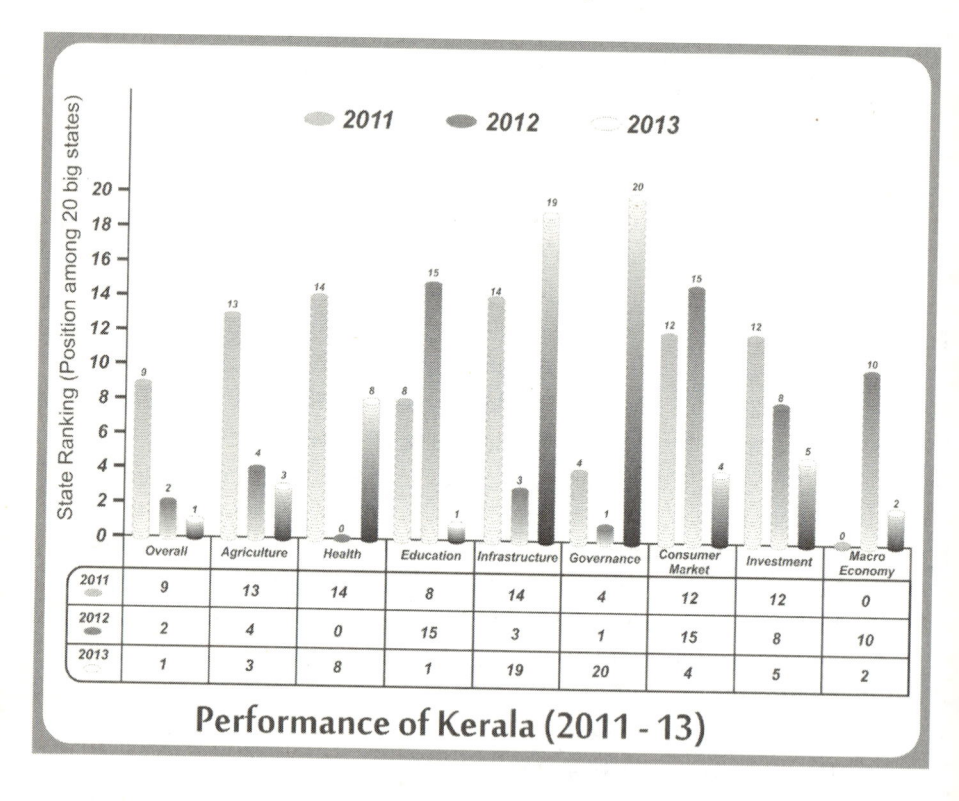

Performance of Kerala (2011 - 13)

	Overall	Agriculture	Health	Education	Infrastructure	Governance	Consumer Market	Investment	Macro Economy
2011	9	13	14	8	14	4	12	12	0
2012	2	4	0	15	3	1	15	8	10
2013	1	3	8	1	19	20	4	5	2

State Ranking (Position among 20 big states)

cent. The 4:100 teacher pupil ratio doubled from two teachers every 100 pupils, while most other states showed negligible improvement. There was a 35 per cent rise in the number of two-wheeler owners, while growth at the national level was 15 per cent.

It not only achieved the first position in overall performance but consistently maintaining improved performance in agriculture, health, education, consumer market, investment and macro economy from 2011. In 2012, it slipped on education, but regained and attained the first position in 2013.

From the graph it would appear Kerala has to focus on improvement in governance, infrastructure and healthcare.

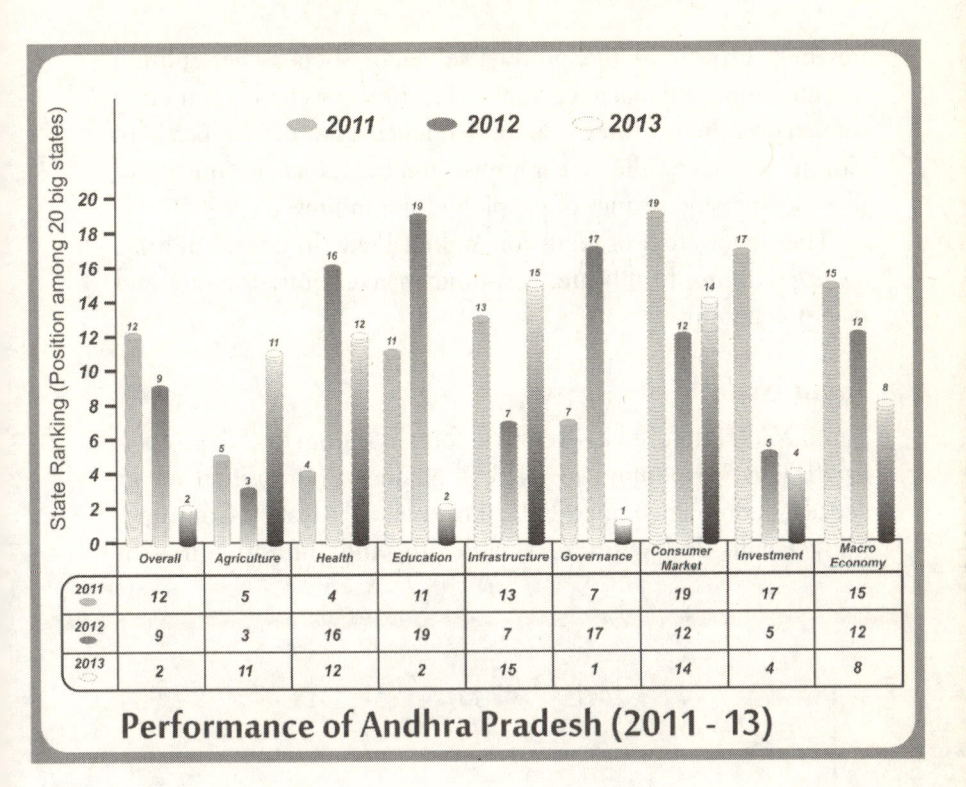

Performance of Andhra Pradesh (2011 - 13)

	Overall	Agriculture	Health	Education	Infrastructure	Governance	Consumer Market	Investment	Macro Economy
2011	12	5	4	11	13	7	19	17	15
2012	9	3	16	19	7	17	12	5	12
2013	2	11	12	2	15	1	14	4	8

Andhra Pradesh

It has attained the second position in overall performance in 2013, climbing from 12th position in 2011. It attained top position in three areas: Governance–1, Education–2, and Investment–4th, but is trailing in five major areas such as Macro Economy–8th, Agriculture–11th, Health–12th, Consumer Market–14th and Infrastructure–15th position. Even though it has attained 1st position in governance, this is not reflected in other sectors for growth. In agriculture, it has slipped from third position to 11th. It has to focus on implementing Smart Waterways Grid to harness the floodwater from Godavari and Krishna to irrigate its water-deficient regions and Telangana region and also connect to the other smart waterways for on-demand water availability from the national waterways grid. Although investment improved from 17th to 4th position, this did not help growth in the productive sector such as agriculture, infrastructure, and macro economy. The health sector continuously slipped over the last three years and touched a low of 12th position. Consumer market did not improve, implying that the quality of life, income, and savings of people did not improve.

The major areas of focus for Andhra Pradesh, one would say, are: agriculture, healthcare, consumer market, infrastructure and macro economy.

Tamil Nadu

Tamil Nadu improved its overall performance from the 5th position in 2011 to 3rd position in 2013. It attained 2nd position for its decadal performance since 2003. It maintained a lead in Consumer Market with 2nd position. Health–6th, and Infrastructure–7th

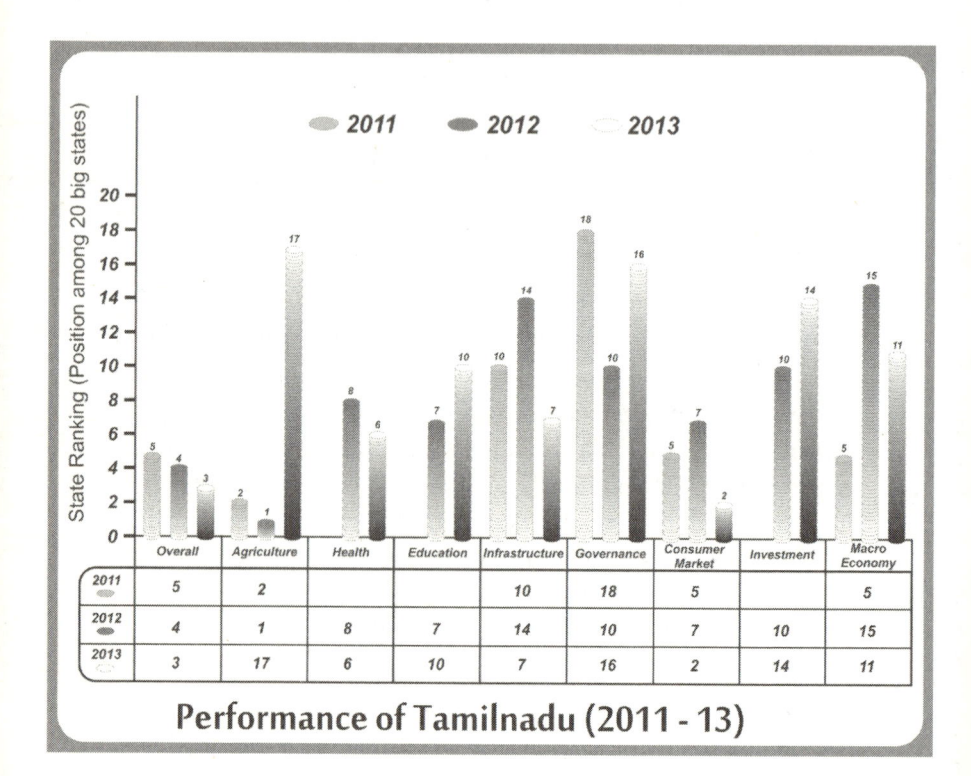

	Overall	Agriculture	Health	Education	Infrastructure	Governance	Consumer Market	Investment	Macro Economy
2011	5	2			10	18	5		5
2012	4	1	8	7	14	10	7	10	15
2013	3	17	6	10	7	16	2	14	11

Performance of Tamilnadu (2011 - 13)

position—but still it needs a lot of improvement in these two sectors. Even though there is slight improvement in infrastructure, it has to concentrate on energy and road infrastructure more for industrial growth. But it slipped far below in agriculture, from 1st to 17th position. In education also it slipped to 10th position. Higher education in the state has to be freed from political interference and it needs able academic leadership and focus on R&D. Governance reached the very bottom by touching 16th position, hence access to government services for fulfilling the basic amenities, ensuring safety and security has to be concentrated upon to improve its performance. It is not able to attract investment and slipped to 14th position, hence proactive governance, real and workable single-window facilitation, accessibility and transparency are the needs of the hour. As macro economy was in 11th position, focus on reducing poverty, increased per capita expenditure, containing the inflation, reducing the per capita debt and improving the GSDP should have priority.

Tamil Nadu has to concentrate on improving agriculture, because it has a core competence in SRI (System of Rice Intensification), SSI (Sustainable Sugarcane Initiative) and precision-farming technologies since these technologies are successfully tested and proven. It has to bring at least 3 lakh hectares into SRI cultivation a year for the next five years. SSI has to be spread to 1 lakh hectare for achieving 1,000 lakh MT of production. It has to implement the Smart Waterways Grid to utilize floodwaters from the Kaveri to equally distribute to other river basins. Out of 40,000 tanks and lakes, it has desilted only around 6,000 tanks. It has to complete this task for better water management.

Gujarat

It slipped to 4th position in 2013 from the 1st position in 2011. But Gujarat is maintaining a lead in Macro Economy (1st), Agriculture (2nd), Governance (4th), Consumer Market (5th) and Health (5th). It slipped to the bottom in Education (13th), Infrastructure

Performance of Gujarat (2011 - 13)

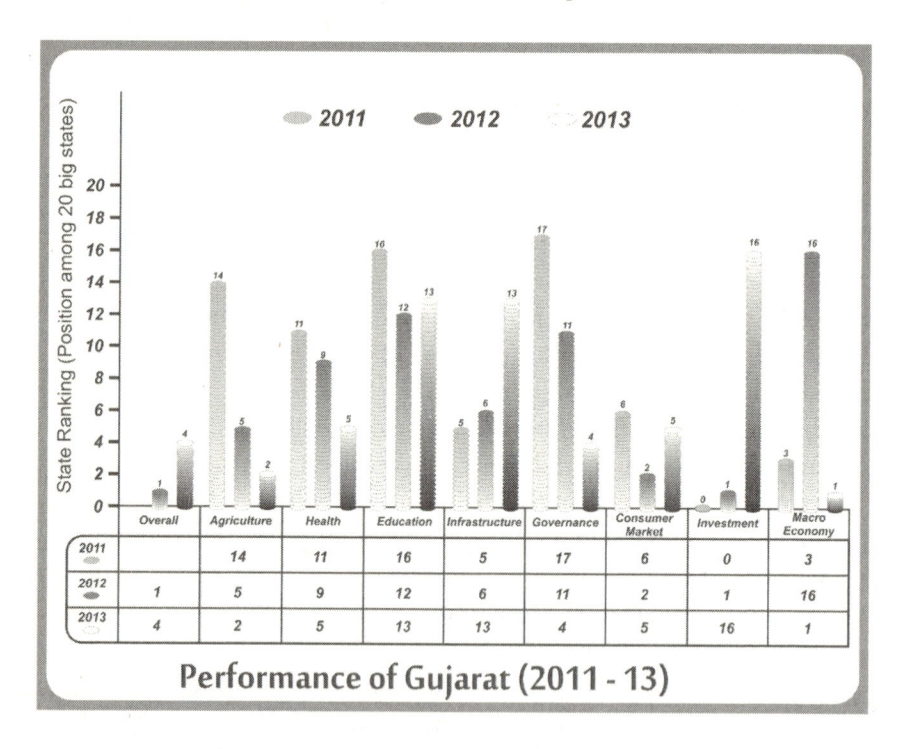

	Overall	Agriculture	Health	Education	Infrastructure	Governance	Consumer Market	Investment	Macro Economy
2011		14	11	16	5	17	6	0	3
2012	1	5	9	12	6	11	2	1	16
2013	4	2	5	13	13	4	5	16	1

(13th) and Investment (16th). It has to focus on education since it is not able to improve its performance in this area for the last three years. The focus should be on elementary education and improving the teacher-pupil ratio. Energy and road infrastructure which were in 5th and 6th position and are now at 13th position have to be brought up. Investment was in 1st position, but in 2013 it touched the bottom and slipped down 16th position. It attained 1st position in macro economy, an indicator that the quality of life improved.

Haryana

It slipped to 5th position in 2013 from 4th in 2011. It maintained the lead in consumer market at 1st position. But it slipped in agriculture (7th) even though it attained 2nd position in 2012. It did well in healthcare (1st), but slipped to 20th position in 2013. In energy and road infrastructure it slipped to 18th position. It should

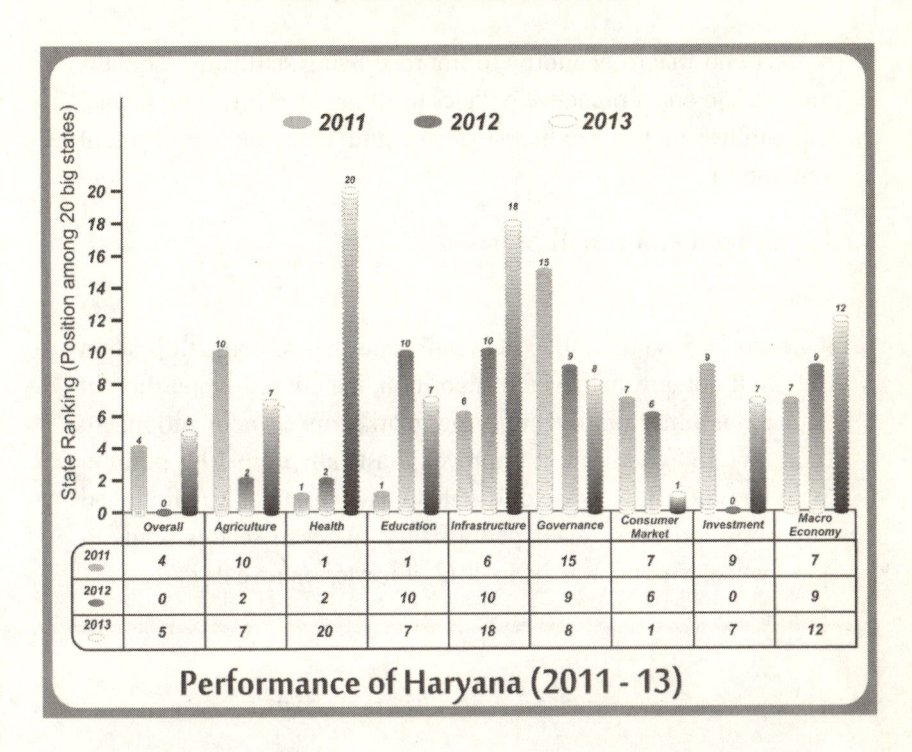

Manifesto for State Assemblies

	Overall	Agriculture	Health	Education	Infrastructure	Governance	Consumer Market	Investment	Macro Economy
2011	4	10	1	1	6	15	7	9	7
2012	0	2	2	10	10	9	6	0	9
2013	5	7	20	7	18	8	1	7	12

Performance of Haryana (2011 - 13)

concentrate on solar energy and other forms of renewable energy sources, and improved road infrastructure to its villages. In macro economy it went down from 7th to 12th position. In governance it has slipped to 8th rank. Hence it has to concentrate on improving the healthcare services such as improving IMR, MMR, safe drinking water, sex ratio, government expenditure on health and quality healthcare services with more outreach. It has also to focus on agriculture productivity. In education its performance is going down and it needs immediate attention in improving the school infrastructure.

Performance of the Rest of the Big States

The rest of the big states achieved higher performance in only one or two areas, but trailed in many areas. They need to adopt a good governance framework and fiscal prudence, and focus on areas such as agriculture, infrastructure, health, education and consumer market and macro economy to improve living standards. Equally, they should enact proactive policies to attract investment for capital expenditure in the productive sector and focus on employment generation.

Performance of Small States

Goa

It gained 1st position (2013) in overall performance from 7th position (2012). It not only achieved first position, it achieved 1st position in education, infrastructure, consumer market, investment and macro economy. In agriculture it improved drastically from 10th position to 2nd position. Goa is the only state to have sustainably maintained improved and accelerated performance in seven sectors. Only in governance, where it was 1st in 2012, it has to improve its rank.

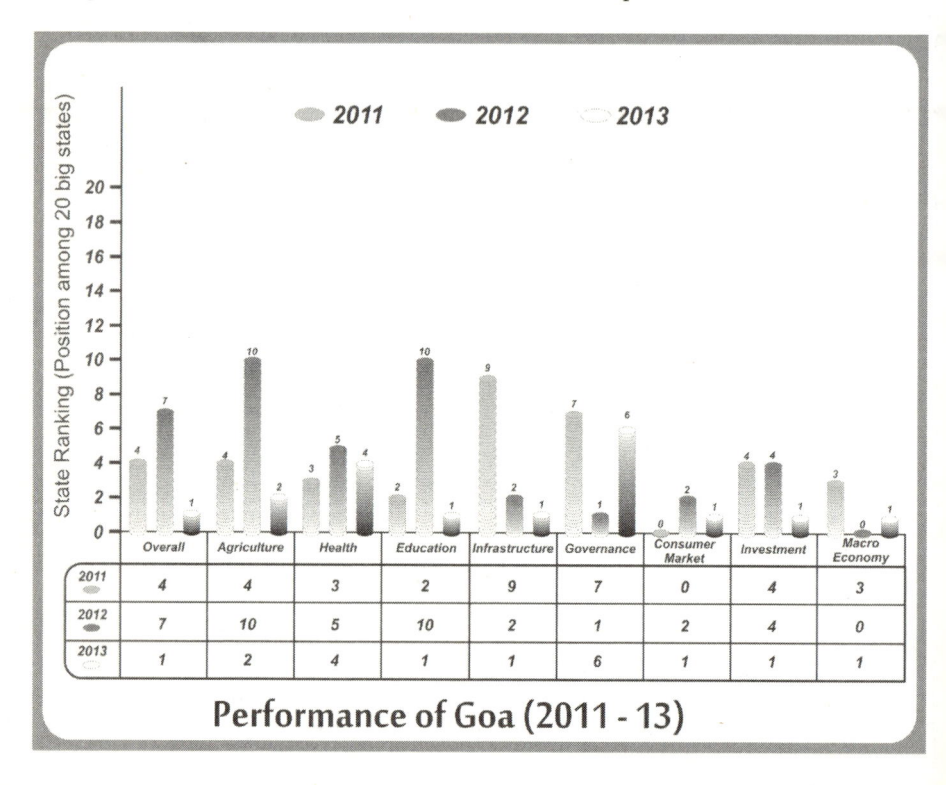

	Overall	Agriculture	Health	Education	Infrastructure	Governance	Consumer Market	Investment	Macro Economy
2011	4	4	3	2	9	7	0	4	3
2012	7	10	5	10	2	1	2	4	0
2013	1	2	4	1	1	6	1	1	1

Performance of Goa (2011 - 13)

Performances of the States

Rajasthan - 2013
Positive:
- Agriculture : 1
- Macro Economy : 3

Negative:
- Overall : 6
- Consumer Market : 6
- Investment : 9
- Governance : 9
- Infrastructure : 10
- Health : 14
- Education : 16

Maharastra - 2013
Positive:
- Health : 2
- Education : 4
- Macro Economy : 5

Negative:
- Overall : 7
- Investment : 6
- Governance : 10
- Agriculture : 12
- Infrastructure : 17
- Consumer Market : 18

Himachel Pradesh - 2013
Positive:
- Investment : 1
- Health : 1

Negative:
- Overall : 8
- Consumer Market : 7
- Agriculture : 8
- Governance : 13
- Infrastructure : 16
- Macro Economy : 17
- Education : 18

Punjab - 2013
Positive:
- Health : 1
- Investment : 2

Negative:
- Overall : 9
- Education : 6
- Agriculture : 9
- Consumer Market : 9
- Macro Economy : 14
- Governance : 17
- Infrastructure : 20

Madhya Pradesh - 2013
Positive:
- Governance : 2

Negative:
- Overall : 10
- Education : 8
- Consumer Market : 8
- Macro Economy : 9
- Health : 10
- Infrastructure : 12
- Agriculture : 15

Bihar - 2013
Positive:
- Macro Economy : 4
- Agriculture : 5

Negative:
- Overall : 11
- Investment : 8
- Infrastructure : 8
- Education : 9
- Governance : 12
- Health : 15
- Consumer Market : 15

Chhattisgrah - 2013
Positive:
- Agriculture : 4
- Education : 5

Negative:
- Overall : 12
- Governance : 8
- Infrastructure : 9
- Macro Economy : 13
- Health : 13
- investment : 15
- Consumer Market : 16

Karnataka - 2013
Positive:
- Education : 3
- Consumer Market : 3

Negative:
- Overall : 13
- Health : 7
- Agriculture : 10
- Infrastructure : 14
- Governance : 18
- Investment : 18
- Macro Economy : 19

West Bengal - 2013
Positive:
- Governance : 3
- Infrastructure : 5

Negative:
- Overall : 14
- Education : 12
- Investment : 12
- Consumer Market : 13
- Agriculture : 14
- Macro Economy : 15
- Health : 17

Assam - 2013
Positive:
- Infrastructure : 3

Negative:
- Overall : 15
- Macro Economy : 10
- Education : 11
- Investment : 13
- Agriculture : 16
- Consumer Market : 20

Uttrakhand - 2013
Positive:
- Health : 3
- Investment : 3

Negative:
- Overall : 16
- Infrastructure : 6
- Macro Economy : 7
- Consumer Market : 10
- Agriculture : 19
- Education : 19
- Governance : 19

Uttar Pradesh - 2013
Positive:
- Infrastructure : 2

Negative:
- Overall : 17
- Governance : 11
- Agriculture : 13
- Education : 14
- Health : 16
- Macro Economy : 16
- Consumer Market : 17
- Investment : 19

Jharkhand - 2013
Positive:
- Governance : 5

Negative:
- Overall : 18
- Infrastructure : 11
- Investment : 11
- Consumer Market : 12
- Education : 17
- Agriculture : 18
- Health : 18
- Macro Economy : 18

Odisha - 2013
Positive:
- Infrastructure : 4

Negative:
- Overall : 19
- Macro Economy : 6
- Consumer Market : 11
- Governance : 14
- Education : 15
- Investment : 17
- Health : 19
- Agriculture : 20

Jammu & Kashmir - 2013
Positive:
- Infrastructure : 1
- Health : 4

Negative:
- Overall : 20
- Agriculture : 6
- Governance : 15
- Consumer Market : 19
- Investment : 20
- Macro Economy : 20
- Education : 20

Positive | Negative

Based on 'State of the States 2013' report from *India Today*

According to the *India Today* report, it took a series of fiscal measures to help the state tide over the financial setback caused by the mining ban. These included a drastic cut of expenses. Auctions of ore lying in mines and at ports and taxing dump sites brought in Rs 800 crore in 2013. Goa plans to increase revenue per tourist and has the ambitious goal to achieve a growth rate of over 10 per cent going forward.

Manipur

It improved its performance and attained 2nd position (2013) from 10th position (2011). It maintained first five positions in Health (2nd), Investment (2nd), Macro Economy (3rd), Education (4th), Governance (4th) and Consumer Market (4th) and Agriculture (4th). It has to improve on Infrastructure (7th). In governance it

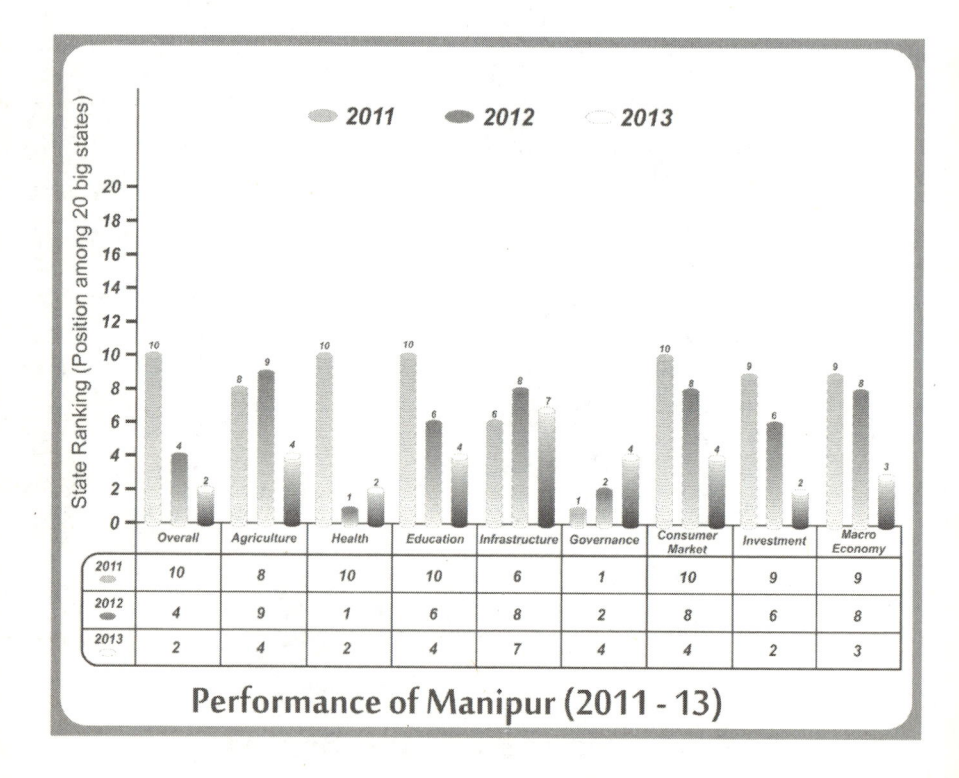

	Overall	Agriculture	Health	Education	Infrastructure	Governance	Consumer Market	Investment	Macro Economy
2011	10	8	10	10	6	1	10	9	9
2012	4	9	1	6	8	2	8	6	8
2013	2	4	2	4	7	4	4	2	3

Performance of Manipur (2011 - 13)

slipped from 1st position to 4th. The Macro Economy improved from 9th to 3rd position. It has to establish necessary irrigation infrastructure to bring more areas under cultivation, adopt hybrid technologies and system-oriented approach for pre- and post-harvesting techniques and implement agro food processing mission in a big way to increase the agricultural GSDP. In education, it has to focus on improving the school infrastructure, increasing the teacher-pupil ratio and ratio of boys to girls in elementary education. The dropout rate needs to be brought down.

Nagaland

It has improved its position from 6th (2011) to 3rd position (2013). It is maintaining first five positions in Agriculture (1st), Health (1st), Education (2nd), Infrastructure (3rd), Consumer Market

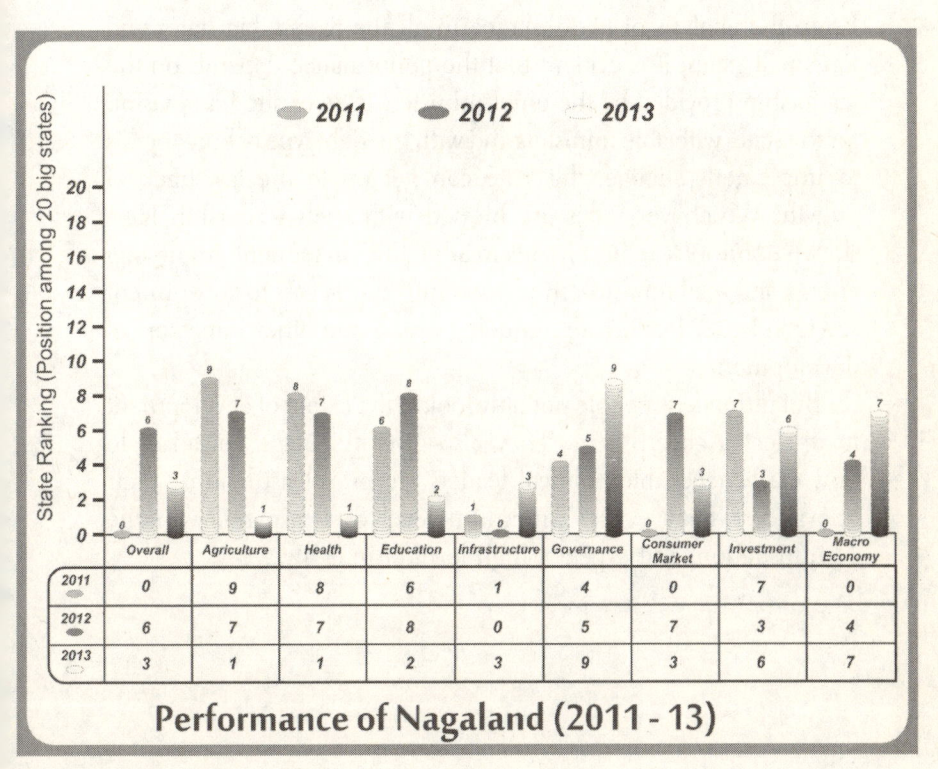

	Overall	Agriculture	Health	Education	Infrastructure	Governance	Consumer Market	Investment	Macro Economy
2011	0	9	8	6	1	4	0	7	0
2012	6	7	7	8	0	5	7	3	4
2013	3	1	1	2	3	9	3	6	7

Performance of Nagaland (2011 - 13)

(3rd). It has also achieved 1st position in agriculture and health. In education it has risen to 2nd position from the 8th. It has a good track record in improving the standard of living of the middle class. But it is not faring well in improving the quality of life of people living below the poverty line and increasing the per capita GSDP. In the following areas it is in negative position: Investment (6th), Macro Economy—(7th) and Governance—(9th). Also it has to attract more investment for capital expenditure, commercial bank credit, gross capital formation in manufacturing, reducing the ratio of factories to number of disputes, ratio of industrial workers to urban populace in the 15-59 age group by creating more employment opportunities, and revive the sick small-scale units.

Conclusion

From the analysis of performance in all the twenty big states and ten small states, it is evident that the performance depends on the leadership provided by the chief minister. If he or she has a vision for the state, with able ministers and with the right type of bureaucrats to implement change, the state can get on to the fast track of growth. Whichever states are blessed with such leadership have shown enormous achievements in attracting investment, improving energy and road infrastructure, providing easy access to government services, better healthcare, reducing crime and other indicators of development.

But ultimately, people not only look at the extent of development to re-elect a government. They also give weightage nowadays to how easily accessible political leaders are in at least hearing their grievances. They expect minimum level of transparency in the administration, and expect a high level of integrity.

SECTION VII

MANIFESTO FOR THE NATION

We have looked at ideas for village and state-wise development. We offer here a manifesto for the nation. For this, I have drawn upon my discussions with intellectuals, experts and researchers from universities in India and abroad, including students and faculty of the IIMs in Ahmedabad, Indore, Bangalore and Shillong and, of course, the 16 million youngsters with whom I have interacted over the years. Our nation's requirements are diverse and numerous. What I have tried in this section is to focus on manifestos for nine important spheres of national life. Missions in these areas, successfully implemented, will bring the nation much closer to Vision 2020.

SUSTAINABLE DEVELOPMENT OF RURAL AREAS

In order to bring sustainable development and prosperity to rural areas, we need to establish 7,000 self-reliant village clusters by Providing Urban Amenities in Rural Areas (PURA), under a public-private partnership model in the next six years. It would be a new and innovative cooperative model to bring about sustainable development to villages and would entail establishing physical, electronic and knowledge connectivity between villages.

The focus would be on development in an integrated manner. Thrust areas under this mission would include providing clear drinking water, generating power through renewable energy sources, bringing down infant and maternal mortality rates, increasing the literacy rate, and improving the functional literacy of self-help groups and unemployed youth. It would also lay emphasis on enhancing villagers' access to technology, legal recourse, communication, internet, quality healthcare services, education, sanitation and a pollution-free environment.

The main difference between PURA and other rural development schemes or the selective intervention of NGOs is that it will be aimed at integrated rural development and inclusive economic growth, unlike independent projects which do not do much to improve the living conditions of villages and check urban migration in the long term.

The ultimate aim of this mission would be to cover more than 6,00,000 villages (6,38,000 as per the 2011 census), which are home to more than 70 per cent of India's population, and to eventually bring the per capita incomes in rural areas to the same levels that are seen in the urban areas. This would create an economy that will not be affected by the vagaries of the global economic situation. Launching PURA as a national mission to create 7,000 PURA clusters will bring us closer to that goal.

Education and Healthcare

Even after spending Rs 3.7 lakh crore for rural development in the 11th Five-Year Plan, access to education and healthcare in rural areas remains inadequate. For a vast majority of villages in the country, higher secondary schools, colleges and ITIs are a distant dream. The same is true of good healthcare access in the form of government hospitals, private hospitals, health centres and even medical shops and general practitioners. Consider this: with every one kilometer increase in the distance to a health facility, there is a reduction of about 4 per cent in the chances of a pregnant woman opting for an institutional delivery.

The establishment of schools, hospitals and PHCs—through proactive government policies under the PPP model—is the need of the hour in rural areas. The government should focus on the generation of good teachers at the school level, while the private sector should jointly help establish a sound infrastructure. The idea is to bring the existing government and aided schools under the PPP model so that both sectors put their best foot forward—the private sector builds state-of-the-art facilities while the government trains teachers and fully subsidizes education so that it remains completely free.

Information and Communication Technology

Did you know that it took thirty-eight years for radio and thirteen years for television to reach 50 million people, but it took only four years for the World Wide Web to reach the same number. The internet revolution is remarkable in terms of speed and the promise it holds. But, according to the Internet and Mobile Association of India (IAMAI), only 2 per cent of rural India has access to the web.

This mission needs to combine mobile-based internet access, infotainment and education to provide edutainment services. The aim would be to provide knowledge- and skill-enabling services to those in rural areas, so that they have functional literacy in banking, financial and legal services and are better informed as to their rights.

Power Supply and Roads

The overall rural electrification in India stands at 94.2 per cent, but the quality of power supply is poor and intermittent. In most cases, there are blackouts of ten to fifteen hours a day. Power shortages have a direct impact on the rural economy, as farmers need power to irrigate their crops or to light their cattle sheds. Also, the availability and quality of power of supply is a major hindrance in setting up industries in rural areas.

This mission's target would be to ensure 24x7 access to 3-phase power supply in rural areas, with connected smart grid services, and availability of green energy through solar, bio-mass and bio-waste energy sources.

In terms of infrastructure, another major requirement is that of roads. Around 40 per cent of India's villages do not have access to all-weather roads. Implementing plastic road technology, which is already proven, will be of immense use. At the same time, we would eliminate the plastic waste accumulated in villages and cities. Road connectivity and rural poverty are directly related, with an increase in roads and other transport facilities leading to a reduction in poverty by providing better market access for rural goods and services, mainly labour. Hence improving the road network should be taken up on a war footing.

Access to Clean, Safe Drinking Water and Sanitation

Over 30 per cent of India's rural population has none or only partial access to clean drinking water. Equally grave is the lack of sanitation. According to a United Nations study, far more people in India have access to mobile phones than to toilets. It is estimated that 597 million people in India defecate in the open, which is more than half the total number of open defecation in the world. Open defecation is one of the biggest problems in rural India. It is estimated that one in ten deaths in rural Indian villages is linked to poor sanitation and hygiene, and diarrhoea accounts for a large proportion of these deaths.

Girls are often forced to miss or drop out of school due to poor sanitation facilities there. Lack of sanitation also has an economic impact in the form of reduced productivity caused by illnesses. According to an estimate of the Water and Sanitation Programme of the World Bank, this loss amounts to Rs 2.4 trillion annually, with a per capita loss of Rs 2,810.

Research and Development of Rural Technologies

The target of this mission would be to encourage universities, engineering institutions and industry to design and develop village silos and farm equipment needed to implement System of Rice

Intensification (SRI),* Sustainable Sugarcane Initiative (SSI)** and precision-farming technologies. Equally important would be the establishment of facilities for the storage of agricultural produce, food processing, seed distribution and other services.

Centralized Drainage System for Clean Power Generation

Here, the idea would be to establish a centralized drainage system in every village, which connects households and buildings. It will not only serve to avoid waste accumulation but also use the waste to create a 100 kW bio-digester/bio-mass plant which will generate electricity for rural industrial activity.

The government could encourage industry to direct its corporate social responsibility initiatives in this direction, while providing grants from its own coffers. The power plants could be managed by local self-help group members and skilled youth, leading to clean energy and employment generation at the same time.

Encouraging Corporates and SMEs

The government alone might not be able to shoulder the mammoth responsibility of transforming India's rural areas. It may need to seek the help of big corporate houses. In this direction, the government could provide an expenditure tax exemption to corporates and industry for adopting villages and doing development work like creating farm ponds, check dams, and water harvesting structures. Apart from the corporates, the SME sector could be encouraged to provide skill development with government support by way of tax exemption and other means. There could be support as well for establishing tele-medicine, mobile diagnostic vans, and mobile pharmacies. Super speciality and district hospitals could be

---

*A low-water, labour-intensive methodology aimed at increasing yields.

**A method of sugarcane production to achieve higher yields which requires less seed and less water.

linked up. Together, the government and social-minded organizations in the private sector would be able to develop large swathes of India's villages to bring sustainable development.

School Infrastructure

Every school should have playground facilities and competent coaches. There is an abundance of untapped local talent which good coaches could groom for international sports events such as the Olympics. Conducting an annual sports meet would be a mandatory provision. The schools should nurture skills in the arts, music, dance, and drama, besides the key habit of reading, and even provide speech training for felicity in self-expression. They could, alongside, develop skills and competence in working with computers which are becoming an integral part of education today. Exposure to disaster and emergency management and legal and constitutional rights and responsibilities at school level would be helpful to students in later life. The school infrastructure should be friendly to girl students and there should be special facilities for differently abled students. Extending the services of university and college professors on loan basis every year to coach the teachers and students might be of help too.

Literacy and Functional Literacy

One way of achieving 100 per cent literacy: implementing Same Language Subtitling (SLS) in films, movies, TV songs and serials as a mandatory provision for broadcasting, as advocated by Prof. Brij Kothari of IIM Ahmedabad and his team, who introduced a concept called 'Positive disruption in Education: Small Innovation, Big Impact'. Evolve an integrated mission for spreading functional literacy among women and unemployed youth on specific skills for entrepreneurship, banking, legal and financial matters. Empowering rural people through Village Knowledge Centres (or CSCs) which provide electronic and knowledge connectivity will ultimately lead to a uniformly high levels of awareness.

> **ENERGY INDEPENDENCE AND CLEAN ENVIRONMENT**

India's Energy Vision 2030 has to be three-dimensional. The first would be ensuring access to energy for all. Second, ensuring that the dependence on depleting fossil fuels is minimized, thereby giving stability to energy supply. Third, our energy needs are to be balanced with the needs of the environment, by stressing on clean energy, both in how we produce it and how we consume it.

By 2030, India's total energy requirement is likely to be around 4,00,000 MW, up from the present 2,05,000 MW. At that time, power generated from coal-based power plants would increase from the existing 80,000 MW to 2,00,000 MW if we follow the present route. This would demand a significant build-up of thermal power stations and large-scale expansion of coalfields. For the rest of our needs, we will have to depend on a mix of other energy sources.

India has tremendous potential to generate hydropower. As per an assessment of the Central Electricity Authority, India has the potential to generate at least 50,000 MW of hydropower by 2030. Large-scale solar energy farms of hundreds of megawatts capacity could contribute around 55,000 MW. These targets are feasible and well within our capability. Moreover, our nuclear scientists have an integrated energy policy with a target of generating 63,000 MW by 2030. In any case, we are sure that we will be able to generate 45,000 MW of nuclear power by 2030. The rest of our electricity requirement should be met by wind energy. We are in a good position in this respect. Within the last decade alone, we have reached a capacity of generating over 11,000 MW through wind farms. I do not visualize many challenges in enhancing our capacity to 45,000 MW by 2030.

We also depend on oil to the extent of around 134 million

tonnes and above every year, 75 per cent of which is imported, and used almost entirely in the transportation sector. We produce only one-fourth of our total requirement. Future exploration of oil and gas may give mixed results. The import cost of oil and natural gas was almost Rs 2,00,000 crore ($40 billion) in 2012-13. Petroleum prices are highly volatile and steadily rising, going as high as $147 per barrel in 2008. This situation has to be carefully addressed as a large proportion of our net imports are petroleum imports alone, and major fluctuations in the international prices of oil and gas have the potential to destabilize our balance of payments.

Power generation through renewable energy sources has to be increased from 5 per cent to 28 per cent. Our dependence on fossil fuels as primary energy sources needs to be brought to under 50 per cent from the present 75 per cent. We need to adopt alternative methods such as mandatory ethanol usage, biofuels and emulsification and reduce the dependency on oil imports. We need to evolve a comprehensive alternative fuel usage policy which will empower the farmers to produce energy crops and mandate their usage from 10 per cent to progressively increase it to 50 per cent before 2030. This means evolving a comprehensive policy which encourages farmers to produce energy crops. Also, the automobile sector has to be mandated to produce flexi-vehicles within a stipulated timeframe and create an alternative fuel distribution system across the nation.

Keeping this situation in mind, our manifesto for the energy independence and clean environment mission would comprise the following aspects:

Formation of a National Energy Commission
This national agency will bring together all policy makers and planners, both at the state and central levels, ministries dealing with various forms of energy such as coal, petroleum and natural gas, the ministry of non-conventional energy sources, and the ministries dealing with irrigation and environment to ensure a

coordinated, speedy thrust to implement our energy policy in such a way that it helps our GDP grow at the targeted rate of 10 per cent annually. The National Energy Commission should evolve Energy Independence Vision by 2030 from the present Energy Security perspective for a greatly expanded use of renewable energy sources. Clear timebound targets are needed to reduce the dependency on fossil fuel use and oil/coal imports.

Research and Development

The country's top academic and R&D institutions in both the public and private sectors need to do the bulk of their research on the science and technology needed for energy independence for the next decade. The thrust of the research would have to be on how to replace petroleum as the primary fuel source for transport by less carbon emitting or completely carbon-neutral renewable fuels. There will have to be an international collaboration on promoting green energy with a flow of ideas and technologies between countries doing path-breaking research in this field.

Reducing Emissions

The vision for energy independence will not be complete without stressing the need for reducing emissions and protecting the environment. My team and I calculated that currently the emission per unit of energy used through various means comes to around 1.3 kg of carbon dioxide per watt of power per year. Through multipronged efforts, this should be brought down to under 0.65 kg in the next twenty years. This will in turn bring down the global emissions of greenhouse gases.

High-Tension Power Grid Infrastructure across the Nation

A vital need for economic development is that surplus energy generated in one part of the country should be available to the other parts if they have a shortfall. Hence, it is essential to establish a high-tension power grid infrastructure across the nation, connecting the southern and northern grids and upgrading them with the latest transformers and wireless smart metering and monitoring systems at the consumer level. This will help reduce distribution and transmission losses, which can be an enormous drain, and, at the same time, ensure proper use of generated power.

Coupling Captive Power and Emulsification for Efficiency

India has 30,000 MW of captive power located in different industries. The suggestion is, we can increase this captive power in various forms to 60,000 MW with a provision to feed into the grid unutilized captive generation capacity for meeting volatile supply needs. All the captive power is powered by diesel fuel. Implementation of emulsified fuel systems in automobiles, boilers and other diesel consumption systems will lead to saving in fuel of the order of 35 to 40 per cent per system. Evolving a policy to use the emulsified fuel coupled with use of captive power and other systems which use diesel could thus generate enormous savings.

Intelligent Buildings

Buildings consume 50 per cent of electricity produced globally and also account for high levels of heat trapping and emissions. Multiple energy efficiency measures can reduce consumption by at least half. The emerging trends of intelligent buildings and green buildings entail the use of smart materials and eco-friendly designs. For example, I have seen building material made out of flyash, which is not only more environment friendly but also a better insulator against heat and cold. Such eco-friendly, cost-effective material can make the building more energy efficient. The future holds a lot of promise as new concepts in nanotechnology, smart materials and design software will open fresh avenues in this field. Such green enterprises will give rise to a new cadre of green corridor jobs—jobs in businesses which supply green power or green power-generating equipment.

Solar Power for Homes

India has approximately 200 million houses, of which 60 million do not have access to electricity. These should be provided with grid-independent solar panels, and the coverage could gradually be extended to 140 million homes. Also, street lights powered by solar panels could be set up in villages, towns and cities. Such use of solar power will release nearly 60,000 MW of electricity for use by various sectors of the economy and bring down distribution losses. The benefits to national growth are obvious.

Renewable Energy Missions

A major objective of India's Energy Independence Vision 2030 would be to bring down our dependence on non-renewable sources of energy and increase the use of renewable ones. Apart from the extensive use of solar power, this mission would involve the expansion of wind energy farms. Micro-hydroelectric power units should be set up along streams and small rivers. There should be a thrust on using municipal waste to generate electricity. All thermal power stations should substitute 20 per cent of their annual electricity output with electricity from renewable energy systems. Lastly, all steel plants and heavy industries should be mandated to use their waste heat to generate electricity to meet their own needs. We need to embark on launching a national solar energy policy mission, which promotes solar energy systems and products manufacturing in the country, and exclusive R&D for nano science and technology for solar energy systems. Launching major projects in solar energy systems and technologies for both large, centralized applications as well as small, decentralized requirements concurrently, for applications in rural and urban areas, is of immediate relevance.

Carbon-Neutral Villages, Cities and States

We need to encourage power generation from waste. We could create 200,000 carbon neutral panchayats before 2020 and carbon neutral municipalities and corporations in towns and cities. The technology is available from the Department of Science and Technology. Only the willpower, necessary fund allocation and implementation through PPP model and CSR will make this mission possible.

> On a visit to Iceland, their president and I travelled in a hydrogen-fuelled bus. We stopped at a hydrogen fuel station, where I saw the tank being filled, and then we continued our journey and discussions. I am aware that hydrogen-operated motorcycles, three-wheelers and small generators have been developed in that country. In addition, Polymer Electrolyte Membrane Fuel Cell (PEMFC) and Phosphoric Acid Fuel Cell (PAFC) technologies and hybrid vans have been developed. Hydrogen production from distillery waste and other renewable methods has also been tried. At present, research is in progress to further improve the performance of these vehicles and generators.

Nuclear Power

Nuclear power generation is a must if we are to attain even a reasonable degree of energy independence. We would need to develop technologies for a wider spectrum of fissile material found around the world. For example, India has one-fourth of the world's thorium reserves, which needs to be protected from export. Therefore, it is essential to pursue the development of nuclear power using thorium. Also, nuclear fusion research needs to be fast-tracked with international cooperation to meet our power requirement when fossil fuels get depleted.

Municipal Waste as a Source of Power

We need to fully use the technologies now available to us for generating power from municipal waste. Today, there is hardly any significant energy being generated from waste. In India, studies indicate that as much as 5,800 MW of power can be generated by setting up 900 electric power plants in different parts of the country, which can be fuelled by municipal waste. Well-established Indian technologies from DST to generate power through bio-digester and municipal waste are available within India. Power generation and creation of a clean environment will be the two big benefits of this initiative.

Hydrogen Fuel

Hydrogen is considered to be the fuel of the future. It is an environment friendly fuel and renewable, thus removing dependence on petroleum resources. In India, an electric car company, in collaboration with the DRDO, has developed a hybrid vehicle which can be run with a fuel cell, a device that converts chemical energy from a fuel, commonly hydrogen, into electricity through a chemical reaction with oxygen or another oxidizing agent. The cost per kilometre will be just 40 paise in addition to the pollution-free operation of the car. Hydrogen can thus be used to run electric vehicles, trains and urban mass transportation. The challenge for the global research community is in areas such as high pressure storage of hydrogen, liquid storage, storage in nano-structure, development of safety codes and standards and development of dedicated engine for hydrogen fuel.

Algae Oil

One of the best and most efficient biofuels available to us is algae oil. It is far superior in terms of yield per hectare and, compared to conventional biofuel crops like corn which generate about 172 litres per hectare, algae oil can generate more than a hundred times that yield. Moreover, it can be grown in marshes and shallow regions of the sea which are otherwise unutilized. The challenge is to develop better technologies which can bring down the cost of generation of algae oil.

Energy Independence as a Global Mission

The challenge of reducing our dependence on fossil fuels and conserving the environment is a global one, which would necessarily require global platforms for evolving and implementing solutions that are efficient and economical in nations across the world. Integrated international platforms for research, development and implementation of solutions for energy independence using green sources need to be evolved. Joint research missions need to be carried across different countries towards finding common solutions which are not only effective but also economical. Global corporate houses should aggressively seek opportunities to support green enterprises, and students should be encouraged to take up entrepreneurial ventures which help spread the mission of energy independence.

We can further consider the creation of a World Energy Independence and Environment Platform, which would facilitate the research, development, marketing and deployment of all aspects of alternative and green energy and lead to a sustainable environment.

The missions for the Global Energy Independence Platform would be:

- High-circulation, low-intensity products
- High-efficiency, green power plants
- Establishing and propagating green practices
- Integrated products.

Such a global platform can have participation from governments, corporates, academic institutions, social organizations and R&D agencies as an integrated international social and environment responsibility mission. The contribution towards this programme could be a nominal 0.1 per cent of the GDP of every member nation. Even this amount will enable the mobilization of over $60 billion at current GDP estimates. Such a platform must address the progressive dismantling of systems which are operated by fossil fuels in a timebound manner and work on the reduction of energy consumption by all household and industrial systems.

Using Space Solar Power

At a time when the world is witnessing a rapid depletion of fossil fuels, it is essential to explore the possibility of harvesting solar energy from space. There are many initiatives and potential research studies in India, the US and other space-faring nations which have now brought together these countries to work on this mission. I cherish sharing my experience with Mark Hopkins, chairman of the National Space Society in the US, and his team during the International Space Development Conference in 2010, where I delivered an address on the topic of 'Harvesting Solar Energy from Space'. I was glad that by mid-2010 we could sign off an understanding to start an international Space Solar Power (SSP) Feasibility Study under the 'Kalam-NSS Space-based Solar Power Initiative'.

> In 1982, I left the Indian Space Research Organization (ISRO) after working there for over two decades and joined the DRDO. There I came across a unique person, Air Cmdr Gopalasamy, who is a well-known expert in system design, integration and management. He was a demanding technologist with innovative ideas backed by professional expertise.
>
> He is still active in the field and pursuing international research in space transportation systems. Based on his preliminary design, the DRDO has designed a Hypersonic Flight Test Vehicle. His vast experience and professional expertise will be of great advantage to further the mission of harvesting energy from space using solar-powered satellites.
>
> I definitely foresee the emergence of technological coherence soon in the space solar power mission, which will benefit the nation and the world in a big way.

In India, the need for space-based solar power stations was identified as far back as 1993 in anticipation of the emerging global energy crisis. Since then, work has been carried out in India on advanced space transportation system design concepts for affordable space solar power. To realize this mission, Air Cmdr (Rtd) Gopalasamy, I and V. Ponraj have evolved the concept of World Space Knowledge Platform and the International Virtual Laboratory for space solar power. This will help bring space-faring nations together to work on space solar power technologies, space transportation systems and transmission of solar power so that harvesting of this energy will be a reality before 2050.

Hence we would like to suggest the following points for realizing this great mission of using space solar power for liveable Planet Earth'

1. Creation of the World Space Knowledge Platform with Virtual Laboratory for Space Industrialization by US and India with other space-faring nations.
2. Identify the Space Virtual Laboratory partners to draw up a detailed feasibility study report on the International Space Solar Power Mission supported by definitive sub-scale technology demonstrations of critical technologies; and fully validate the critical concept of reusability of space transportation systems on which the whole mission concept rests.
3. There are choices for space solar power wireless transmission including microwave, millimeter wave (W band), laser wave or 'nano energy packs' and visible sunlight deflection through space mirror approach. In three years' time, the virtual laboratory for space solar power can bring an optimum, workable and possible solution for transportation of the power to its terrestrial stations.
4. We need to bring out a workable research document for marketing the concept to space-faring nations, especially among the G8 or G20 nations.

SMART WATER MANAGEMENT

Today, only half of the global population of 6 billion people has a satisfactory supply of water. It is estimated that 33 per cent has no access to sanitation, and 17 per cent has no access to safe water. By 2025, the world population is going to rise to 8 billion, but only 1 billion will have sufficient water. About 25 per cent will have no access to safe water, while 62 per cent will have no access to sanitation water. Going forward, we need to give utmost priority to our water situation and manage it well to ensure there is enough water available for drinking and irrigation purposes.

For economic development, India has adopted multiple route since the inception of the Five Year Plans. India has adopted two

---

WATER: AN ACTION PLAN

Water is a precious resource. Experts warn of severe shortages in the years to come. In India, we should foresee the problem and avert it as a top priority before the situation worsens.

Here is an action plan:

- Schemes which will ensure availability of 25 kilolitres of water per citizen.
- Water sufficiency for producing 400 million tonnes of foodgrains per year.
- Water harvesting must be made mandatory for all buildings, as too recycling of water in particularly hotels and industries with high consumption.
- There are many schemes for interlinking of rivers. The Ministry of Water Resources has to consolidate the best ones and bring out a cost-effective project report. On the whole, interlinking of rivers has to be a mission mode project.

It should be remembered, water availability makes the nation.

fundamental routes for promoting agriculture and water management, which is the foundation for various phases of economic development. The first route for the three decades after independence was to build major hydro dams, reservoirs, tanks, lakes for better water management and hydro power generation to accelerate development in the three sectors of the economy. This initiative has resulted in the building of eighty-four major dams and reservoirs which can store only 150 BCM (Billion Cubic Metres) of water every year. The next route was initiated by Dr K.V.L Rao and Captain D.J. Dastur on Interlinking of Rivers and Contour Canal. Subsequent to the national discussion, various studies brought out that there would be a lot of technological, environmental, financial and political challenges involved, hence it has not taken shape so far, even though it is a vital and important project for the nation. With the experience of these two routes and its challenges known to the nation, we the authors were searching for a new and innovative solution.

We receive approximately 4,000 billion cubic metres (BCM) of water every year from all natural sources in India. Of this, 700 BCM of water is lost to evaporation and another 700 BCM to flow on the ground. Groundwater recharge accounts for 430 BCM per year, and the present utilized surface water is just 370 BCM. A large part, around 1,500 BCM, flows to the sea during floods. Our aim should be to channelize this so that it can be supplied to drought-affected areas and sufficient water can be made available to the whole country during the non-monsoon months.

In India, a new thought is emerging as a third solution called National Waterways. After studying all these options, we have come to the conclusion that the right solution for India is to establish the National Smart Waterways Grid Mission, which will connect the rivers, dams, reservoirs and catchment areas at a particular height to use the flood water and to supply it on demand to deficient regions in the country. Our analysis of National Smart Waterways Grid for India gives a possible solution for water management in all conditions for India.

Characteristics of National Smart Waterways Mission of India

An expert team headed by A.C. Kamaraj conceptualized the National Smart Waterways and also built the working model with zero slope to demonstrate how, using differential pressure this waterway can recharge water during floods and feed the water to any deficient region.

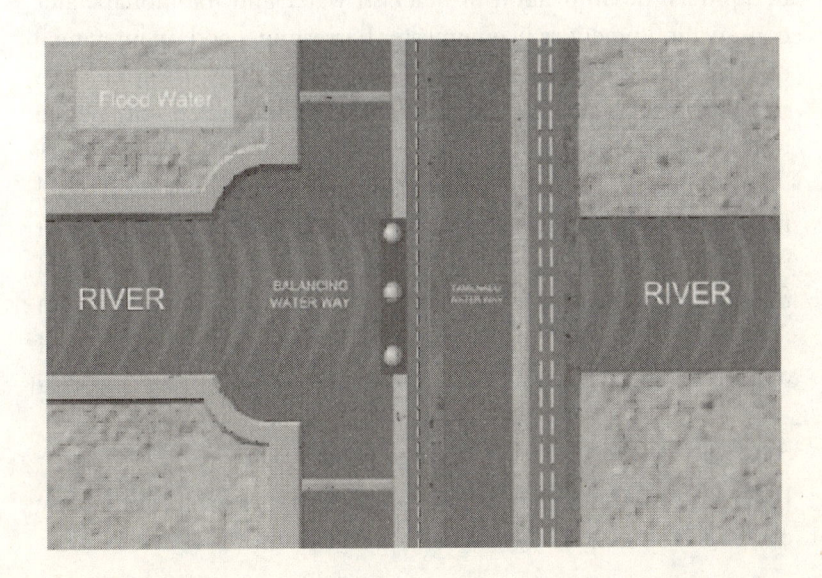

A smart waterway will have characteristics such as: It will be constructed at the height of ~250 metre MSL (Mean Sea Level) across the nation at Zero Slope and connect the rivers, dams and catchment areas on a single plane, so that due to differential pressure the water flow dynamics is effectuated. This will be called the National Reservoir. It will have sufficient navigable depth and width in the balancing waterway to hold at least minimum 300 BCM to 600 BCM of floodwater at any point of time. Floodwater from the rivers in the catchment areas/dams will feed this reservoir. Since it is going to act as a waterway grid, water can be released at any deficient place and recharged during floods. It will also pave the way for navigation, irrigation, agricultural productivity and power generation. It will be an all-season waterway grid, with conditions permitting navigation throughout the year, smooth bends and minimum siltation, adequately lighted and equipped with modern navigational and communication aids. This facility will enable the state to take advantage of the energy efficiency of transportation through waterways, which is double that of railways and eight times that of the road transportation system for a given load. This will also reduce the congestion on the roads, improve environmental conditions and afforestation and create jobs on a very large scale. Hence, there is a need to embark on a mission mode programme to make the waterways operational. This has to be a joint effort between the state and central governments. Land acquisition and resettlement problems will be very, very minimal, because the route is mainly at 250 metre MSL.

The high demand for water now and going forward brings forth the urgent need for effective management and development of water resources using methods like inter-basin water transfers, smart waterways, check dams, river water wells, artificial recharge of aquifers, desalinization of brackish water and traditional water conservation practices like rainwater harvesting, good maintenance of irrigation systems, and promoting efficiency through drip irrigation/sprinklers. We should evolve an integrated sustainable water management mission.

One major plus point is that the national smart waterways grid mission is non-controversial, unlike the proposal for interlinking of rivers. The waterways grid will only need central government financial support to the states, which would implement it within five to seven years to empower Indian youth with huge employment opportunities.

Access to Water

India is a seriously water-stressed nation, with per capita availability of water falling sharply from 5,177 cubic metres in 1951 to 1,545 cubic metres as per the 2011 census.* India's per capita water availability will reduce sharply to 1,340 Cu. M by 2025 and further down to 950 Cu. M by 2050, according to some projections.**

India, however, has done precious little to conserve water for off-season use. Rich countries like the US have built water storage capacities of 5,000 cubic metres per capita and middle-income nations like China and Mexico store about 1,000 cubic metres per capita.†

As per various reports, India needs to formulate new indices to measure the available water resources as the calculations per capita water availability do not include disparity in water allocation and access. Severe water shortages have led to growing number of conflicts between users in the agricultural and industrial sectors, as also the domestic sectors. The lack of water availability and poor management practices have also manifested in poor sanitation facilities, one of the biggest environmental and social challenges India faces today.

Under these circumstances, as of now India's storage capacity is a mere 200 cubic metres per capita. The challenge is, which are the water management systems and practices that will increase availability. The target: 2,500 cubic meters by 2025, rising further to 5,000 cubic meters by 2050.

Hence we strongly believe and recommend the National Smart Waterways Grid Mission which will increase the per capita availability of water to an expected target level by 2025 and 2050. Is it possible to accomplish such a mission? We would like to narrate a few examples of river basin management which we have witnessed and researched.

---

*http://pib.nic.in/newsite/erelease.aspx?relid=82676

**http://www.frost.com/prod/servlet/press-release.pag?docid=238980815 Frost and Sullivan.

†http://articles.timesofindia.indiatimes.com/2012-06-26/edit-page/32410118_1_water-crisis-water-supply-water-resources.

In April 2010, I was in the US to take a course at the Gatton College of Business and Economics. University of Kentucky. Apart from the teaching assignment, I was curious to know how the Ohio and Mississippi river basins have been managed for flood control and smart navigation. In this context, we studied how the Corps of Engineers of the US Army has played an integral part in the development of the country's infrastructure.

The Corps has constructed more than 400 major artificial lakes and reservoirs, more than 8,500 miles of levees, and implemented hundreds of smaller local flood protection projects. The Corps of Engineers' lakes store more than 372 BCM of water.

In Canada, a large proportion of goods are transported over water for some part of the journey. The inland shipping routes are dominated by the 2,342-mile (3,769-km) St. Lawrence–Great Lakes waterway, which provides navigation for vessels of 26-foot (8-metre) draught to the head of Lake Superior.

With 6,000 km of navigable waterways, the Netherlands offers one of the most extensive such networks in Europe.

England makes extensive use of a network of canals for transporting goods and recreation, and Ireland has been in the forefront of European efforts to restore long-abandoned canals for the same purpose.

Brazil's Inland waterways have high potential but are currently underused (60,000 km of inland waterways and only 13,000 km used).

The Magdeburg Water Bridge in Germany deserves special mention. Opened in October 2003 and part of the Magdeburg crossing of waterways, it connects the Elbe-Havel canal to the Mittelland canal, crossing over the Elbe River. At 918

metres, it's the longest navigable aqueduct in the world. All these nations are blessed with plenty of water, and they have great experience in constructing the waterways mainly for irrigation, navigation, trade and tourism. Possibly, ISRO's NRSA can provide less than 1 m pixel resolution of India, which would help identify the optimal path for a smart waterway.

Indian Inland Waterways Authority

India has inland waterways with great potential. Their length varies depending on the seasonal concentration of rainfall. Kerala, which is blessed with backwaters and inland water resources, is an exception to this dependence on rainfall. I have witnessed by helicopter survey in Goa, how the state linked Zuari river with Kalay river in Mandovi basin through installation of pumps and gravity flow. Gujarat which has large areas that are water-deficient has already taken steps for interlinking of rivers and completed the first link.

Similarly, many other states might have initiated such programmes such as the Ken-Betwa link in UP and the Tamiraparani, Karumeniyar and Nambiyar link in Tamil Nadu. The Tamiraparani link should potentially benefit the drier regions of Thirunelveli and Tuticorin districts, which are expected to utilize the 13,000 million cubic feet surplus water in Tamiraparani river. But mostly, the projects have not seen much progress.

While addressing state legislative assemblies, I have suggested to them to focus on the creation of smart waterways within the states to manage floodwater. As a first phase, our focus was on Bihar, Kerala, Andhra Pradesh, Tamil Nadu and Karnataka.

Bihar Smart Water Management Missions

Bihar is not short of water. Many times Bihar gets much more water than it can handle. The Bihar CM used to tell us that even though they got surplus water, they did not have a mechanism to store it for further use. Properly harnessed, the floodwater could help Bihar become the granary of India through the development of an inland water transport system. The smart waterways system could help control floods and manage the river basins and also generate electricity.

When we study the map of Bihar, we find that the Ganga runs in the middle of Bihar as it is a valley. The level being around 70 meters above MSL and the ground on both sides, north and south, rising to nearly 100 to 300 meters MSL. Hence, the Ganga water as such cannot be used for irrigation in Bihar due to height difference. However, in many years, there is heavy flooding in the river causing severe damage to north Bihar. The solution for this is to build a smart waterway which is at a higher level at around ~250 meter MSL for around 500 km using the water from the tributaries of the Ganga for irrigation. This will provide irrigation facility to over 5 million acres, enable generation of 1,000 MW of power and provide employment for 9 million people. These measures could also reduce the severity of floods by fast disposal of floodwater and ensure storage of surplus water for future use. The Bihar government has taken initial steps to evolve a Bihar Waterways Management project plan and initiated an SPP (Special Purpose Vehicle) for undertaking the feasibility studies and implementation. We were told that it is in the process of obtaining permission from the Planning Commission and the Central government for its implementation.

Layered Wells: In the Gangetic region, we have recommended construction of layered wells in the entry points of Kosi River. Normally the floodwater has certain dynamic flow conditions. The layered wells assist gradual reduction in dynamic flow velocity after filling each storage well. The water thus stored will be useful during periods of scarcity. Similar solutions can be found for the north-eastern region.

Southern Smart Waterways Grid: The next priority is to create a Southern Smart Waterways grid which will connect Tamil Nadu,

Andhra Pradesh, Karnataka and Kerala and make all the four states fertile in all seasons irrespective of flood and drought. These states face acute water shortage for irrigation during the drought season. They are heavily dependent on the Krishna, Godavari, Cauvery, Tamiraparani, Mullai Periyar, Vaigai and Pallar rivers for irrigation. Whenever floods occur, the water-deficient states get the water that spills over the dams from water-sufficient regions.

Name of Reservoir	Capacity (BCM) Live FRL at	Current Storage (BCM) Live as on 31 Jan 2013
Southern Region		
Andhra Pradesh	20.044	5.916
Karnataka	23.323	8.415
Kerala	3.605	1.26
Tamil Nadu (Only 6 major Dams)	4.229	0.493
Billion Cubic Meter Available	**51.201**	**16.084**

During the flood season, we were informed, from the Godavari and Krishna rivers in Andhra Pradesh alone around 2,000 to 3,000 TMC of water goes into the sea after filling all the connected dams, reservoirs and tanks. At the same time, many parts of Andhra Pradesh and Telangana region reel under drought in dry weather. During the drought season, all these states face acute shortage of water. There is tension among the southern states leading to disputes over water. Ultimately, it is the farmers and the people in these states who are the worst affected.

With a waterways grid in place, the floodwater can be shared among Andhra Pradesh, Karnataka, Kerala and Tamil Nadu whenever there is a drought. Andhra Pradesh and Telangana smart waterways and Tamil Nadu smart waterways would connect on the same contour near Vellore. This southern waterway grid can easily get 2000 TMC feet of water during floods, which can feed all the southern states in all seasons.

The Possible Solution: National Smart Waterways Grid

As a national mission, the government could consider preparing the DPR for the implementation of National Smart Waterways Grid across India with the following characteristics to harness the 1500 BCM of floodwater. This grid will become a national reservoir and will use at least 600 BCM out of 1,500 BCM of floodwater which flows into the sea every year. It will act as a national reservoir of 15,000 km length, provide drinking water to 600 million people, irrigation to 150 million acres and 60,000 MW of power generation. Waterways transportation will provide 10 to 20 per cent fuel saving compared to road transportation. Each state can implement this mission with an outlay of around Rs 50,000 crore from the annual budgetary support for five to seven years, alongside central government and private consortium assistance. It is a dream that can be realized within a decade. The golden quadrilateral highway project is a major step towards infrastructure which became a reality because of a visionary leadership at the Centre. We should evolve such a vision for a smart waterways grid.

Smart Waterways Project Is a Major Economic Accelerator

During a visit to Canada in September 2010, I had detailed discussions with Canadian leaders and an expert group on water management and infrastructure development for the Indo-Canadian joint venture missions. The whole initiative was spearheaded by the Canada India Foundation (CIF). During the visit we presented the smart waterways proposal and held discussions which resulted in possible action to create inland smart waterways in at least two states (Tamil Nadu and Bihar).

After the visit, I had written to the Prime Minister to constitute an expert team to study the proposals for necessary action. Regarding this initiative, an official delegation from Canada also met the concerned secretary and officials of state governments and at the Centre. A.C. Kamaraj, a proponent of the Smart Waterways programme, was present too. I deputed V. Ponraj for further discussion on this topic during December 2013. Follow ups continue.

Manifesto for Water Management

In light of this situation, I would like to suggest some points for sustainable water management:

- Launching the National Smart Waterways Grid Mission to harness the 1,500 BCM of floodwater which flows into the sea every year.
- Helping state governments plan for statewide Smart Waterways Grids with budgetary support from the central government and the World Bank.
- Undertaking a detailed project report for the grid and also planning for environmental improvement by planting trees on the banks of the waterways and the navigation canals to improve the forest cover.
- Allowing FDI for design, development and implementation of the grid under the PPP model.
- Launching a Nationwide Water Harvesting Mission for homes, villages, cities, towns, municipal corporations and also for private and public institutions, ensuring compliance under an appropriate legal framework.
- Setting up a special purpose vehicle to establish 40 million new farm ponds to cover 170 million hectares of irrigation land to improve the water table and irrigation potential. Fishing in the ponds can also be encouraged to generate revenue for farmers.
- Building wells along rivers to store water and also to increase

the groundwater table. Simultaneously, all water bodies need to be saved from encroachments using satellite maps. All village ponds also need to be immediately de-silted. This mission may be implemented by taking note of the Siruthuli model pioneered in Coimbatore, Tamil Nadu, where the people, NGOs, government and industry came together to revive around ten lakes from encroachments and pollution, thereby improving the water table considerably.
- Protecting cities by creating channels on both sides of river embankments. This will also help create a clean and green environment with a potential to attract tourists. Diversion channels should be built upstream to provide water to regions where it is required.
- Using the Mahatma Gandhi National Rural Employment Guarantee Scheme and other government schemes to create sustainable water bodies and to de-silt lakes, canals and tanks. The government could rope in incorporates under their CSR initiatives while providing matching grants and necessary tax exemptions for their support.

INTEGRATED SUSTAINABLE AGRICULTURE, INDUSTRY AND SERVICE SECTORS

The Indian agricultural sector employs about 50 per cent of India's workforce but accounts for only about 17 per cent of its GDP. In real terms, agriculture's contribution to the GDP has increased from around Rs 1 lakh crore in 1950-51 to Rs 5 lakh crore now. But the GDP per agricultural worker is currently around only Rs 2,000 per month. The 11th Five Year Plan (2007-12) witnessed an average annual growth of 3.6 per cent in GDP from agriculture and allied sector. The growth target for agriculture in the 12th Five Year Plan is estimated to be 4 per cent. Whereas the agriculture and allied sector's contribution to the GDP was 41.66 per cent in 1970-71, which came down to 13.68 per cent in 2012. On the other hand, the service sector's contribution to GDP has grown from 33 per cent in 1970-71 to 59 per cent in 2012-13, of industries from 23 per cent then to 27 per cent now, and manufacturing sector's from 12 per cent to 15.24 per cent. This shows India has spent all its efforts on service sector growth, neglecting agriculture—wherein lies its core competence—industry and manufacturing.

According to a World Economic Forum report, over the past few years, food insecurity and the global economic crisis have highlighted the urgent need for developing sustainable agricultural systems. Nearly 1 billion people—one out of six globally—lack access to adequate food and nutrition. By 2050, the global population will surpass 9 billion and the demand for agricultural products will double. Thus, the sector has two interconnected dimensions: a '9 billion future' and a '1 billion problem'. Economically speaking, the agro-food sector is more promising than any other, given its size, global reach and that food security is a basic need of us all.

India's core competence is agriculture, and we have every opportunity, and the technology and resources, to increase productivity in the sector. The time is right for India to concentrate on increasing agricultural productivity by three to four times and develop food processing, manufacturing and marketing. If we evolve an integrated policy which brings together food processing and agro industries and service, we can certainly target and dominate the global market and make our economy stronger.

Normally, in India, we have separate missions for agriculture, industry, manufacturing and service sectors carried out by the respective ministries. As a result, every mission is going in a different direction leading to staggered growth. An 'Integrated and Sustainable Agriculture, Industry and Services mission' would, however, bring about an additional 10 per cent growth in these three sectors by 2020. This is the need of the hour. Our ultimate aim should be to capture at least 40 per cent of the global agri-food market by 2050. This would require an annual investment of around $50 billion.

It would entail development of the areas that follow.

Second Green Revolution

India now has to embark upon a Second Green Revolution which will enable it to further increase its productivity by three to four times in the agricultural sector and concentrate on value addition through food processing. The second green revolution is indeed a graduation in our knowledge and practices, from characterization of soil to the matching of the seed with the composition of the fertilizer, and involving water management and the use of improved harvesting techniques. The domain of a farmer's work would enlarge from grain production to food processing and marketing. While doing so, utmost care would have to be taken for various environmental and people-related aspects. By 2020, India would need to produce over 340 million tonnes of foodgrain in view of population growth and increased purchasing power. The challenges here would be:

- *Land:* The requirement of land for the increasing population as well as for greater afforestation and environmental preservation activities would create a situation in which the present 170 million hectares of arable land would not be fully available. It might shrink to 100 million hectares by 2020.
- *Water:* In addition, there would be a shortage of water due to competing demands.
- *Technology:* Our agricultural scientists and technologists, in partnership with organizations like the Indian Farmers Fertiliser Cooperative (IFFCO), have to work towards enhancing the average productivity per hectare from 1.1 tonnes to more than 3.4 tonnes with less need of water. The type of technologies needed would be in the area of the development of seeds that would ensure high yields even under constraints of water and land. Technologies such as System of Rice Intensification (SRI), Sustainable Sugar Initiative (SSI) and precision farming will more than double

agricultural productivity and ensure a 30 per cent contribution of agriculture to GDP by 2020, up from the present level of 15 per cent.
- *Sphere of Work*: The domain of a farmer's work would enlarge from grain production to food processing and marketing.
- *New Approaches*: The government could introduce an innovative new community cooperative farming model for specific crops in some regions and help ensure the availability of inputs at the right time.
- *Better Equipment*: Industry has to be empowered with inclusive growth-oriented policies to set up farm-level silos, a cold chain, refrigerated transportation, strategic distribution centres linked to retail super markets, and a food processing industry. This will help develop the agri-food sector to grow in tandem with other sectors, such as services.
- *Budgetary support*: Agriculture will need budgetary support of Rs 60,000 crore per year for rural infrastructure development, which would include creating silos at farms, warehousing and cold chain facilities along with viability gap funding to set up modern cold storage facilities. The aim will be to shorten the gap between the farm and end consumers. In addition to this, there will be need for a budgetary allocation of Rs 1,000 crore for R&D, design and development of food processing technologies, precision irrigation systems, pre- and post-harvesting equipment, genetic engineering and biotechnology-based seeds, fertilizers, and pesticide-resistant crops, doubling the biomass, and for formulating mission-based consortiums in association with agriculture universities, engineering institutions, and service sector companies. The government should also encourage an FDI inflow of $200 billion for agri-food processing to be achieved within three years.

Stakeholders and Their Roles and Responsibilities

- *Government:* The government needs to do the following in order to bring about synergy between the three sectors of the economy: draft and implement a public policy for inclusive growth, draft and implement an FDI policy for agro-food processing and industry, chalk out a mission management structure, revamp and restructure FCI, IFFCO and other agriculture-oriented public sector bodies and their processes, draft and implement an innovative growth-oriented policy for funding through agro banks, revamp agriculture insurance, and implement a smart waterways grid.
- *Agriculture and Engineering Universities and Public-Private Industry:* Their role will be related to R&D on seeds, farming practices and technology infusion, agriculture implements, pre- and post-harvesting equipment manufacturing, micro irrigation, farm silos, cold chain, modern storage and godowns, food processing machines, refrigerated transportation and packaging.
- *Farmers:* They have to become knowledge partners, agro-industrial partners with their land as investment, agro cooperative mission society members, and community farming partners.
- *Services Sector:* Its role will relate to seed-testing centres, agri transportation and logistics, managing import and export of agri commodities, agri service and extension centres using ICT technologies, business schools to start socio-economic business models for agriculture growth, packaging and brand building, and sales and global marketing among other things.

Sustainable Economic Infrastructure

The indicators of development are the per capita consumption of energy, water, coal and steel. The consumption of these ingredients is directly proportional to the developmental status of any nation. The consumption pattern here clearly shows that India is far behind in achieving the target for infrastructure development. Our economic policies should help increase our use of these elements to the world average and above. What do we need by way of infrastructure?

- *Steel*: We are lagging behind the world average in terms of steel production. India's total steel consumption in 2011 was 67.8 million tonnes, up from 64.9 million tonnes a year ago, according to the World Steel Association. But China's consumption the same year was the highest at 623.9 million tonnes. India's economic policy encourages the sale of raw material to other countries instead of using it for domestic consumption or turning it into finished steel. We need to convert iron ore into finished steel and reduce our imports, in the process increasing our per capita steel consumption by ten times by 2020.
- *Coal:* India ranks twenty-fifth in the world in per capita consumption of coal while China ranks first. India's total coal consumption stood at 298.3 million tonnes in 2012, and it recorded an annual growth of 9.9 per cent in 2012—the sharpest growth seen since 1981. In the year ending March 2013, India imported 20 per cent of its total coal requirements, which is expected to grow to 23 per cent by 2017, according to data analysts Bloomberg. We need to increase our coal production and consumption by seven times to 2,000 million tonnes by removing legal bottlenecks through parliamentary laws and by following transparent and proactive policies to make efficient use of our natural resources.
- *Energy:* India's per capita power consumption was 684 kWh as of 2011 and we ought to increase it by at least five times by 2020. One suggestion would be creating a high-voltage

- *Water:* In India, the per capita consumption of water is 135 litres per person per day. The per capita water availability is reducing progressively due to an increase in population. The average annual per capita availability of water, taking into consideration the population of the country as per the 2001 census, was 1,816 cubic metres, which reduced to 1,545 cubic metres as per the 2011 census. This will reduce sharply to 1,340 cubic metres by 2025 and further to 950 cubic metres by 2050. Estimates by the ministry of water resources indicate that by 2050, India's overall water demand will double, growing at a compound annual growth rate of 1.5 per cent. It is reported that almost half of our annual rainfall occurs in just two weeks. But India has done precious little to conserve water for off-season use. As mentioned before, high demand for water brings forth the urgent need for effective management of water resources by various means.

power grid to productively use the power being generated and reduce transmission and distribution losses.

QUALITY EDUCATION SYSTEM

Creative School Education System for Generating Bright Students

Education is a lifelong learning with three components: (a) learning to learn (b) learning to live (c) learning to survive. A school student is twelve years in class, from the first to the twelfth, 25,000 hours in all. Of the three, we would need to reform the source of education, that is, primary education. Primary education is the foundation for all education; it brings out the creativity of the child at a young age. Hence, a primary school has to have a creative syllabus, a creative teacher and a creative classroom. Changes are needed in all three areas: teaching, syllabus and teacher. How to do that? Again, there are three aspects: capacity building in students, imparting skills sets, and the third is moral leadership.

What Do We Mean by Capacity Building?

When the students come out of the educational institutions, they require certain capacities to be able to deal with the real world, particularly to grow in their professional career and participate in national development. We suggest that the ingredients for capacity building must be embedded right from the beginning of the student's life. A good educational model is the need of the hour to ensure that the students develop as enlightened citizens and also participate in national development missions.

For participating in the nation building tasks, the capacities that need to be developed among students in their formative years by the educational institutions are: the capacity for research or inquiry; the capacity for creativity and innovation; the capacity to use high technology; the capacity for entrepreneurial leadership; and the capacity for moral leadership.

The ASER 2011 (Annual Status of Education Report) points out that the levels of reading and mathematics at every level were not only poor but declining in many states. With one more year of data, this observation is strengthened. The chart below brings out this fact. Fewer and fewer children in successive batches reaching 3rd and 5th standard are learning basics of reading and math. Unless someone can show that children are learning something else better, this indicates an alarming degeneration. In 2008, the proportion of children in Std 3 who could read a Std 1 text was under 50 per cent, which has dipped to nearly 30 per cent. A child in Std 3 has to learn to do two-digit subtraction, but the proportion of children in government schools who can even recognize numbers up to 100 correctly has dropped from 70 per cent to near 50 per cent over the (2009) last four years, with the trend downward

> According to the ASER Report 2012, 'Learning declines do not happen in one year. They are the result of a cumulative effect of neglect over the years.'

turning distinctly visible after 2010, the year RTE came into force. These downward trends are also reflected in Std 5, where a child would be expected to be able to at least read a Std 2 text and solve a division sum. Private schools are relatively unaffected by this decline but a downturn is noticeable, especially in math beyond number recognition, as per ASER.

People are aware of the difference between government and private schools, with or without assessment. It drives the demand for private schools and results in an exodus from government schools, like it or not. Of course, all this is about very basic indicators and education is much more than just basic skills. At the same time, if we can get these basics right, much more can be done, but not without them. Government and private, both types of schools have a long way to go. In the meantime, private school enrolment is growing rapidly at the primary stage. The states' contribution to the overall decline in learning levels is not uniform either for the government or for private schools. In some states, the situation is unchanged or steady, which may be good news under the circumstances. The reasons for deterioration of learning outcomes in other states need to be explored by leaders and officials of each state. Whatever the cause, this trend has to be reversed urgently.

The big states where the learning levels are low and unchanged but do not contribute significantly to the overall decline in government schools are Karnataka, Tamil Nadu and Andhra Pradesh. There are three other states, Himachal, Punjab, and Kerala, which have high learning levels on the ASER scale and are largely steady. Other big states contribute heavily to the overall declining learning levels. However, the contrast between government and private school performance is easily visible in every state.

It is reported in ASER 2012 that 35 per cent or more of India's primary schoolchildren in both urban and rural areas are attending private schools. The best example of this may be Tamil Nadu, which is now 48 per cent urbanized, according to Census 2011. DISE (District Information System of Education) reports that in 2010-11, 59.4 per cent of all (urban and rural) children in Std I-V attended private schools in Tamil Nadu. Only a third of these were in aided private schools. ASER 2010 estimated that the rural private enrolment in Std I-V in the Tamil Nadu was around 28.5 per cent, and rose to 34.8 per cent in 2012. One of the estimates says that anywhere between 80 and 100 per cent children in Std I-V in urban Tamil Nadu are in private schools and less than a fifth of these are government aided.

A glance at the DISE 2010-11 private school enrolments shows that in the southern part of India—Kerala, Tamil Nadu, Puducherry, and Goa—there is 60 per cent or more enrolment in private primary schools. Andhra Pradesh, Maharashtra, and Karnataka are all above 40 per cent and moving up. All these states are highly urbanized and urbanizing further. Madhya Pradesh and Gujarat are at around 30 per cent. Rajasthan, Haryana, Punjab, J&K and Uttarakhand are between 40 and 50 per cent. Uttar Pradesh rural is already at about 50 per cent and it is quite likely that urban Uttar Pradesh is not far behind. Of the North-Eastern states, Tripura has low private school enrolment but nearly 70 per cent of government primary schoolchildren go to tutors. Assam and Arunachal are at about 25 per cent private enrolment and Meghalaya, Mizoram, Manipur, and Nagaland are between 30 and 50 per cent. Of the most rural states, Bihar and West Bengal have low private school enrolment but 40 per cent and 60 per cent government schoolchildren in Std. 1-5 respectively go to tutors. That leaves the highly rural Odisha and somewhat urban Chhattisgarh among the bigger states which have low private school enrolment of about 10 per cent and 20 per cent. It appears that no matter who is in power, private school enrolment will go on increasing till it hits family budget constraints. As this happens, unless the quality of government schools improves substantially, the gap between children who attend one or the other will create a big divide in every aspect of life and opportunity.

Much of our developmental planning is rural focused and in education the tendency in government is to think of government-run schools as 'our' schools. It is time to start looking at private schooling more carefully and to regulate it without taking away the essential strengths of the private school. Government-funded and regulated, but not controlled, private schools like the aided or 'charter schools'—replacing government-run schools seems to be the way of the future. The RTE has already introduced the concept of funding private schools on a per child cost basis. This can be extended further. Aided schools exist in large numbers in Kerala, Tamil Nadu, Maharashtra, Goa, and Meghalaya. Existing practices can be looked into to create new governance mechanisms so that there is a right balance of freedom and accountability, and eliminate nonperformance in the government schools.

In short, big changes are happening in education and they are happening rapidly. Any long-term plans of building or strengthening institutions must take these changes into account or else we will end up creating more dysfunctional white elephants all over the country that are not suitable for the next half a century and longer. There is a need to keep a close watch and have a vision of the future with feet firmly planted on the ground today.

India spends 3.5 per cent of GDP on education which there are plans to increase to 6 per cent. The 11th Plan placed high priority on education for achieving rapid and inclusive growth. The allocation in the plan showed a fourfold increase over the 10th plan. In order to achieve the goal in higher education by 2015 as per the 11th Plan, we need 1,500 universities. Hence there is a major role to play for public-private partnership in this sector. Many years ago, before we amended our Constitution, it was common to say that political will was needed to give India's children their fundamental right to education. The Constitutional amendment in 2002, imposition of education cess in 2004 leading to increasing financial allocation for elementary education, and finally the passage and enforcement of the Right to Education Act after a long wait were all step-wise demonstrations of increasing political desire, although not quite the will. For a country that is undergoing huge economic, social, and demographic changes, education requires a much more resolute political direction. One of the key requirements of the Indian education system is a focus on granting a vocational skill along with basic education.

A *Manifesto for Creative School Education for Generating Quality Input*

1. The objective of school education should be an empowered education system. Our school education needs a transformative educational reforms policy for producing quality human resources. This policy should focus on developing high IQ- and EQ-based creative classroom, creative syllabus and creative laboratory. This classroom environment with the teacher and students should be interactive, collaborative and participatory. State-level independent accredited agencies should rate the schools annually and the ratings should be freely available.
2. At present, only after 10th standard are students allowed to choose their streams, such as science, math or computer science, economics, commerce and vocational courses. The system is loaded with a huge syllabus burden whether the students adopt the particular system or not. This puts stress on the students, leading to dropouts. Till the 8th standard, the same foundation level is needed for all the students. Hence we need to design multiple course options and choice of subjects based on the higher education system opportunity available and accordingly we need to bring in a four-year stream after standard 8. For that four-year stream

in many disciplines, we need to introduce only the mathematics needed. Similarly, the necessary syllabi needed in science, physics, chemistry, biology, zoology, economics, commerce and other domain subjects have to be introduced. The idea is that students shouldn't be burdened with loading of full syllabus and they should study what is needed, not everything which is not useful in their higher education.

3. Normally if a child develops a skill gap in the first standard, he or she is carried forward to the second standard with the same skill gap. In the second standard he or she is forced to learn the new skills with the existing skill gap. Either they fail to pass the standard or simply carry the gap further forward to the next class. As the skill gap widens the child comes under increasing pressure, and either begins to hate the school system or drops out at an early stage. This becomes an unending cycle and a reason why 88 per cent dropped out at the various stages of their school education.

4. Instead of concentrating on the syllabus-based approach, basic learning outcomes and skills need to be set for each standard from the primary to secondary level (6-8th standard) on all the subjects for all the state, central and other boards.

5. What are the skills the students should possess needs to be established for every standard from 1st to 12th, and evaluation of that skill gap assessed every six months and remedial steps taken. Every year each student should be assessed on the basis of the learning skill outcome rather than the syllabus-based questions. Accordingly, the syllabus for the next year should be decided dynamically by the school management. Skill-based sections based on the grading should be formed from the second standard onwards so that more emphasis is given to impart the skills required to bridge the gap with caring and experienced teachers helping to impart the skills needed in the next standard. The teachers who help students with skill upgradation should be given special incentives

based on the students' performance on an annual basis within three months of the school results being announced. The process should be followed from 1st to 12th standard.

6. A suitable course curriculum should be evolved incorporating ethics, integrity, honesty, aptitude, moral values, culture, communication, collaborative interaction skills, inter-personal skills and ultimately leadership qualities in schools. Good scores in these subjects would be needed for admission into higher education. Teachers who can be role models should be selected for these course.

7. Sports facilities of international standard should be made available at the district level. Coaches and consultants of repute should be appointed at an attractive compensation to coordinate with physical education teachers. There should be a transparent selection mechanism by an unbiased group of people which includes student representatives to identify talent among the village and city schools. Sports events conducted regularly will help improve standards. Physical education marks should also be considered as an additional grade for higher education.

8. There is much to distract student's attention in today's world, with both parents working. Television, cinema, social networking sites and lack of parental or school support often lead to poor performance and indiscipline. Populist steps to pass all students, disallow even minimal punishment and allow filing of criminal cases against teachers on the basis of a complaint by some misled students have led to teachers bring afraid to exercise the duty of teaching with a certain level of discipline and strictness. In order to punish some rare cases of abuse by the teacher, for which the law should take appropriate action, the whole system of maintaining discipline should not be rendered ineffective.

9. As envisioned, we need to have a creative classroom, creative syllabus and creative teachers. We can have a creative

classroom and also a creative syllabus, but the challenge is how to find creative teachers. Finding such teachers is the hardest task.

10. We would like to make the following recommendations for teachers' education based on studies and inputs from people with an interest or experience in the field. Those who have completed teacher training for primary and secondary school and B.Ed/M.Ed programme for higher secondary schools when they clear the Teacher Eligibility Test or other qualifying examinations, have to go through two years of practical training. This comprises training under experienced teachers in schools for six months, three months' training in a university environment, three months training in psychology and counselling and again twelve months of training in schools to teach the low performers to become better. The methodology and practices in the training have to focus on the following approaches.

a. Attitude, skill and knowledge development approach
b. Practice-oriented and enquiry-based learning process
c. Research—teaching—research methodology
d. Reflection-oriented approach in learning—studying—learning process.
e. Interactive, collaborative, participative and creative approach in classrooms.
f. Identify the potential of each student and encourage them to tap into it.
g. Help the student to absorb the vast information available on the internet in a meaningful way.
h. Teachers should pass on the following skills to students:
- toleration of and respect for differences.
- an ethical mindset so that they learn to think beyond individual self-interest.
- problem solving ability.
- creative thinking.

- working collaboratively.
- communicating cogently both orally and in writing.
- flexibility and adaptability
- ability to have a great aim, to acquire knowledge continuously, and perseverance.

Teachers who can teach such abilities are special. The teachers who train students in these should be respected in society and accorded preferential treatment and other benefits befitting a special category.

11. Evolution of a National Creative Education Policy: A National Creative Education Policy with a focus on developing a body of students who can match the best in the world can be prepared drawing experts from the education system, government and various professional associations and societies. The evolution of such a policy in a timebound manner will generate quality, knowledge and skills needed by all sectors of the Indian economy and globally employable human resources. The aim of the education system should be to create employment generators rather than employment seekers, apart from building research capability.

Quality inputs generate quality output. The primary foundation for such action is the capability of the teachers at the school level from primary to higher secondary level and creation of a revamped national quality teacher education system.

> An OECD (Organization for Economic Cooperation and Development) International Approaches to Teacher Selection and Recruitment study emphasizes that the most effective mechanisms for selecting candidates for ITP (Initial Teacher Preparation) 'acknowledge that for a person to become an effective teacher they need to possess a certain set of characteristics that can be identified before they enter teaching. These include a high overall level of literacy and numeracy, strong interpersonal and communication skills, a willingness to learn, and the motivation to teach'.

Research-Oriented Higher Education with Skill and Knowledge Development

In ancient times, India was a hub for science and trade. Nalanda attracted scholars from all over the world. We gave the world the zero. We knew the sun was the centre of the solar system (Aryabhata correctly insisted that the earth rotates on its axis daily, and that the apparent movement of the stars is a relative motion caused by the rotation of the earth, contrary to the prevailing view that the sky rotated). We knew about blood circulation. Traders from all over the world swarmed our nation. Where are we now? What is the situation now? The US and China publish more than 200,000 research papers every year. We from India publish a mere 40,000, with few referrals. Since the inception of the Noble Prize, the US has given 338 Nobel laureates, the UK has given 119, Germany has given 101 and France 65. India has given only 7. We rank poorly in the Global Competitive Index and in Ease of Doing Business. So we have already spent six decades in managing the present education system without radical transformation. Many reforms proposals are gathering dust. What ails us? Is it regulations? Is it governance? How are we going to ignite the young population? What apex bodies are needed? What polices need reforms? What needs to be restructured? There are many such questions in everyone's mind.

It might be worthwhile to consider a manifesto for research-oriented higher education with global skills.

1. Higher Education System

The system has to be reoriented towards research by giving autonomy to universities and decoupling them from political control in deciding the quality of syllabus, quality of teachers, and quality of laboratory and other aspects. Instead of a national accreditation and regulatory bill, we need to evolve a national accreditation and facilitation bill which will empower our universities and institutions to be globally competitive in teaching and research standards. A bill (the right to research oriented higher education with global skills bill) has to be introduced which will be binding on all.

2. Decoupling the Controlling Institutions

Decoupling or decommissioning the existing monitoring, controlling and guiding institutions has to be the starting point of any move to rid the higher education of corruption. The universities and institutions have to be made autonomous to decide on their own syllabus. The government should announce standards for establishing an institution, college and university. Syllabi should be set which are on par with global standards. These could be updated periodically by academic experts and adopted by universities after vetting. This should be applicable to all existing and new institutions teaching the arts, science, management, engineering, medical and other professional courses.

There is no need to check whether they adopt the syllabus or not or follow the guidelines for academic infrastructure set by the controlling bodies. Instead they need to be evaluated, ranked and accredited by three independent agencies on parameters such as their syllabus, research facilities, infrastructure including laboratories and library, e-governance system, sports and other extracurricular activities, participation in NSS, NCC, etc.

As with the universities, the independent or joint venture (academic and industry) research proposals by faculties from universities, colleges and institutions also should be rated by the three independent agencies based on their originality, content and relevance. Colleges having core competence should be encouraged to do research independently or in association with a university with adequate research grants to find local solutions. Once a university, college or institution has been rated, it would be eligible to get the funding from the government without any further administrative and bureaucratic control. Accordingly, the funding support for research (like the funding grant based on referral ranking of published papers) and infrastructure development grant has to be released by the government within three months of the ranking announcement.

3. Academic and Research Administrative Services for Higher Education

In the UPSC, another service, the Academic and Research Administrative Services for Higher Education, should be established. Eligibility criteria for vice chancellors, registrars, and controllers of examinations need to be set. Based on the eligibility criteria, a selection process has to be initiated every year for selecting people to these posts after an interview and presentation by them. Based on the interview a list would be announced of the selected candidates to these key posts. Such a system would reduce the political interference and corruption in the appointment of top administrative positions of the academic and research institutions, which is the root cause of the dismal performance of the university system at present.

4. Higher Education and Research Policy

The research policy should be so designed that India's R&D spending goes up from less than 1 per cent to 6 per cent of GDP. We should attain the first five levels in the H index which is used to calculate the impact and productivity of scientific work. The policy should be designed in such a way that a research environment is created to attract the young talent from India and other parts of the world to do quality work and generate patents. India should find a place among the top twenty countries in respect of patents. According to an ISB 2011 report, a dismal 13 per cent of the overall R&D spend of the top 100 companies in India goes towards partnerships with universities.

5. Multi-disciplinary Research Universities

Concentrating significant resources in high-potential institutions and faculty through competition will help in creating exemplars of global excellence. Multi-disciplinary research universities can be created within the existing universities. We should convert research institutes into small-sized research universities, aggregating various CSIR research labs under a common university system. We should make the process of applying for research or grants easy and attractive. Students should be allowed to select guides from across academic institutes for joint research. We could also collaborate with foreign research centres and universities through MOUs.

6. Involving Indian Private Sector in Research and Development

This holds enormous potential for results too. There could be possibilities of converting research institutes into business enterprises by commercializing university R&D. The involvement of the private sector could help bring in innovative practices and skill development, as also synergy between academic institutions and requirements of industry in drawing up the curriculum.

7. Improving the Gross Enrolment Ratio

India's GER of 16 per cent is much below the world average of 27 per cent and is the lowest among the BRICS countries. The GER for higher education was 12.3 per cent in 2006–07 and increased to 17.9 per cent in 2011–12 during the 11th Plan. In India, private institutions provide the major chunk of enrolment in higher education with 59 per cent, whereas the state and central institutions provided 38.5 per cent and 2.5 per cent respectively in 2011-12. During the 12th Five Year Plan, the enrolment in central institutions is expected to grow at 16.34 per cent, where the main focus of these institutions will be on research. The future growth in higher education enrolment should not come from adding more institutions but by increasing the capacity in existing institutions. During the 12th Plan we need to increase enrolment capacity and raise the GER broadly in line with the current global average from 17.9 per cent (estimated for 2011–12) to 30 per cent by 2020.

8. Central Institutions as Quality Research Institutions

Only research and innovation-based institutions or exemplar institutions would be established in the central sector. Central institutions should become catalytic role models for other institutions in all aspects including governance, infrastructure, faculty and curricula.

Accreditation of Institutes: As of March 2010, only 32.3 per cent (159) of the total number of Indian universities and 13.1 per cent (4,094) of the colleges in the country had been accredited by the National Assessment and Accreditation Council (NAAC). As of March 2010, NAAC had rated 62 per cent of the universities and 90 per cent of the colleges as average (B) or below average (C) on specified quality parameters.

World Rankings: Two Indian higher education brands featured in the QS World University Rankings 2011-12 of the top 500 global universities. Of the forty-eight countries studied, India ranked last in the U21 rankings of national higher education systems. (*These are the findings of assessments such as the U21 Rankings of National Higher Education Systems 2012 report, the QS top universities website, and the UGC report on higher education India: Strategies and schemes during Eleventh Plan period [2007-2012] for universities and colleges.*)

9. Independent Evaluation, Ranking and Accreditation: The following reforms are some of the other key initiatives for evaluation, ranking and accreditation which we believe will have a lasting impact on the Indian higher education sector:

   a. Creation of an independent Top 100 Indian University Ranking by three independent agencies, one government, one a private agency and the other a global agency of

repute, periodically. (Note: Punjab University was recently ranked better than the IITs this year by THE Rankings. India has many such examples; unfortunately, they have not been highlighted.)
- b. A choice-based credit system.
- c. We need some quality liberal arts universities—students must be given the freedom to select their subjects of interest and excel in the same.
- d. Funding based on assessment. Well-performing institutions must be given increased funding to encourage them. This will lead to rural institutions performing better and gaining greater funding.
- e. *Encourage Private Accreditation*: High quality non-profit bodies must be licensed to perform accreditation as per global standards. Accreditation must be compulsory.
- f. *Curriculum Development*: These must be in sync with industry needs. The curriculum must go through rigorous reworking every three years. Industry must play an active role to ensure that institutions turn out candidates suitable for their requirements.
- g. *Admission Procedure*: This must be based on Access, Inclusion, Equity and Quality. There must be total transparency and credibility in admission procedure. Management quota must be done away with. All education institutions must be brought under RTI.
- h. *Continuous Internal Evaluation*: The current system of evaluation puts undue pressure on students, especially during the examination season, resulting in increase of stress-related tragedies. To discourage rote learning, a continuous system of evaluation must be undertaken to assess real learning instead of depending on just the written content of exam papers.

10. **Foreign Universities Bill:** Empowering Indian higher education and research with necessary infrastructure, and appropriate ranking

and accreditation mechanism, facilitating autonomy, funding innovation and research potential of institutions for scientific research are among the steps that should be in place before bringing foreign universities into the Indian education system.

AFFORDABLE AND QUALITY HEALTHCARE

The state of healthcare in India can be gauged from the fact that about 70 per cent of our doctors live in urban India, whereas 70 per cent of our citizens live in rural India. In healthcare, India ranks way below China, Brazil and Sri Lanka, just below Bangladesh and Nepal and, in some cases, even Pakistan. If India sets up 100 medical colleges a year for the next five years, we may address shortage issues by 2025. According to the 2001 census, there is a shortage of 4,477 primary healthcare centres and 2,337 community healthcare centres. India would require 1.75 million beds by 2025. We also need to double the number of doctors from 0.7 million to 1.5 million and triple the number of nurses from 0.8 million to 2.5 million. India registers some of the highest figures of maternal, newborn and child deaths for any country in the world and accounts for 21 per cent of the world's global diseases. India is losing more than 6 per cent of its GDP annually due to premature deaths and preventable illnesses, according to a World Bank 2010 report.

We can also get a clear picture of our standing by comparing our expenditure on healthcare with that of other countries. India spends 1 per cent of its GDP on health, whereas France spends 10.4 per cent and Japan 8 per cent. According to the WHO's World Health Statistics 2010, public sector spending on healthcare in India is 26.20 per cent, while private sector spending is 73.80 per cent. Globally, the public-private spending ratio is 59.6:40.4. In China, it is 44.7:56.3, while in the UK it is 81.7:18.30. The per capita spending on healthcare in India is $40, while in the US it is $7,265, $3567 in the UK, $108 in China, $608 in Brazil and $802 globally.

Lifestyle Diseases in India

We have had success in controlling communicable diseases like malaria, cholera and polio. However, there is a new epidemic coming up, that of lifestyle diseases. A lifestyle in which there is less physical effort, and youth are at risk from vices like smoking and alcohol. Unhealthy processed foods and drinks pose their own problems. India has 61.3 million diabetics—a stupendous figure—and the incidence of heart disease is also very high. The economic burden of these non-communicable diseases in India is estimated in trillions of dollars ($6.2 trillion from 2012-30)—many times more than the health expenditure ($710 billion over the previous nineteen years).

A nation which has to give its young a bright future cannot ignore quality healthcare going forward.

Medical Education

It would be of interest here to consider that the quality of the education imparted is of great importance too, and not just having the requisite numbers on paper. Thus, a 2012 survey in Delhi and in rural Madhya Pradesh to assess the quality of primary health services found that in Delhi, the rate of correct diagnosis was as low as 22 per cent, and the rate of correct treatment was less than 50 per cent. In rural areas in Madhya Pradesh, the study by *Health Affairs*, an international journal, found that in 42 per cent of the cases, unnecessary or even harmful treatment was prescribed.

Worse still, the 305 healthcare providers tested were asked to diagnose illnesses with clear-cut symptoms such as unstable angina, asthma or dysentery, for which there are treatment checklists developed by the National Rural Health Mission. The study showed that only 11 per cent of rural care providers had any medical education. As many as 67 per cent had no medical qualification whatsoever, according to the report in the *Hindu*. While there are many more colleges and doctors, it is important to ensure there is no fall in the quality of the doctors produced, on account of poor standards among the newer colleges or lack of student ability due to lax admission standards.

The government has taken a number of measures to set up more medical colleges and nursing institutions, improve the doctor/nurse to population ratio in general and also correct the urban bias in the availability of doctors/nurses. A sum of Rs 1,350 crore has been earmarked for providing financial assistance to strengthen and upgrade state government medical colleges, while measures to set up six AIIMS-like institutions are in progress. The government has also liberalized the Medical Council of India's norms related to land, bed strength, etc. to enable the opening up of new medical colleges. The ratio of postgraduate medical teachers to students has been relaxed from 1:1 to 1:2. It has been proposed to upgrade existing schools of nursing to colleges of nursing.

But these actions have not yielded the desired results to reduce the doctor-patient ratio and extend quality healthcare services to rural areas. Today, no doctor likes a rural posting, and the government has to force them to take up such assignments. As medical education becomes costlier, meritorious students are not able to get into private medical colleges due to high capitation fees that are charged. Moreover, the highly uneven distribution of medical colleges has resulted in an unequal availability of doctors.

Setting up new medical colleges over the next ten years in the underserved districts with populations of more than 1.5 million should be a priority. Hence, we suggest that the government launch a quality medical education mission under a PPP model and increase the doctor-patient ratio to 1:400 by allowing private medical colleges to adopt government district hospitals, tertiary hospitals and PHCs to improve the healthcare infrastructure and services instead of opening new hospitals. This will make fresh resources available every year in government hospitals. There should be guidelines to maintain a level of quality in the services provided as well.

The other major challenge is the lack of quality teachers. This may be better handled using high definition tele-education, as in the successful Pan African e-network programme, which is providing education to more than 5,000 doctors in Africa from twelve super-speciality hospitals and medical universities in India. The government should study this programme and allow this type of teaching, which is more practical and more effective. It also has the potential to reach a lot more students than the conventional method. This should not be a video conferencing mode but should be an augmented virtual reality teaching methodology.

Cardiac Disease Management and Prevention

Indians are three times more prone to heart disease than Europeans. But India produces just eighty cardiologists a year against 800 in the US. There are just nine hospital beds per 10,000 people in India, compared with forty-one per 10,000 in China. We need to perform 2.5 million heart surgeries a year but we do only 90,000.

We need to include physical education as a mandatory subject from the school level up to graduation. As part of this, meditation, brisk walking, gymnastics, aerobics, sports, games, athletics, trekking, swimming, and good dietary habits would be taught. Acquiring good grades in this subject should be essential. This will result in healthy students and will in turn reduce the incidence of heart disease at a later stage. The government should also announce 100 per cent tax exemption for corporates to set up and maintain good physical education infrastructure in schools everywhere.

Strengthening Public Health Systems in Rural Areas

Strengthening the public health system, its facilities, and working and living conditions in rural areas is an immediate need. About 149 districts in fourteen states do not have any nursing school or nursing college as of 2009. It is essential to set up new nursing schools and colleges there over the next decade.

We need to ensure equitable access to functional beds to guarantee secondary and tertiary care in rural areas. An increase in bed capacity to at least two per 1,000 people by 2020 would be ideal. An emphasis on early interventions, prevention, and promotive health practices is likely to progressively reduce the need for hospital beds. The investments required for the same can come from public-private partnerships, FDI, private equity and mergers and acquisition activity. There should be a mandatory requirement for the private sector to reserve seats and establish PHCs in surrounding areas.

We should make available optional integration programmes and legal registration for AYUSH doctors to strengthen primary care. Start umbrella medical colleges in each district, with modern medicine, AYUSH, Nursing, and Paramedic institutes in one campus to bring about functional and systemic integration in training and in health care delivery.

We also need to provide quality healthcare outreach through mobile hospitals and diagnostic services to 50 per cent of all villagers who don't have access to healthcare providers. Tele-medicine and tele-radiology services could also help patients get second opinions from super specialist doctors. A 24/7 tele-medicine nodal centre should be established at district level government/ private hospitals connecting 50 per cent of PHCs for 24-hour access through tele-medicine in each district. Electronic medical record sharing should be promoted through the private sector. Private hospitals should take up such ventures for primary level consultation. Cable TV, mobile phones, chip-embedded Aadhaar cards and m-Money can be used to revolutionize the field of rural medicine.

Sanitation in India

Poor quality drinking water and improper disposal of sewage water and industrial waste create hazardous life conditions, especially among children, leading to malnutrition, stunting, premature death and other problems. Open defecation due to a lack of toilets and latrines is one of the most improper practices of sanitation responsible for many health-related issues. It is also an unsafe practice for women and girls. To improve sanitation, what we need is:

- *Centralized Drainage System with Bio-digester Power Generation:* Since 33 per cent people in India have no access to toilets and a large percentage defecate in the open, it is essential to plan and implement a centralized drainage system in 2,00,000 village panchayats and urban municipal areas, coupled with a bio-digester plant in each village panchayat/city municipal unit to generate at least 60 to 100 kW of electricity to be fed to the power grid or micro grid, thereby ensuring 100 per cent sanitation and clean and green villages.
- *Special focus on women and girls:* All sanitation-related initiatives should have a special focus on women and girls as they are the ones who bear the brunt of a lack of sanitation facilities. We need to create micro-credit options for women to build individual latrines connected to the centralized drainage system. Another initiative that needs to be undertaken is the creation of dedicated cooperatives for constructing and maintaining toilets. This can be included in the MNREGA scheme.
- *Technological Innovation:* This would include developing a low-cost model that re-uses waste water in households. We also need to use recycled waste material from industries to generate renewable energy. Such initiatives should be subsidized by the government for individuals undertaking them. The government could also introduce a rating system for industries and provide incentives for re-using waste water after purification. Awareness about the need for technological innovation needs to be inculcated in children from a young age by holding workshops and awareness campaigns.

- *Good health:* We need to ensure good health, especially among children below the age of five. Prevention of contact with waste and untreated sewage water will keep water-related diseases like diarrhoea away. Many children are forced into rag picking in hazardous conditions and in hospital waste sites for a livelihood. Hence it is necessary to segregate plastic waste and incinerate hospital and hazardous waste from the industry by enacting laws. Hospitals and other hazardous industries should ensure their waste is not transported to dumping sites.

Pharmaceutical and Drug Price Regulation

To maintain quality of medicine and ensure availability on a larger scale, we need to extend the coverage of generic medicine, thereby reducing the unit cost of treatment per person. The agencies involved here and their responsibilities would be:

- *Trusts/NGOs:* These organizations can maintain and run Jan Aushadhi stores outside hospitals and in villages. Sufficient margins need to be built into the MRP.
- *Private Sector:* It should be expected to make available unbranded generic medicine and surgical products at a low cost and nominal profit.
- *National Pharmaceutical Pricing Authority:* Should create awareness through multimedia publicity, design of a comprehensive policy and periodic review of the scheme.
- *State Governments:* Should provide space in government hospitals for stores and ensure that state government doctors prescribe non-branded generic medicines.
- *Jan Aushadhi:* The initiative should ensure the availability of quality medicines at affordable prices for all. It is essential to improve the feasibility and visibility of this programme by creating an adequate number of outlets and instituting a facilitation mechanism that ensures proper prescription and

administration of drugs. It should also look at improving medical education among the masses. Jan Aushadhi could be a self-sustaining business model not dependent on government subsidies by striving to make just minimal profits.

Empowering Healthcare Services through Innovative Policy

Some innovative policy interventions in the field of healthcare and medicine would be:

- *Healthcare FDI through ECB:* One of the ways forward in healthcare is FDI through external commercial borrowing (ECB). The global financing market is a huge source of credit. Foreign lenders provide far more flexibility in terms of security. Such borrowing may lead to a PPP model of investment in the healthcare sector.
- *PPP Model for Improved Healthcare Infrastructure:* This will ensure the direct involvement of super speciality hospitals, wider coverage of the BPL population, insurance schemes for the poor, self-sustainable business models with avenues for profit, involvement of a larger section of people, and innovative proposals like cooperative funding.
- *Improving the Community, PHC and Sub-centres in Villages:* India has a 40 per cent shortage in healthcare sub centres, 41 per cent shortage in PHCs, and 16 per cent shortage in community health centres. More than 50 per cent of public spending should be on primary care. By directing health financing mainly into tertiary care, we are not providing the population or providers with any incentive for preventive care. We need to set up low-cost, single specialty or even single micro-specialty primary and upgraded secondary care facilities and low capital cost day-care centres. The government, on its part, needs to support these efforts by providing subsidies on land and medical equipment and tax

benefits to professionals working in such organizations, especially in rural areas.
- *The Way Forward for Health Insurance Policies:* A continued and significant rise in claims can threaten a scheme. Insurers would be forced to hike premiums. In the voluntary private health insurance markets, an unsustainable hike in premiums would have deleterious effect on individual policies, as individuals may be forced to opt out of the scheme while employers may cut back on the contributions. While publicly funded health insurance schemes may factor in rising premiums in the short run, high hospitalization rates along with rising premiums are likely to drain government coffers.

The government needs to integrate the Central Government Health Scheme, the Rashtriya Swasthya Bima Yojana and the Employees' State Insurance Scheme under one umbrella. A combined entity would create a ready pool of about 138 million people with a budget of roughly Rs 4,000 crore and a per capita expenditure of Rs 290 per annum. Also, any strategy which attempts to achieve universal health care must take into account the entire population, or at least the poor and vulnerable, who account for over three-fourths of the population.

The present healthcare insurance system mostly covers government employees. Its share of public financing in total health care is just about 1 per cent of the GDP. Over 80 per cent of health financing is private financing, much of which is out-of-pocket payments and not by any pre-payment schemes. The government should enact an innovative healthcare insurance policy which covers the rest of the middle class, the unorganized sector and those below the poverty line with a layer of subsidy so that 65 per cent of the total population is covered by the public insurance scheme. With the subscription amount generated, all government hospitals can be better equipped than private ones. Diagnostic services and hospital management services may be handled by the private sector with the highest quality of service ensured, so that people are provided with a clean and neat hospital environment.

INCLUSIVE GOVERNANCE FOR SUSTAINABLE ECONOMIC DEVELOPMENT

It is the government's job to bring smiles on the faces of a billion people by enacting appropriate policies and laws and facilitating societal transformation. We have been working with policies and procedures that are mostly based on mistrust. These led to framing of extractive policies in almost all departments.

Underlying the policies was a control mindset instead of a facilitating mindset. This dampened motivation and empowerment at all levels of governance in productive sectors and among the people. The irony is that Indians have shown enormous resilience and achieved phenomenal success when provided with an environment of trust and confidence in the working space.

Whenever there has been a programme run in mission mode through a specially conceived management structure we have had very satisfactory results, whether in government, quasi-government or the private sector. We have examples to show that even for governance-related items there are models where a focused mission mode operation has helped. I recall an example from my ISRO days. When a failure occurs in a programme, normally the person who is in charge of the programme will be the target for censure, even for removal. In my case, when the first SLV3 launch failed in 1979, the ISRO chairman, Prof. Satish Dhawan, defended our team and took the failure upon himself. Within a year, when we achieved our goal, he gave the credit for the success to his team members. This quality of creative leadership, I have never witnessed anywhere.

> Some obvious examples of extractive policies:
>
> - An ordinary passport had a cumbersome procedure lasting several weeks. The same procedure has now been made much quicker, recognizing that the common, law-abiding citizen deserves a better deal. Getting an online appointment can still be a herculean task, but overall the process is more convenient.
> - Holding the file for years together to obtain a permission to start a high value project citing various reasons, sending applicant running to dozens of departments and delaying clearances for umpteen reasons makes setting up new industry an ordeal.
> - Many youth who became first-time entrepreneurs executing government projects feel that getting the payment for the work done from the officials becomes a tedious task leading to loss in their projects, getting into trouble with their banks, ending up paying service tax to the government for the invoice they have raised from the high-interest loans they have taken, finally having to close the company and go abroad to work as employees for someone.

The vision for inclusive governance is to transform us into a knowledge society. The prohibitive mindset which was formed based on mistrust stifled growth in all sectors of the economy. A new approach will help achieve sustainable GDP growth for a decade to make us reach developed status.

Governance Deficit: 'If the Central government releases one rupee for the poor, only 10 paisa reaches them.' These famous words by former Prime Minister Rajiv Gandhi made during the Congress Plenary Session in Bombay more than twenty-five years ago are as pertinent today as they were then. In October 2009, the Planning Commission deputy chairman, Montek Singh Ahluwalia, told a seminar that the former PM was correct about the extent of leakage. He said a Plan panel study of the public distribution system found that only 16 paise out of a rupee was reaching the targeted poor. He went on to suggest that 1 per cent of the funds for every scheme be earmarked for monitoring and evaluation.

In plan after plan, the main part of the fund allocation is marked for welfare schemes. While the funds have been regularly allocated, it is evident from the lack of access to safe drinking water, habitation, electricity, roads, healthcare, education and employment opportunity among a large number of people that the results have not matched requirements. Thus, the flaws prevailing in the system have to be corrected.

When corruption permeates all the layers from top to bottom, everybody in the chain is benefited. Ultimately, however, while individuals benefit, the nation fails. Government after government is interested in announcing subsidy schemes rather than empowering people to create a self-sustaining model of growth. Why not work at improving agriculture and energy infrastructure to create opportunity and employment. Waiving of agricultural loans due to drought and floods is a temporary solution. But what are the long-term measures which can activate the economy?

Some of the immediate short-term achievable targets are: enacting sustainable and inclusive economic policies; shedding the old archaic laws, rules, regulations and procedures which are a stumbling block; creating a single-window facilitation centre fixing the responsibilities and QoS parameters for clearing projects; removing abrasive tax structure to allow the industry and service sector to thrive and encourage the people to save; restructuring and resizing the ministries; and implementing a secured dynamic workflow-based e-governance system to provide accelerated and efficient governance. In addition, establishing agro-food processing to market eco-system; creating an industrial investment eco-system to empower small and medium enterprises and skill development to provide more employment generation in agro-food processing, industry and service sectors; an enabling environment for establishing modular solar farms and sea water desalination plants; announcing the immediate implementation of ethanol policy to promote sugar cultivation and reduce oil imports; activating tourism, hospitality and rural sector development with corporate tax exemption and to create more job opportunities would be other achievable targets.

Implementing networking of rivers, creating national smart waterways grid, improving the water management infrastructure, and establishing high-tension power grid, launching second green revolution mission and achieving energy independence goals by 2030 are among the long-term goals which can yield enormous benefits and take the country to a different level of development altogether.

Scams	Year	Presumptive loss in Rs Crore
Bofors pay-off	1987	65
Securities Scam	1992	5000
Fodder Scam	1996	950
Stock Market Scam	2001	1,15,000
Stamp Paper Scam	2003	30,000
Satyam Scam	2008	10,000
2G Spectrum loss (presumptive)	2008	1,76,000
Commonwealth Games Scam	2010	40,000

The phenomenon of corruption is not new. However, the past few years have seen an upsurge in major cases. As per the Transparency International ranking of nations based on the level of corruption, India slipped to 87th spot in 2010 from 84th in 2009. The World Bank also argued in a recent report that 'India aid programmes are beset by corruption, bad administration and under-payments.' As per the Doing Business in India report, India ranks 134 out of 183 countries on the World Bank's index of ease of doing business.

After corruption, the second most talked thing today is black money parked by Indians in tax havens abroad. With no consensus on the amount of money deposited abroad, everyone has a different conjecture. The estimates range from $2 billion to $500 billion to $2 trillion (more than India's GDP) or above. However, assuming that the sums are substantial—$500 billion by CBI's own estimates submitted in court—the money if retrieved could obviously be used to great benefit in core areas like health, education, and housing, pressing issues that need funding on a large scale to make a difference.

Black money has a direct impact on public finance, economic growth and ultimately the society. We can only reduce the black money in a major way if we bring some structural changes in the administrative and governance system through measures such as a strong Lokpal Bill, convert income tax into expenditure tax, bring the hidden money out through an amnesty scheme, and so on.

The large amounts of money involved are a result of the policies and governance system followed over many decades, which stunted growth but made some rich through corrupt means. Hence, inclusive governance will focus on developing the capabilities of political and economic institutions to perform the increasingly complex and demanding tasks expected of them by enacting policies which do away with bottlenecks. We have three pillars of democratic governance (Legislature, Executive and Judiciary) and three tiers of government (Centre, State and Panchayats). The capabilities of these institutions to deliver on their mandate need to be greatly improved. The gaps are most evident at the lowest level of PRIs (Panchayati Raj Institutions), where trained personnel are lacking and the training systems are also inadequate. It is also true at higher levels, where trained personnel may be available, but the capability of the systems is poor because they are not performance oriented and motivation is low.

Sustainable, Inclusive and Productive Use of Natural Resources

In recent years, the mining industry has suffered from a series of setbacks on account of environmental and policy issues. As a result, from being an exporter of certain ores India became an importer, with huge outflows of foreign exchange. The issue has to be looked at anew in seeing the problems industry has faced in harnessing natural resources.

Policies have to be evolved that enable productive use of coal, iron ore and other minerals and reduce the dependency on imports within the next three years. At the same time, any classified minerals including mineral sand should be mined only by the government and be used for strategic industrial growth within India. Export should only be done with value addition without impinging on our own requirements and interests.

Sustainable land use bill 2014: It is essential to transform the Land Acquisition, Rehabilitation and Resettlement Bill, 2011 into the Sustainable land use policy bill 2014. As per the 2011 bill, minimum compensation would be at least four times the market value for the land acquired in rural areas, and two times the market value for the land acquired in urban areas, besides other benefits enlisted in the bill.

For growth, India does not need a land acquisition policy, it needs a sustainable land use policy. Thus, Indian business, public or private, and MNCs should be allowed only to lease the land or make the farmers partners and not to buy the land. They should ensure yearly revenue to the farmers out of the revenue/profit. The bill primarily has to make the farmers partners in the project according to the level of land contribution at the market rate. The farmers and their wards need to be empowered with skills to get gainful employment. An industry had to reorient itself every three decades or so earlier. Now the cycle has come down to three to five years, as technology changes at a rapid pace. In this situation why should the government allow outright sale of farmers' land. It should be either leased or a farmer become the partner of the industry being set up, investing his land as his share of the equity.

Urban Land: Urban land needs use of vertical space to accommodate rising population. Increasing FSI and opting for township development are other ways of meeting the demand. Land supply may be increased for urban cities by amending laws and creating townships along the golden quadrilateral.

Forest and Tribal Land: Forest land in the country is about 21.5 per cent out of which dense forest is barely 1.66 per cent and there is hardly any tree cover on 8.8 per cent of the forest land due to encroachments. Forests should be essentially dense with tall and wide canopy cover and their productive use must be explored through forest agriculture. Many steps have been taken to improve the lot of tribals who should be brought into the modern economy through special tribal land development that offers sustainable livelihood.

Transforming Protection to Enrichment of Environment

Enacting an environment enrichment act instead of environment protection act might be a better way of serving the purpose of saving our environment. The environment ministry and other regulatory ministries should work in cohesion with agriculture, manufacturing, industry and service sector ministries for any new industry or technology adoption for speedy clearance and targeted action.

FDI in Agriculture and Food Processing Sector

The priority should be to create an enabling environment for growth in agriculture. From that perspective, FDI could be encouraged in agro-food processing. This will enable Indian industry to invest heavily with the support of FDI to create value addition through food processing and other industries that make use of agriculture produce.

What do we mean by value addition? Value addition can cover everything from a refrigerated transportation network to enhanced seaways, inland waterways, railway, and other means of transporting agricultural goods to investment in packaging industry and quality seed.

According to the draft report of a working group—Food Processing Industries for the 12th Five Year Plan, every Rs. 1 crore invested in the agro food processing industry creates value-added skilled employment for thirty people directly and forty-five people indirectly. But so far the MNCs who came here set up assembly plants in automobiles, electronics and other high-tech industries that generated low-value service jobs. They have not done enough by way of value addition in employment considering the worth of the incentives given to them in the form of policies to provide infrastructure such as water, energy, land and tax exemption.

India has given much importance in bringing FDI into various low-end service sector industry segments which have not generated large-scale value-added employment, when compared to the agriculture sector which is still providing 50 per cent employment. Such policies result in skewed growth which is irregular rather than sustainable.

Tax Reforms

A uniform GST (Goods and Services Tax) Act across the country would dispel the confusion among the investors regarding the tax structure. We need to evolve a user friendly law, which should facilitate the willingness to comply.

Personal income tax should be transformed into expenditure tax and then merged with GST. It would be a game changer that would bring multiple benefits is another idea which has been around for some time.

Mines and Minerals Act

Mining and related activity has the potential to contribute $250 billion to GDP and create 15 million jobs. However, the contribution of the mining sector to GDP is just 1.2 per cent. In countries like Chile and Australia mining contributes 6 per cent to their GDP. Some of the problems and solutions are given below.

Problem 1: India's spend on exploration projects is as low as 0.3 per cent of the global spend compared to 19 per cent for Canada, leading to stagnant reserve base for all mineral categories.

Solution: Sign MoUs with countries like Australia and Canada which are well advanced in using technologies related to mining for bilateral research cooperation and knowledge sharing.

Problem 2: It takes five to eight years to get mining lease in India whereas in Australia, it takes just about a year.

Solution: Set up clear timelines for each intermediate step like: Opinion on forest land: 5 months. Revenue opinion: 5 months (land records need to be updated frequently). Recommendation by state: 4 months. Approval by ministry of mines: 3 months. Approval by IBM (Indian Bureau of Mines): 3 months.

Setting up the responsibility matrix coupled with QoS delivery for the officials with necessary penalty has to be mandatory if they keep the file pending for more than the stipulated time. A facilitation officer has to be appointed at the secretary level to get these clearances on time and ensure strict compliance.

Problem 3: Logistical inefficiencies and lack of infrastructure that cause a loss of billions each year.

Solution: The development of infrastructure will require collaboration with railways, ports and surface transport ministry to pursue projects for the mining sector. The use of local development funds would be required for socio-economic infrastructure creation, management and maintenance. Co-operation with the department of shipping to develop key coastal corridors and expand capacity of major ports would be needed as well.

Problem 4: Shortage of human capital in mining.

Solution: Work with the HRD ministry to increase the engineering and management seats in mining.

Land use for mining should get priority over others, as minerals cannot be shifted and we cannot afford to lose mineral wealth. Sand export on the southern sea shore has to be brought under control since that belt is rich with thorium deposits that are disappearing. Minerals and coal are basic inputs and any shortage has a direct impact on manufacturing and the power sector. The mineral sector is under great stress and it should be relieved and normalized by removing hurdles. Restrictive laws and politicization of the minerals sector have created a huge shortage of this resource.

Manufacturing Sector

Manufacturing has been recognized as the engine for economic growth. We should focus on developing the Agro food processing Industry, Biomedical engineering, Transportation, Oil and Gas industry, Defence, Aerospace, ICT electronics, and hardware in this sector. The share of manufacturing in the GDP is only 16 per cent over the last decade and a major reason for this appears to be the lack of sufficient power, lack of infrastructure, lack of efficient process adoption, lack of state of the art machinery and ultimately the lack of automation. The manufacturing sector has to be empowered to achieve 25 per cent GDP contribution by 2020 by increasing the depth in manufacturing, focusing on the level of domestic value addition, enhanced global competitiveness through appropriate policy support and sustainability of growth particularly with regard to the environment. As per a recent McKinsey report, India's manufacturers have a golden chance to seize a larger share of the global market. It further says that the rising domestic demand together with the multinational companies' desire to diversify their production to include low-cost plants in countries other than China would help India's manufacturing sector grow sixfold by 2025 to $1 trillion, while creating up to 90 million jobs.

Transportation Challenges

The 12th Plan outlay for transportation should be increased to Rs 25 lakh crore for achieving 9 per cent growth. A minimum of 50 per cent investment should come from private funding. Composite transport services are likely to grow nearly 1.2 times of GDP growth. Private investments need facilitation and protection against regulatory and political risks

Roads: State and rural roads are in either bad condition, or non-motorable and require frequent repairs or relaying due to the poor quality of construction. Extra dependency on road transport increases freight cost. Checkposts, restrictions on movement delay turnaround time thereby adding to costs. Urban transport is overstretched. Rural roads have to be made in mission mode using plastic road technology with higher strength to make them withstand weather conditions.

Railways: Indian Railways needs major restructuring like the air travel sector. Private players should be allowed to compete in railway passenger and freight services. The railways could monetize their surplus assets and outsource the non-core activities. They need to modernize signalling, security, bio-toilet and entertainment system, maintain cleanliness and neatness and upgrade station services to the level of airports. They need to increase track length by another 25,000 km. The train speed should increase to a maximum of 300 km per hour.

Air: Promotion of air connectivity to tier two and three cities should be undertaken in a timebound way. Helicopter tourism can be improved to create a devotional, entertainment and cultural circuit.

Defence and Aerospace Industry

India should focus on the design and development of the following defence missions either indigenously or through joint venture missions. We need to give impetus and special attention to indigenous R&D and create an investment eco-system for private sector participation to fulfil our defence requirements. Allocation of 3 per cent of GDP for the aerospace and defence missions is essential to develop our indigenous capability and also provide large-scale professional employment to youth. Lean systems to enhance the productivity and efficiency of the defence manufacturing and production sector need to be brought in immediately. Similarly, streamlining the procurement policy for military hardware and software is the need of the hour. At the same time, we should regulate and change the 30 per cent defence offset to benefit Indian private and public companies rather than go back again to foreign-origin companies, which doesn't serve the avowed purpose of empowering Indian R&D.

Aerospace: We should develop a 70-100 seater passenger jet aircraft capitalizing on the spinoff technologies developed for the light combat aircraft Tejas. A hypersonic reusable cruise system for achieving low-cost access to space and launching solar-powered satellite missions are some of the next big challenges.

Among the possibilities:

Space: Achieving higher level of reliability in design and development of cryogenic engines and higher payload GSLV rocket systems for Moon, Mars unmanned and manned missions. Launching of SDMB (Satellite—Digital Mobile Broadcast) satellites for mobile services. Accelerating the deployment of navigation satellites and remote-sensing satellites for identifying natural wealth.

Defence: ICBMs, underwater missiles, anti-ballistic missiles that can intercept the target at multiple levels of trajectory, stealth technology for missiles, low-intensity warfare systems; design and development of aircraft engines, nuclear submarines, helicopters with night flying capabilities are some of the important mission which need to be restructured, accelerated with higher research and development focus and leaned. The focus should be on convergence of technology: Info+Bio+Nano+ Ecology.

We have to have a long-term defence strategy and a vision for defence industry growth involving large private industries as production partners is the order of the day. Industry partnership with renowned global companies enables flow of new manufacturing techniques and process to our industries that will result in high technology products. R&D is an important component and the government should allocate more funds for it. The determination and commitment of the government to use weapons made indigenously will definitely accelerate the growth in this field.

The need of the hour is to establish a Military Industry Complex (MIC) at the national level enlisting large and medium industries to be the partners along with defence PSUs as members of MIC. Procedures are to be formulated which will enable participation of cluster of industries to design, develop and produce systems (irrespective of private or public). More thrust has to be given to government funding for R&D even to private companies to strengthen R&D capabilities. Encouraging high technology tie-ups / JVs between Indian and other global defence industries will achieve not only competitiveness but also open up prospects for export. India cannot afford to lose any more time in pondering the issue.

Shipbuilding

India today builds ships for oil exploration, service vessels, port operations, self-propelled barges for river transport and cargo ships up to 92,000 DWT (dead weight tonnage). In addition, we build warships for the Indian Navy. Today India has shipyards for building vessels of capacity 100,000 to 150,000 DWT. Going by the current global trend in the shipping industry, we have to create facilities for vessels ranging from 150,000 to 300,000 DWT with much larger output of ships per annum in terms of total tonnage. Shipbuilding used to be a labour-intensive industry. Presently, the technology has undergone a sea change. With the ships growing larger and larger shipyards have to plan for automation and computer-aided design and manufacturing right in the beginning. South Korea and Russia are two countries building ships for us.

The time has come, India has to increase its capacity of shipbuilding of large vessels for both civil and military applications. A major part of the design office tasks can be reduced substantially through the application of design software. Good design and quality control for safety have to be the focus. These actions will enable the industry to build capacity for shipbuilding of 30 million DWT creating a market worth $30 billion a year by 2020. However, proper planning, action-oriented decisions and investments have to converge.

All the above systems and areas may need to deploy collaborations nationally and internationally for design and development.

Other Industries

The following is a sampling of some industries and the kind of issues they face and steps that can help bring them on top.

Oil and Gas as Industrial Growth Promoters: It goes without saying, we need to focus on higher domestic production. Enact energy conservation policy. Develop substitutes like biofuel, ethanol, and emulsified fuel and their associated automobile and transportation logistics consumption policy. We need to phase out petroleum subsidy. Alongside, there should be a policy on developing substitutes and ensuring alternative fuel availability to all consumers. This could go a long way to spur growth.

Gold Industry: Reduce gold import by hiking custom duty and reduce public buying of gold through an ETF (Exchange Trade

Fund) scheme. As suggested by many economic experts, if an appropriate scheme is evolved to attract the deposit of domestic gold for long-term savings, with minimal interest, people may come forward in large numbers, thereby bringing in a huge investment unmatched by even FDI. This may be used for building major infrastructure projects.

Fertilizer Industry: We need to reduce the fertilizer subsidy. This could be coupled with an R&D policy for production of alternative organic fertilizer made available to farmers by completely revamping its distribution network using an innovative business model.

Plastic and Glass Industry: We need to evolve a policy for plastic use. Since plastics can only be down cycled, usage has to be reduced to cut down on the growing pollution and the danger due to heaps of plastics thrown on the streets and in water bodies. We need to evolve a policy which enables the use of items which are recyclable and encourage biodegradable materials. Appropriate legislation and strict compliance with restrictions on plastic use are an immediate requirement.

IT and Software: We need to empower, accommodate and provide necessary venture capital and cash flows for small and medium (SME) Indian enterprises to make them competitive in global IT services. They should be able to compete in government tenders as a consortium. There could be 40 per cent allocation of government IT services to small- and medium-scale Indian enterprises to promote them to be globally competitive and create a level playing field. An allocation of 60 per cent contracts to companies in consortium mode would further help small units develop their competence.

Improving Economic Efficiency

We need to achieve a trade surplus in goods and services. If we achieve that target the foreign exchange inflow will support growth and infrastructure spending in a big way. As per the experts, we need to come out of our domestic internal economy crisis and external sector challenges. Internal reforms and improvement of economic efficiency will certainly help to reduce both trade deficit and inflation.

Public Finance

Expenditure reforms should get priority over revenue generation. Subsidy should be less than 25 per cent of revenue receipts. Interest cost should be reduced and short-term debt replaced with long-term debt for reducing the debt service burden. The defence budget should be focused on indigenization, R&D, joint venture design and development of technologies. Domain-based ministries may be merged together to reduce the size of the government and the position of minister of state under a cabinet minister may be abolished. Outsource the common/routine/periodic services to bring in more efficiency and productivity in all the departments and ministries thereby ensuring quality of services to the people. Capital expenditure needs enhancement in terms of GDP. External borrowings must be used exclusively for productive infrastructure.

Encouraging Savings

The country's savings provide resources for investment, which is the foundation for economic growth. Savings touched 36.8 per cent of GDP in FY 2008, but dropped down to 30 per cent GDP in 2013. Our aim should be to make them touch 40 per cent of GDP. Savings should be channelized into financial products instead of physical assets like gold and precious metals. They should be utilized for productive investment and not for expenditure funding. Cash at home is like dead money which should be brought into the system by extending banking network with relaxed KYC (Know Your Customer) norms. The misconceptions about corporate saving should be removed, as these are the key drivers for public income and growth. Our dependency on foreign savings will continue till domestic savings reach 40 per cent.

Transparent, Responsive and Corruption-free Governance

A new, independent Lokpal bill (not in its present form) empowering an independent CVC, independent CBI, and independent Special Court with a checks and balances mechanism built-in to deal with corruption cases with constitutional authority status similar to that of the Election Commission is needed. Evolving an efficient public administration and bureaucracy by enacting or reforming policies to promote creativity, efficiency, excellence in the administrative system in all Civil Services, protecting honest officers who have a 'what I can give you' attitude towards the people is another requirement. There should be unbroken tenure without transfer due to political considerations and accountability for lack of performance.

Sustainable Policies for Inclusive Development

Non-sustainable policies such as extractive policies pose a challenge to the growth of our economy. Challenges include closure of small and medium industry due to lack of proper supportive infrastructure such as supply of power or finance, a non-competitive public sector due to lack of visionary leadership which cannot rise to market demands due to rigid structures and bureaucratic control; and closure of traditional industries. There is no policy which promotes small and medium industry to compete locally for large projects either individually or in collaboration with multinationals. Except for a handful of big industries and corporates other companies don't get an opportunity to compete. When they don't get an opportunity to compete within India, how can they compete globally?

The challenges have not changed even after the economic liberalization, but at the same time, our productive sector is made to compete with advanced global companies and loses out on many opportunities due to rules that benefit the MNCs.

Inclusive Governance

Stringent regulations for the productive sector due to pre-liberalization mindset that always preferred to regulate than to facilitate continue to hold back development. Good economic policies are replaced by regressive laws and regulations. Any non-compliance is equated with grave criminal offence leading to the belief that being in productive sector itself is a criminal activity among the young entrepreneurs. This affects the investment sentiment and growth reversal has started already. Economic policy shouldn't be influenced by electoral politics, rather it should be based on economic prudence only for long-term benefits to the people.

Priority should be given for improving the performance of the existing productive sector by relieving the pressure on it. Political consensus should emerge for enabling new reforms and legislations. Law and regulations must be reduced and simplified by forming a constitutional bench to revisit all the archaic acts and procedures. Plant closure may be the last option and it shouldn't be exercised as a first option (for example, in the Satyam fraud case, the company was revived as Tech Mahindra Satyam).

Facilitation should prevail along with regulation. Taxation should be simpler to promote wilful compliance. All government officials should be trained on the economic needs and policies of the country. Everybody is a team member in the growth process. Good policies alone cannot deliver the result unless they are implemented by the right people with the right team spirit at the right time.

SMART E-GOVERNANCE FOR TRANSPARENT ADMINISTRATION

Good governance is being recognized as an important goal all across the world. Many countries have taken up specific initiatives for open government. Freedom of information is being redefined and supported by detailed guidelines. The internet revolution has proved to be a powerful tool for good governance initiatives. Along with this, there is a conscious effort to make the citizen the focus of governance.

As part of governance, the government needs to provide many facilities and services to the people. Also, these services require to be constantly upgraded. The government budgets and expends a large amount of funds to fulfil this goal. The money for the work comes from people themselves in the form of taxes. It is this money collected from the people which is spent for their benefit, particularly that of the poor and needy.

> e-Governance means, a transparent smart e-governance with seamless access, secure and authentic flow of information crossing the inter-departmental barrier and providing a fair and unbiased service to the citizen.

However, when it comes to ensuring that the benefits reach the common man, the value of the services which reach the citizens is much below the expected level in far too many areas, be it education, healthcare, sanitation, water, power or roads. Even to make timely payments, receiving certificates for certain services, citizens have to struggle and sometimes pay bribes. Information is a wealth, as long as it is non-transparent, the corruption is bound to exist from top to bottom. As long as there are no QoS (Quality of Service) parameters evolved for the government services such as G2G, G2C, and G2B, corruption is bound to exist.

Indian people have shown enormous resilience and have achieved phenomenal success when provided with an environment of trust and confidence in the working space. Whenever there has been a programme run in mission mode through a specially conceived management structure we have been realizing very satisfactory results whether in government, quasi-government or the private sector. We have examples which show that even in governance-related items, there are models where a focused mission mode operation has helped. How are we to develop the requisite empathy among our administrators? Our administrators have to imagine the people they administer at work: farmers tilling a field, fishermen in the rough seas; workers in industries; teachers in schools; health workers in healthcare institutions—before they take political and administrative decisions or when they give judgement. It might help them better appreciate the problems the people they administer face. I would consider our government machinery corruption-free only if the purpose for which it was set up is fulfilled, in letter and spirit, with honesty, sincerity and purposefulness.

This is possible only under an e-governance mechanism. No country has so far implemented such a system for 1 billion people and so it will be a big challenge for us. Most importantly, e-governance has to be citizen friendly and enable seamless access to information and flow of information across states and the central government. Let us explain the kind of e-governance which we visualize through some typical scenarios, along with some suggestions for implementation.

e-Elections

I visualize an election scenario in which a candidate files his nomination from a particular constituency. Immediately, the election officer verifies his/her authenticity using the national citizen ID (UIDAI/National Population Register ID/any other citizen ID) database. His/her civic status is reflected by the crime record with the police. His property record comes from the land authority; income and wealth sources from the income tax department; education credentials from university records; employment record from various employers; credit history from various credit institutions like banks; and legal records from the judicial system.

All details automatically show up on the election officer's

computer screen within a few minutes, thanks to an e-governance software which scans state and central government directories. The election officer immediately decides on the candidate's eligibility, and the election process starts. During the election, voters having mobile phone with their national ID can use a secured and authentic election mobile app to vote for the candidate of their choice in their constituency, besides the option of going to a polling booth.

Is such a system possible? If so, when will it turn to reality? Will the political parties believe in such an advanced system? Will the bureaucrats allow it to be implemented? As far as the technology goes, it is feasible. It is for the leadership to have the courage to implement such a transparent system for elections, which will attract near 100 per cent voting and reduce the pitfalls in the election system. Also, this would only be a starting point. We would need to replicate such systems across the board. Can we provide good governance to our 1 billion people? Can such governance speed up the delivery system? Can it differentiate between genuine and spurious transactions? Can it ensure immediate action in genuine cases such that all standards of quality on a checklist are met? Can the cost be affordable for our nation? If we can implement such a system, I will call it a true e-governance system.

Challenges in e-Governance

We are trying to seek an answer for the questions mentioned above by asking another set of questions. Do we have the required e-governance framework? Do we have a complete national citizen database which will be the primary unit of data for all governance applications across state and central governments? At present, India has multiple registration authorities, the UIDAI and the National Population Registry, creating confusion among ministries and leading to duplication of efforts.

Do we have standards for the secure exchange of information? Do we have a secure delivery framework by means of a virtual private network connecting state and central government departments? Do we have data centres in the central government and state governments to handle departmental workflow automation, collaboration, interaction and exchange of information? All states have a State Wide Area Network and a State Level Data Centre, but still there is no e-governance system in the country which smoothly connects all the citizens with everyone in the administration from top to bottom. No state has implemented such a system. In the kind of scenario which exists today, with the complex web of government—citizen interactions and rising requirements to ensure good governance and implement programmes, it is time to face these challenges and reform and empower administrative systems to accelerate decision-making.

Transparency in Administrative Services

In order to bring about transparency in governance, I would suggest the following:

- Establishment of an e-Governance Commission or Empowered Board for total e-governance system to ensure Quality of Service in G2G, G2C, G2B, and G2I. Establishment of an e-Governance grid across states and the Centre connecting ministries and departments.
- Many state governments have already established a data centre and State Wide Area Network. But a full-fledged e-governance cloud system connecting the chief minister's office to the collectorate up to the Village Administrative Officer and accessible to all its citizens would be optimal.
- While adopting e-governance with secured digital and electronic signature for bringing down corruption, doing away with paper file movement in all government offices is a must.
- Setting up a multipurpose, secure, citizen ID database as the primary source of data for all e-governance services.
- Online issue of National Citizen ID cards based on Aadhaar

or NPR data collected for authenticating multipurpose government services including election ID.
- Creation of Wi-fi hotspots to reach out government services at the village level with higher bandwidth connectivity backbone.
- Ninety per cent of the work related to e-governance should be outsourced to native Indian IT companies and consortiums for propelling their growth competitively and the government should only manage data centres/its private cloud and maintain those for online e-governance application.

e-Judiciary

It is my experience that the computerization of a large organization or mission is successful only if the processes themselves are re-engineered to realize the full benefits of automation. In a connected world, e-courts or a 'Justice Cloud' should lead to an e-judiciary by linking various organs of society, government, institutions and citizens. The objective of an e-judiciary should be to ensure the smooth flow of information across the various units of government, judiciary, institutions and citizens to ensure: availability of authentic information on the fly; linkages established between all transactions; improvement in overall productivity; and reduction in multiple levels of appeal.

The typical scenario under an e-judiciary system would be one where, for instance, a litigant in a land dispute case comes with his national ID card to an e-court service centre in a district court with all the documentary evidence he possesses. The e-court service centre electronically helps him identify a civil lawyer to present his case. The lawyer files the case in a prescribed format in the e-court. Once the case is filed, the e-court web service agent scans the state and central e-governance grid and collects the relevant information from the land records registry and gets the encumbrance certificate details of litigants and defendants. If necessary, the agent also collects the credit history of the parties from the banking grid, criminal records if any from the police grid, litigation records if any from the other courts, property tax and service tax payment data for the disputed land from the state e-governance grid, legal heir verification from the registrar of deeds and classification and conversion details of the land from the district e-governance grid.

The judicial officer now has the documentary evidence submitted by the litigant and defendant and the certified and authentic documentary evidence collected from various government units which have relevance to this case in front of him. This will enable the judicial officer to apply his or her mind objectively with optimal examination and cross-examination of the witnesses, leading to a fast decision in the particular case.

I would like to make the following suggestions so that the planned e-judiciary system can be integrated with the national e-governance grid system to ensure a robust, transparent and fast judiciary process.

- The e-judiciary system may work with the ministry of communication and information technology to ensure information flow.
- Consider the creation of a judicial e-governance grid/cloud, supplemented by a police e-governance grid, state and central e-governance grid—particularly for land records, service and property tax—a knowledge grid, healthcare grid and institutional grid to provide support document services.
- Consider establishing e-judiciary service centres in all court complexes for digitizing court records and feed into secured dynamic workflow from there onwards in the judicial process.
- The aim of the e-courts should be to bring down the pendency rate by more than 80 per cent in district courts from the existing 2.5 crore, in high courts from the existing 36 lakh, and in the Supreme Court from the existing 41,000 cases by the year 2020.

- To ensure timely implementation of the e-judiciary system, certain actions related to the process and education are essential to bring about functional literacy among the masses.

Prevention of Cybercrime

Though information and communication technology (ICT) has been a tool for speeding up the justice system, we would soon witness in our digital economy more and more crimes being committed using ICT itself. These are now known the world over as cybercrimes. The problem with the digital world is that the crime may originate anywhere in the world beyond our own shores but will damage organizational wealth in digital form in multiple locations in the country. Judges, lawyers, the police and law officers should be trained to be aware of such possibilities in much the same way as they have been trained to understand crime in the physical world. In this globalized world of connectivity, every new technology advancement comes with its associated crime as well. However, to stop, deny or block the information traffic would not be a suitable option.

It is essential to maintain information flow, set up a monitoring, filtering, tracking and capturing mechanism and update the technology regularly with research inputs. The objective would be to make the system non-vulnerable to any external attack with malicious intent or with an intent of bringing bad reputation to any individual or organization or country or meant to destroy the economic assets of the nation. We need appropriate laws to handle the increasing cybercrime and its technology advancements. We need to establish a 'cybercrime eco-system' to detect, monitor, locate and act to prevent the cybercrime before it causes damage.

Multiple Dimensions of the Right to Information

Apart from e-governance, another tool to ensure transparent administration is the Right to Information (RTI), which came into effect in 2005. For the effective implementation of the RTI Act, we need to embark on a mission to strengthen the administrative setup and accelerate its processes. Thus, in sum, we have the following suggestions with regard to improvements in governance.

    a. Providing transparent governance with administrative reforms.
    b. Responsibility coupled with accountability.
    c. Capacity building in specialized and technical areas of expertise.
    d. Bringing transparency in cadre management.
    e. Performance-oriented career advancement.
    f. Transformation of the government machinery into a government facilitation service, and that of a government officer into a government growth facilitator.
    g. Making RTI more responsive and accelerating its processes.

Right to Quality of Service Act

Right to public services legislation has been enacted by many state governments. The RTS focuses on statutory laws which guarantee timebound delivery of services by the government to citizens. It provides a mechanism for punishing the errant public servant who is deficient in providing the service stipulated under the statute. *(Ref: Punjab clears Right to Services Act. 8 June 2011 [Chennai, India: The Hindu]. 8 June 2011).*

Some of the common public services which are meant to be provided in a fixed timeframe as a right include the following: issuing caste, birth, marriage and domicile certificates, electric connections, voter's card, ration card, copies of land records, etc.

It is necessary to bring out Right to Quality of Service Act instead of the RTS Act. It has to include not only G2C services, which pertain to the services to citizens and involve low-level corruption, but the G2G, G2B, G2I, G2I dealings which involve higher level corruption. Hence, RT QoS (Right to Quality of

Service) has to ensure the quality of service from the government officials with transparency and speed in all their dealings. RT QoS should ensure penalty and demotion, if the official holds up or delays the file beyond the realm of QoS parameters laid down for corrupt purpose.

Initiating number of these smart measures will certainly bring down the corruption to minimum levels in all government dealings and ensure quality of service in its dealings with all parties, whether individuals or institutions.

STRATEGIC FOREIGN POLICY FOR PEACE AND PROSPERITY

India needs to evolve a new strategic external affairs policy. Some key principles would be:

Promoting Peace and Prosperity in the Neighbourhood

European civilization has a unique place in human history. For hundreds of years, the continent had been a theatre of conflicts, with a number of wars between civilizations and nations, including the two world wars which originated in Europe before pulling the rest of the world into their vortex. The European Union came into existence against that backdrop, with a vision for peace and prosperity. It has become an inspirational model and an example to emulate for every region in the world such as the African Union. The Union is an example to developing countries to show how they can come together to work unitedly challenging established global norms and reshape trade, commerce and security.

In this context, I am reminded of the words of a Tamil poet, Kaniyan Poongundranar, who said 3,000 years ago: 'I am a world citizen; every citizen is my own kith and kin'. When European countries, which fought among themselves for centuries, can come together and form the EU without losing their individual national identities, why can't SAARC (South Asian Association for Regional Cooperation) nations come together and form a SAARC Union Parliament? Poverty and disease are the common enemies of all SAARC nations. We should evolve a foreign policy which can remove these.

A nation's outreach begins from its neighbourhood and for India we are lucky to belong to a region rich in civilization, resource and potential. Together the SAARC countries Afghanistan, Bangladesh, Bhutan, Maldives, Nepal, Pakistan and Sri Lanka represent 1.50 billion people or 25 per cent of the world population. The inspiring and unique aspects of SAARC countries that we share, are: first, the high intensity of bio-diversity in our region; second, we have the largest population of youth in the world; third, our combined purchasing power has the potential to be the highest in the world; and also we are blessed and interconnected with a civilizational heritage that goes back for thousands of years. What better environment can any region in the world have, which is more favourable for development and peace in the region, if we share a common vision and work together to realize our vision through dynamic missions.

In spite of these major structural advantages, there is an impression among the people of the SAARC nations that we have yet to make a distinctive contribution that can make a difference to lives of people in our region. Can we now together make an attempt to change this impression? I would like to share with you, if you agree, two experiences that relate to the impact of connectivities and rural development that are actually making a difference.

Vision for SAARC

Let me start with my visualization of SAARC countries ten years hence.

a) The people living below poverty line will become near zero from the existing 25 per cent.

b) The per capita income of the SAARC region as the whole will increase from the present $2,777 to $10,000.
c) Infant mortality rate will become less than 10 per thousand from the present 260 per thousand prevalent in some of the countries.
d) All the SAARC countries will be free from waterborne diseases and receive affordable, quality healthcare.
e) The SAARC countries will realize the goal of 100 per cent literacy from the existing less than 40 per cent in some of the countries.
f) All citizens of SAARC countries will be empowered with quality education, healthcare and employment potential leading to overall enhancement in prosperity and happiness.

Core Competence of SAARC Countries

The main objective of SAARC is to provide a platform for the peoples of South Asia to work together in a spirit of friendship, trust and understanding for accelerating the process of economic and social development of member states. SAARC countries have several core competencies and every country has a vision to become a developed nation in a timebound manner. Let us now focus on some of them which can be collectively pooled for mutual benefit. Afghanistan is endowed with natural resources such as untapped oil and natural gas, minerals and metals. The Grameen Bank concept of Bangladesh which has made a difference to the life of many people has received international attention and acclaim. Bhutan is known for its hydel resources and is a model for the promotion of the concept of Happiness Index. India over the years has established itself well in IT and e-connectivity. Maldives is known for its innovation in tourism. Nepal for its biodiversity and hydel resources. Pakistan has created a name for itself in cotton, textiles and apparels. Sri Lanka is known for tea and rubber processing. Let us see how these national competitive advantages can be harnessed for accelerating the transformation of the region as a whole.

Social and Economic Development—Transforming SAARC into a Fully Developed Region

Since over one billion citizens of SAARC countries live in villages, there is an urgency for all of us to improve the conditions of rural life through better physical connectivity, electronic connectivity, knowledge connectivity, which together will lead to comprehensive economic connectivity. For this mission, we have to ensure that the overall GDP growth rate for SAARC countries has to reach 8 per cent to 10 per cent, and is maintained at this level for the next ten years. For this, employment generation, particularly in the rural areas, is essential, which can only come if the development process is carried there.

India has a nucleated programme called PURA (Providing Urban Amenities in Rural Areas) involving geographically co-located clusters of multiple villages with four connectivities, as mentioned above. India with its 6,00,000 villages needs to have 7,000 PURAs. The specific needs of the PURA for different SAARC countries can be worked out by the specialists based on terrain and socio-economic conditions prevailing in the particular region. Each PURA cluster, apart from concentrating on reinforcing agriculture, will emphasize agro processing, development of rural craftsmanship, dairy, silk production and fishing in the nations having coastlines, so that the non-farm revenue for the rural sector is enhanced, based on the competitive advantage of the region.

It is also essential that the rural economy should be driven by renewable energies such as solar, wind, biofuel and conversion of municipal waste into power. With this approach, the core competencies in the rural sector would be harnessed for sustainable development of the economy as a whole.

SAARC Knowledge Platform and Its Missions

We need to evolve the SAARC Knowledge Platform which will combine the core competencies of the SAARC nations and will become the launch pad for many innovations that are waiting to be unleashed by the combined power of scientists and technologists of the region.

The convergence of bio, nano and ICT is expected to touch every area of concern to humanity. The SAARC Knowledge Platform will take up the missions in some of the areas given below which are of utmost urgency to all of us.

1. **SAARC Nations' e-Network:** Creating e-Partnership in education, healthcare, business and trade similar to Pan-African network.
2. **Energy:** Transforming energy security to energy independence for the region.
3. **Water:** Enhancing the quality of existing resources, efficient recycling technology, rainwater harvesting, interlinking of rivers, seawater desalination using renewable energy.
4. **Healthcare:** Vaccine for HIV/AIDS, malaria, tuberculosis and other diseases in the region; using traditional medicine while working towards molecule to drugs programme.
5. **Agriculture and food processing:** Increasing the per capita yield from agriculture, new technologies for preservation, developing varieties of crops for semi-arid and arid regions.
6. **Capacity building:** Capacity building in internationally competitive skills development and higher education with research as a focus through partnership among the educational and R & D institutions of SAARC countries through direct and virtual classrooms.

India is conscious that GDP alone does not fully reflect in the quality of life of a large number of people, particularly in rural areas and even in urban areas. This may be true in SAARC nations also. For a comprehensive and inclusive approach to a measure of true socio-economic development, we have evolved what is called a National Prosperity Index (NPI), which is a summation of (a) annual growth rate of GDP; plus (b) improvement in quality of life of the people, particularly those living below the poverty line plus (c) the adoption of a value system derived from our civilizational heritage in every walk of life.

It may be noted that the concept of National Prosperity Index includes the factor of the International Human Development Index. That is NPI=a+b+c. Particularly, 'b' is a function of availability of housing, good water, nutrition, proper sanitation, education, healthcare and employment potential, 'c' is a function of promoting the joint family system, creation of a spirit of working together, following a righteous way of life, removing social inequities, and above all promoting a conflict-free, harmonious society. This will be indicated by peace in families and communities, reduction in corruption index, reduction in court cases, and elimination of violence against children and women and communal tensions. There should also be progressive reduction in the number of people living below the poverty line leading to poverty becoming near zero. All our efforts in improving the national economic performance should be guided by the National Prosperity Index of the nation at any point of time. Based on this or a similar model let us evolve a SAARC Prosperity Index which will represent the overall quality of life of the people in the region.

Trade and Business Growth

India has trade agreements with its neighbours and is seeking new ones with East Asian countries and the US. Examples of these include the India-Sri Lanka Free Trade Agreement; the trade agreements with Bangladesh, Bhutan, Sri Lanka, Maldives, China and South Korea; the India-Nepal Trade Treaty; and the Comprehensive Economic Cooperation Agreement (CECA) with Singapore. There are agreements with the Association of Southeast Asian Nations (ASEAN) and further afield Chile as well.

According to the department of commerce, the fifteen largest trading partners of India represent 62.1 per cent of Indian imports and 58.1 per cent of Indian exports as of December 2010. These figures do not include services or foreign direct investment but only trade in goods. The largest Indian partners, with their total trade (sum of imports and exports) in $ millions for 2012–13, are given here:

Country	Exports	Imports	Total Trade	Trade Balance
UAE	36,265.15	38,436.47	74,701.61	-2171.32
China	13,503.00	54,324.04	67,827.04	-40,821.04
United States	36,152.30	24,343.73	60,496.03	11,808.57
Saudi Arabia	9783.81	34,130.50	43,914.31	-24,346.69
Switzerland	1,116.98	29,915.78	31,032.76	-28,798.80
Singapore	13,608.65	7,754.38	21,363.03	5,854.27
Germany	7,244.63	14,373.91	21,618.54	-7129.28
Hong Kong	12,278.31	8,078.58	20,356.89	4,199.74
Indonesia	5,331.47	14,774.27	20,105.75	-9,442.80
Iraq	1,278.13	20,155.94	21,434.07	-18,877.81
Japan	6,099.06	12,514.07	18,613.14	-6,415.01
Belgium	5,506.63	10,087.16	15,593.80	-4,580.53
Kuwait	1,060.80	16,569.63	17,630.43	-15,508.83
Iran	3,351.07	11,603.79	14,954.86	-8,252.72
South Korea	4,201.49	13,461.25	17,662.73	-9,259.76

This list does not include the Gulf Cooperation Council (GCC), which includes two (UAE and Saudi Arabia) of the above states in a single economic entity. As a single economy, the GCC is the largest trading partner of India, with almost $160 billion in total trade. This list also does not include the European Union (EU), which includes two (Germany and Belgium) of the above states in a single economic entity. As a single economy, the EU is the second largest trading partner of India, with Euro 40.5 billion worth of EU goods going to India and Euro 39.4 billion of Indian goods going to the EU as of 2011, totalling approximately Euro 79.8 billion ($104 billion) in total trade.

India is also the largest export and/or import partner of the following countries:

Exports		Imports	
Guinea-Bissau	56.0%	Nepal	51.0%
Nepal	55.7%	Mauritius	23.7%
Tanzania	14.1%	Sri Lanka	21.3%
Togo	13.7%	Kenya	20.7%
Guinea	10.3%	UAE	17.0%

Apart from maintaining good relations with the other countries, Indian missions have to become much more proactive and suggest new ideas for business in their respective locations. Indian envoys abroad can play a greater role in advising ministries about trade opportunities, as too the factors that can help Indian business become more competitive.

Creating World Knowledge Platforms

I firmly believe that nations can collaborate on the basis of their unique core competencies, leading to the development of a system or product which benefits both the nations and the world for attaining global economic empowerment. I call this 'World Knowledge Platform'. One such example is the emergence of BrahMos, in which India and Russia have jointly invested $150 million each to create a world-class supersonic cruise missile using their core competencies. Today, it has generated a business volume of $10 billion for both the nations.

Another such example is a Pan-African e-network, which I

envisioned and announced during my address to the Pan-African Parliament. V. Ponraj is the system architect of the mission initiated by India in association with the Ministry of External Affairs, the PMO and ISRO. The e-network benefits fifty-three African nations by providing tele-medicine, tele-education and e-governance services from Indian and African educational and healthcare institutions with an investment of $125 million to meet the millennium development goals of African countries. This project has won a top international award, Hermes Prize for Innovation—2010, for innovation in the field of sustainable development.

Similarly, India and South Korea have joined hands and created a World Knowledge Platform for nano science and technology systems at the Indian Institute of Science. On 18 May 2011, I was in Sydney, where I interacted with a team of doctors, ophthalmologists and vision experts from the Brien Holden Vision Institute at the University of New South Wales. For eliminating avoidable blindness from the world, there is a mission called Global Vision 2020. It is presided over by Prof. G.N. Rao of the L.V. Prasad Eye Institute, one of the most renowned ophthalmologists in India, and Prof. Brien Holden of the institute mentioned above. Both these institutes are conducting research and trials in areas such as identifying and preventing genetic eye degradation and developing low-cost and robust vision correction devices. These missions are examples of World Knowledge Platforms, how the competencies of nations are converged for mutual benefit.

One of the next important global missions is to create a World Space Knowledge Platform for the development of an International Virtual Space Laboratory. This platform will become an advisory body for space industrialization. It will take the form of a coalition of leading academic institutions in space and energy—which will work on a feasibility study for Space Solar Power.

There are several threats and opportunities that can be taken up by the World Knowledge Platform for Global Action:

- The first global threat is environment degradation and climate change. Energy independence based on environmental impact mitigation and selecting the right energy mix, and finally harnessing space solar power, could be an answer.
- The second threat is trade deficit and global economic recession, which is affecting many nations. In such a scenario, my suggestion is to evolve regional cooperation based on the core competencies of the collaborating nations to work on the missions of energy, water, healthcare, infrastructure and employment generation.
- The third threat is poverty. Around 3 billion people across the world need improvement in their quality of life and help with finding employment through systems such as PURA.

Addressing problems such as these would have a wide-ranging positive impact on society as well, and offer opportunity to youth, our most powerful resource.

A Place in the Security Council

India is a charter member of the United Nations and participates in all of its specialized agencies. It has contributed troops to UN peacekeeping efforts in Korea, Egypt and the Congo in earlier years and in Somalia, Angola and Rwanda in recent years. India has been a member of the UN Security Council for six terms (a total of twelve years), and was a member for 2011-12. India is also a member of the G4 group of nations, who back each other in seeking a permanent seat on the Security Council. India has been elected seven times to the Council. Only three countries have served longer (Japan, Brazil, and Argentina), except for the permanent five, while Colombia has served the same amount of time.

India has been seeking a permanent seat on the council as a

member of the G4, a body composed of Brazil, Germany, Japan, and India, all of whom are currently seeking permanent representation. According to their proposal, the Council should be expanded beyond the current fifteen members to include twenty-five members. If this actually happens, it would be the first time that permanent Security Council status is extended to a South Asian nation. Supporters of the G4 suggest that this will lead to greater representation of developing nations.

Although the US and other permanent members have not been very supportive of expanding the Council, in his visit to India in 2010, US President Barack Obama offered his support for India to become a permanent member. However, the reactions from other council members are not very clear, particularly China.

The points discussed in this section could be part of external affairs strategy. And if we focus on the nine fulfilling manifestos discussed in this section, assuredly India will get its rightful place in the Security Council and the G8 Group of Nations.

SECTION VIII

VISION FOR INDIA

We have discussed nine manifestos for the nation which help bring about inclusive growth. They are pointers to appropriate policies and action that can be taken to achieve our goals.

In the context of evolving a vision for our country, I wish to share with you my experience of addressing the Beijing Forum in November 2012. The Beijing Forum is an international platform that seeks to promote social progress. I met a large number of Chinese youth at this forum. I discovered that all aspiring political leaders in the country have to take a course at the China Executive Leadership Academy in Pudong, Shanghai (CELEP). It includes modules on Chinese political philosophy and on politicians' role in China's development. It is only after doing this course that officials can graduate to taking on political responsibilities, including ministerial ones. The school—and other similar schools—it is said, was established because the Chinese government became impatient with the lack of what it called the quality of local cadres and their inability to govern their localities or institutions effectively, according to Prof. Frank Pieke, the author of *The Good Communist: Elite Training and State Building in Today's China*.

The message here is that it is important to engage and train young minds with an inspiring vision for the country. As I often say, the ignited minds of India's youth are the most powerful resources on the earth, above the earth and under the earth.

Birth of a Vision

Transforming India into a developed nation entails a vision of a country whose citizens live well above the poverty line, their education and health are of high standards, national security is assured, and core competence in certain major areas enables the production of quality goods—for competitive exports as well—bringing all-round and inclusive prosperity to the country, ultimately bringing smiles to the faces of billion plus people. Any long-term vision needs at least ten to twenty years' time. Normally, any political party is elected to Parliament for a five-year term. But how to draft a long-term vision and how to implement such a vision for over a decade or two without losing its focus is the question. Normally, if Parliament discusses each aspect of the vision and adopts it, then there will be at least minimum assurance for the next government to implement it, even though it is not mandatory for it to do so. But as long as the vision and its targets are clear, then every government can have its own way of implementing it. But ultimately, evolving the public policy which brings sustainable development with inclusive growth is the challenging task. Providing leadership to lead the billion-plus people in a challenging democratic environment is the need of the hour.

The process of chalking out such a vision was set in motion more than two decades ago. Let me share with you my experience from the mid-1990s about the formulation of a vision for India for the year 2020. I was given the task of chairing the Technology Information, Forecasting and Assessment Council (TIFAC), an autonomous body set up in 1988 under the Government of India's department of science and technology (DST) to look ahead in technologies and support innovation in select areas of national importance. At the first meeting itself, council members decided that TIFAC must evolve a plan for India's transformation into an economically developed nation by 2020.

But it was a time when the economic liberalization initiated by Prime Minister P.V. Narasimha Rao had just begun to take effect, and everybody on the council wondered how we could evolve a long-term mission under the prevailing economic and social conditions which could very well be completely different from those twenty years later. At a time when the economy was growing at around 5 per cent to 6 per cent per annum and the population was around 840 million, we had to envisage a growth rate of at least 10 per cent consistently for over ten years in order to realize the development of a billion-plus people with diverse backgrounds and needs.

In spite of the initial doubts, the council, with many young members, met the idea head-on and discussed how we could translate the vision into action. This really ignited the minds of all of us on the council. The members of TIFAC at the time included the principal secretary to the prime minister; nine secretaries to the Government of India; chiefs of the Confederation of Indian Industry (CII), the Associated Chambers of Commerce and Industry of India (ASSOCHAM) and the Federation of Indian Chambers of Commerce and Industry (FICCI); chairpersons of IDBI and ICICI banks, the Industrial Finance Corporation of India (IFCI), and several public sector corporations; chief executives of a number of private sector institutions; vice chancellors of different universities; and scientists from the DST. We debated and formed seventeen task teams with over 500 members, who in turn had consultations with over 5,000 people in various sectors of the economy.

The teams worked for over two years and produced twenty-five reports. These included visions for such diverse areas as agro-food processing, civil aviation, electricity, waterways, road transportation, telecommunications, food and agriculture, engineering industries, healthcare, and life science and biotechnology. These projections are still valid and the targets set are yet to be achieved to their full potential.

Distinctive Profile of a Developed India

Now, let me tell you what an economically developed India should look like by 2020:

1. A nation where the rural-urban divide has been reduced to a thin line.
2. A nation where there is an equitable distribution of, and adequate access to, energy and quality water.
3. A nation where agriculture, industry and the service sector work together in symphony.

4. A nation where education with a good value system is not denied to any meritorious candidates because of societal or economic discrimination.
5. A nation which is the best destination for the most talented scholars, scientists, and investors from around the world.
6. A nation where the best of healthcare is available to all.
7. A nation where governance is responsive, transparent and corruption-free.
8. A nation where poverty has been totally eradicated, illiteracy removed, crime against women and children is absent, and no one in the society feels alienated.
9. A nation that is prosperous, healthy, secure, devoid of terrorism, peaceful and happy, and continues on a sustainable growth path.
10. A nation that is one of the best places to live in and is proud of its leadership.

Integrated Action for a Developed India

In order to realize this distinctive profile, we have to transform India in five areas where India has core competence:

1. Agriculture and food processing
2. Education and healthcare
3. Information and communication technology
4. Infrastructure development, which includes reliable and quality electric power, surface transport and infrastructure for all parts of the country including rural and urban areas under PURA
5. Self-reliance in critical technologies.

Challenges Involved in Realizing the Vision

The India Vision 2020 document was prepared at the time of Prime Minister P.V. Narasimha Rao. It was given to his successor, Atal Bihari Vajpayee, who announced in Parliament as well as in one of his Independence Day addresses that India will become an economically developed nation by 2020. At a governors' conference during my presidency, Manmohan Singh announced that his government, too, will carry forward the task of economically developing the nation.

As any national vision takes at least fifteen years for its realization, a minimum of three democratically elected governments have to work on it. National missions cannot be party agenda, but they can be part of their election manifestos. The methodology of the party in power may be different from that of its predecessor, but the vision would be supreme. For this reason, it has to cut across party lines and be approved by Parliament to ensure continuity in its realization irrespective of the government of the day.

Vision 2020, too, does not belong to any single party, government or individual. It is a national vision. Once the government commits to realizing it, it has to be discussed and debated in detail by all elected representatives in Parliament so that a national consensus—incorporating the concerns of all stakeholders such as the executive, the judiciary, the political class, media, intellectuals, academia, business, industry, teachers, doctors, farmers, and the youth of the nation—emerges.

Hence the elected leader of the nation—the driving force behind the vision—should be a creative leader who walks an unexplored path of developmental politics with the cooperation of other parties, using the core competences of other leaders, intellectuals, able and creative minds from all disciplines irrespective of their party affiliations, to realize the vision.

'Why Nations Fail'

I recently read a book called *Why Nations Fail: The Origins of Power, Prosperity and Poverty* by Daron Acemoglu and James Robinson. It analyses the socio-economic and political policies of developed and developing nations, and offers some insights which are as pertinent to India as the other nations discussed.

For example, England, after the Glorious Revolution created the world's first set of inclusive political institutions. As a consequence, economic institutions in the UK also started becoming more inclusive. The English state aggressively promoted mercantile activities and worked to promote domestic industry, not only by removing barriers to the expansion of industrial activity but also by lending the full power of the English navy to defend mercantile interests. By rationalizing property rights, it facilitated the construction of infrastructure, particularly roads, canals and waterways, and later railways, that would prove to be crucial for industrial growth. The British government adopted a set of economic institutions that provided incentives for investment, trade and innovations like the steam engine.

The rebirth of China came with a significant move away from one of the most extractive set of economic institutions and towards more inclusive ones. Market incentives in agriculture and industry, followed by welcoming aggressive foreign investment and state-of-the-art technology adoption and development, have set China on a path to rapid economic growth.

Now it is time for us to ask ourselves what are the impediments to the economic development of our nation? Indian political institutions are inclusive, or at least partially so, based as they are on a democratically elected Parliament and democratic political parties. The question to ponder is whether these political institutions have created inclusive economic institutions. From the results of the economic situation we see around us today, the answer for now is 'no'. India's economic growth is not sustainable.

India needs to transform its partially inclusive political institutions and extractive economic institutions into fully inclusive political and economic institutions. Internal reforms and improvements in economic efficiency will help reduce both trade deficit and inflation.

Instead of consumption spending, we need to increase infrastructure spending. Imports of agricultural produce, minerals, coal and petroleum products have to be considerably reduced, and inclusive economic policies should empower Indians to attain competitiveness in the agriculture, industry and services sectors. We need to skill-enable and knowledge-enable our youth by fostering private sector initiatives. It is essential to develop sustainable systems in every domain, so that fluctuations in the world economy do not have a direct impact on the Indian economy.

What India Has Achieved

We have only six years to achieve the goals of Vision 2020. The nation should take it up as a primary task and facilitate all stakeholders to contribute to realizing the goals of the developed India mission.

India has made substantial progress in enhancing agricultural productivity and increasing per capita income. According to NASSCOM, the IT–BPO sector in India aggregated revenues of $100 billion in FY2012, with export and domestic revenue standing at $69.1 billion and $31.7 billion respectively. India has become the world's second-largest mobile phone using country, with 900 million users, and the Indian automobile industry has become the third largest in the world. In addition, rural and urban development missions have created large-scale infrastructure such as a national quadrilateral highway, world-class airports in metro cities, and all-weather rural roads. The literacy rate in India stood at 74.04 per cent in 2012. India's healthcare sector is projected to grow to nearly $40 billion. And we are aspiring to provide clean green energy and safe drinking water to all the citizens of the nation.

Against the backdrop of this growth, we have to assess where we stand in terms of what we aspired to in the 1990s and see if and why there is a gap. It is time for the nation and its leaders to take up a review mission and suggest methods by which we can accelerate progress so that by 2020 India can become a developed country with zero poverty, 100 per cent literacy, quality healthcare for all, quality education embedded in a sound value system for all, and value-added employment for every citizen consistent with his education and professional skills. If we channelize our integrated efforts towards Vision 2020, the economic development of our nation is certain.

Conclusion

It is only our political system that gives the required support to farmers, scientists, engineers, doctors, teachers, advocates and other professionals alike to enable this nation to achieve success in the green revolution, white revolution, the space mission, defence mission, science and technology mission, and infrastructure development mission. What we are today is because of our political system. India's youth should not keep away from politics but enter it to inspire, guide and lead to make this nation great in all disciplines.

The ignited minds of the youth are bubbling with the spirit of 'I can do it' and the belief that 'India will become a developed nation'. If you all feel that you can do it, India will certainly get the necessary creative leadership at all levels from panchayat to Parliament. These ignited minds will sing the song of youth and lead the nation towards sustainable development. I strongly believe that the youth of my nation, by entering politics, will build a brand of integrity, honesty, value system, courage, commitment and responsibility with accountability around them and practise development politics.

SONG OF YOUTH

As a young citizen of India,
Armed with technology, knowledge and love for my nation
I realize, small aim is a crime.

I will work and sweat for a great vision
The vision of transforming India into a developed nation
Powered by economic strength and a value system

I am one of the citizens of the billion;
Only the vision will ignite the billion souls.

It has entered into me;
The ignited soul compared to any resource is the
Most powerful resource on the earth,
above the earth and under the earth.

BIBLIOGRAPHY AND REFERENCES

Abdul Kalam, A.P.J. with Y.S. Rajan. *India 2020: A Vision for the New Millennium*. New Delhi: Penguin Books India, 1998.

Abdul Kalam, A.P.J. *Turning Points: A Journey through Challenges*. New Delhi: HarperCollins Publishers India, 2012.

Abdul Kalam, A.P.J. *Ignited Minds*. New Delhi: Penguin Books India, 2003.

Abdul Kalam, A.P.J. *Target 3 Billion: Innovative Solutions towards Sustainable Development*. New Delhi: Penguin Books India, 2011.

Acemoglu, Daron and James Robinson. *Why Nations Fail: The Origins of Power, Prosperity and Poverty*. New York: Crown Business, 2012.

Gupta, R.P. *Turn Around India*. New Delhi: Himalaya Publishing House, 2013.

Kulkarni, Sudheendra. *Music of the Spinning Wheel: Mahatma Gandhi's Manifesto for the Internet Age*. New Delhi: Amaryllis, 2012.

Pieke, Frank. *The Good Communist: Elite Training and State Building in Today's China*. Cambridge: Cambridge University Press, 2009.

*

In writing this book, we used resources from the following: PRS Legislative Research, National Election Watch, Association for Democratic Reforms, 11th and 12th Five Year Plans, United Nations Human Development Report 2013, Central Water Commission, National Waterways, 'River Interlinking in India: The Dream and Reality' by S.R. Singh and M.P. Shrivastava, Trends in Maternal Mortality: 1990-2010 (estimates developed by WHO, UNICEF, UNFPA and World Bank), central government budgets (2011-12, 2012-13, 2013-14), Raghuram Rajan panel report on determining new index of backwardness, National Sample Survey Organization's report for 2002, World Bank Report on Power and Road Infrastructure for 2000, Energy Independence Vision 2030 by A.P.J. Abdul Kalam, International Space Development Conference 2010, reports from the Tamil Nadu Agriculture University, U21 Rankings of National Higher Education Systems 2012 report and Transparency International reports. We also used reports from publications such as *India Today*, *Times of India*, *Hindu* and *Malayala Manorama*.